D1601158

BRE-X

GOLD TODAY, GONE TOMORROW

Anatomy of the Busang Swindle

BRE-X

Gold today, Gone Tomorrow

Anatomy of the Busang Swindle

Vivian Danielson

James Whyte

The Northern Miner

Canadian Cataloguing in Publication Data

Danielson, Vivian, 1951–
        Bre-X: gold today, gone tomorrow

ISBN 55257-003-7

1. Bre-X (Firm). 2. Gold mines and mining – Indonesia
3. Fraud
I. Whyte, James, 1958–   II. Title

Published by The Northern Miner
1450 Don Mills Road
Toronto, ON M3B 2X7

Contents

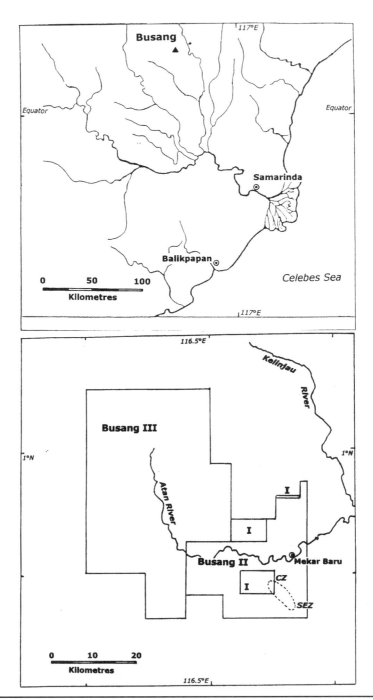

Top: The location of the Busang property in southeastern Borneo.

Bottom: The areas covered by the Busang contract of work applications (I, II and III), with the Central zone (CZ) and Southeast zone (SEZ).

PREFACE

Doers and dreamers,
Scoundrels and schemers

Mining history is a nugget-laden vein, running near surface, that pinches and swells its way across Canada. The country is young enough, and mineral wealth so important to the economy, that tales from the gold-rush days have not lost their allure and relevance. The characters who brought life and color to the Yukon and Cariboo gold fields, and to Ontario's Kirkland Lake and Timmins mining camps, have modern-day counterparts in the diamond projects of Canada's North and the Voisey's Bay nickel camp of Labrador. Prospectors and miners are still to be found in Nevada, California and other western states, reviving the historic mining districts that opened up and built the American West.

North America owes much to its mining pioneers. Their legacy is kept alive by new generations of miners, prospectors, geologists and engineers who bring wealth to local and national economies, along with improved operating and environmental standards. These honest, hard-working men and women — the doers — are the backbone of the mining industry. Behind them are the dreamers, with little to show for their efforts but hard-luck stories. And lurking in the shadows are the rogues and scoundrels who make up the mining industry's underworld, just as their predecessors did decades earlier. Their skulduggery is part of mining lore and legend because mankind has always had a curious fascination for the devious characters who profit from grand-scale speculation and nefarious adventure.

The story of Bre-X Minerals and its Busang "gold" project in Indonesia is about all these things, and more. It is about greed and gullibility, about broken dreams and bitterness, about corporate power and backroom intrigue, about deception and disillusionment, about lessons hard-learned and about how good judgment can be swept away by mass euphoria. It is another cautionary tale of gold's power to seduce and blind not only sinners, but saints and scientists as well. Stories of other infamous gold scams are woven through the book to show that Busang truly was without precedent.

This book is dedicated to the mining professionals who not only set the standards of the industry, but who embody them as well. It also is dedicated to future generations of mining analysts, journalists and investors, with the hope that they will be able to see for themselves when the emperor has no clothes.

INTRODUCTION

'This skulduggery must end'

It all seems so ridiculous now; the feverish excitement, the arm-waving hype, and the slavish adulation that once surrounded Bre-X Minerals. The company that had gone to the jungles of Borneo in 1993, found a gigantic gold deposit, and beaten off rough corporate suitors from the upper floors of the gold industry to hold on to its project, is, at the time of writing, under court protection. The hard-drinking promoter and the chain-smoking geologist who found this treasure are no longer on speaking terms. Their field man is missing, presumed dead, having failed to complete a helicopter flight to the company's jungle property. And the shareholders, who formerly thanked Bre-X executives for putting their children through school, are suing.

The Cinderella story has vanished, along with the golden riches and the gushing superlatives that once described the junior company's Busang project in Kalimantan. Bre-X's $6-billion success story has been exposed as a cruel swindle played out on the world stage by a handful of desperate men who had, in more ways than one, hit rock bottom.

Bre-X President David Walsh is no longer a modern-day David who fended off Goliath to save a hard-won prize, but a disgraced stock promoter whose sole task now is to convince the world that he is every inch the dupe he appears to be. Walsh's partner-in-shame, John Felderhof, is no longer an award-winning minefinder, but a rogue geologist in the throes of denial, hiding from the world, from the truth and from his own training as a scientist. Michael de Guzman is the conveniently dead "fall guy." And Busang is no longer "the world's biggest gold deposit," but the most daring and best-executed "salting" scam in world mining history. Investors went from rich to poor overnight, while analysts and mining professionals who had been heroes one day were perceived as fools the next.

But Busang was more than an ordinary gold scam with a few zeros added, caused — once again — by gullibility and the lure of riches. It was an extraordinarily popular delusion, adding yet another chapter to that great and awful book of human folly. Busang was a tragic triumph of ego and emotion over reason and science, as well as a triumph of timing, for it might well have remained a small, low-grade scam had it not been picked up and carried along by a Bay Street juggernaut with more cash than common sense and an army of investors predisposed to believe. The stars may never line up for a junior company quite that way again.

For the mining industry, where salting is viewed as the stratagem of scoundrels, Bre-X was a mammoth embarrassment, not only because it overshadowed the good work carried out by honest geologists and engineers, but because it had become one scam too many. Mining, particularly junior mining, is an industry that needs public support to survive. The trust built up over decades by honest mining men had been undermined too often by unscrupulous characters out to make a quick dollar through deceit and trickery. Enough had become enough.

In late May 1997, a group of mining men gathered for lunch in the Engineers' Room of Toronto's Ontario Club, as they often do to catch up on the latest news. As the topic turned to Bre-X and several other companies whose samples had been subjected to tampering, a veteran mining engineer stood up. "This skulduggery must end!" he said, his voice shaking with emotion.

But it will never end if gold swindlers remain unpunished. It will never end until the tricks of the trade are dissected and stripped bare for the world to see. It will never end until we learn to see them coming, instead of going.

How do they con you?
Let us count the ways . . .

They do it with smoke and mirrors, with geological gobbledygook or with weird, proprietary assaying techniques. Sometimes they do it with loosey-goosey geostatistics, with sprinkles of yellow fairy dust, or with high-grade gold averaged over long intervals of otherwise barren core to give the illusion of ore grades over minable widths.

They are the silver-tongued scoundrels and pseudo-scientists of the mining underworld; the bit players who sell their souls and reputations for beach-front properties and Armani suits. They are here today and gone tomorrow because they are too greedy to be subtle, too stupid to know when to shut up, and too sloppy not to get caught. Only rarely do men surface who are daring enough to mine pockets, rather than gold, by ways and means that are truly scientific in their insidiousness.

Until the boys from Bre-X Minerals began spinning their tales of millions and millions of ounces of gold in the jungles of Kalimantan, mining industry scoundrels were, for the most part, crude and their scams easily detected. Amateurs and short-term thinkers, these unconfident confidence men lacked the skill and stamina to make it more than one or two notches up the credibility curve. They stuck to the sidelines and to their own kind. They avoided the scrutiny of hard-nosed mining analysts and, instead, cozied up to the type of broker or newsletter-writer who would recommend shares in Hell Incorporated, as long as the pay matched the challenge.

These old-school rogues knew their place in the overall scheme of things and would never have had the temerity to get up on stage and lecture the mining establishment to "go find your own gold," as Bre-X Vice-President John Felderhof did in March 1997 when he accepted the prestigious Prospector of the Year award from the Prospectors and Developers Association of Canada, for his role in the Busang "discovery."

Such high-profile grandstanding is avoided by most rogues, for deep down inside, few are comfortable in their own skin. Their unease is often manifested by compulsive behavior, such as heavy drinking or other excesses, which keep at bay the moments of truth that illuminate their failings and defects of character. But scoundrels are alluring creatures too. Some are surprisingly likable, charming and entertaining, and the complexity of human nature is such that most have a redeeming quality or virtue that keeps them within the human family and restores their self-worth.

The hard-bitten swindler rationalizes his acts and condones his failings by focusing on the unfortunate circumstances that occasioned them, and thereby manages to excuse in himself what he would not excuse in others. So begins the process of self-delusion which, like crime and perversion, is a progressive affliction culminating in anti-social behavior and mental illness. The embittered, self-deluded swindler is perhaps most effective, because, having turned his back on humanity and fooled himself, he is better equipped to fool others. It means less wear and tear on his conscience.

Scoundrels and swindlers should not be confused with promoters, who play an important role in the mining industry. A good promoter knows that early-stage exploration is a risky business not suited for widows and orphans, and conducts himself accordingly. He realizes that where there is potential for high reward, there is corresponding high risk. Investors should too.

Turn-of-the-century gold huckster George Graham Rice makes this point in his book, *My Adventures With Your Money*: "Don't think, Mr. Speculator, because a promoter represents the chances of profit making in a mining enterprise to be enormous, and you later find his expectations are not realized, that the promoter is ipso facto a crook. Big financiers are apt to make mistakes and so are little ones. Undoubtedly grave misrepresentations are made every day, and insidious methods are used to beguile you into forming a higher opinion regarding the merits of various securities than is warranted by the facts. But mine promoters are only human, and honest ones not infrequently are carried away by their own enthusiasm, and they themselves lose their all in the same ventures in which they induce you to participate."

Chapter One:
A SLOW ROAD TO NOWHERE

The lust for comfort, that stealthy thing that enters the house a guest, and then becomes a host, and then a master.
Kahlil Gibran

Unwinding at the Royal York

With 7,500 delegates in town from all over the world, the 1997 annual convention of the Prospectors and Developers Association of Canada spilled out of its traditional home, Toronto's Royal York Hotel, into the modern glass-and-concrete Metro Convention Centre a few blocks away.

The old-timers grumbled about the change of venue, just as their predecessors did decades earlier when the convention was moved to the Royal York from the King Edward Hotel, yesteryear's "home away from home" for mining men. But they were mollified to hear that social events such as the awards ceremony and "Kirkland Lake Night" would continue to be staged in the dimly lit ballrooms of the Royal York. And they were happy, too, that the beer and spirits flowed as freely as ever in the hospitality suites sponsored by the mining companies at the stately hotel.

Mining engineer Stanley Hawkins had done a fair bit of "suite-hopping" in his younger days. But as president of Tandem Resources, a junior company with mineral properties in Canada and Indonesia, he presided over one of his own during the March convention. A horde of people had passed through the elegantly appointed room to shake hands and congratulate Hawkins' old friend, David Walsh, president of Bre-X Minerals. The Calgary, Alberta-based junior had taken the mining world by storm with its Busang project, frequently described as "the largest gold deposit in the world." Walsh, who raised funds for drilling at

Busang from the basement of his house, was the rags-to-riches hero of the convention.

But business was business, and Hawkins wanted a few minutes of Walsh's time to ask about the progress of work on three gold concessions in Kalimantan, where Tandem was a partner with Walsh's other junior, Bresea Resources.

The easygoing engineer was frustrated by the lack of news coming from Bre-X, which managed the work on behalf of the joint venture on a cost-plus-15% basis.

Hawkins was irritated by other things as well. Tandem had made a $100,000 cash-call payment to Bre-X, which was supposed to be for work carried out on the concessions in the past year. "They finally gave us an accounting, which was dreadful," he later told *The Northern Miner*, the newspaper of record of the international mining industry. "They told us the $100,000 was just the entry fee [and not for work done], which was not my understanding at all."

The unexpected cover charge did not sit well with Hawkins, who had already picked up the tab for other areas Bre-X had purported to manage on behalf of the joint venture. "I had to make up the agreement that we had, which I sent to David, along with the maps for the concession that I myself had to get from Indonesia."

But his main frustration was lack of news for Tandem shareholders. The company had other projects, but investors were keenly interested in the ones being explored by the master himself, Bre-X geologist Michael de Guzman.

"For quite a while, I had been trying to get information on just what the hell was going on over there and what results we had," Hawkins complained. "I bugged David on the phone a few times . . . and he told me to call Indonesia, so I talked to his guy over there, Greg MacDonald, but I didn't get a helluva lot out of him either."

Hawkins brought the issue up again at the mining convention, but Walsh brushed him off and said: "Talk to Felderhof." The comment did not surprise Hawkins, or anyone else, for it was well-known that Walsh's time and attention were fixated on how the stock markets were doing, how the share prices of Bre-X and Bresea were holding up, and on keeping his investor relations team pumped and excited about the Busang story.

John Felderhof was not an easy man to pin down. The world-famous geologist had just picked up the prestigious "Prospector of the Year" award for discovering what almost everyone was calling "the largest gold deposit in the world" and was basking in glory, surrounded by his family, friends and a crowd of well-wishers.

Persistence did not pay off for Hawkins, who did manage to contact Felderhof by phone. "But all he said was: 'Jesus, I'm not up on the day-to-day stuff; phone de Guzman.'"

Reaching de Guzman, or his trusty sidekick, Cesar Puspos, during the convention also required patience. The two Filipino geologists had rooms in the Royal York Hotel but were spending much of their evenings at an apartment shared by two girls who worked as exotic dancers at a local bar.

Eventually, de Guzman returned Hawkins' call and a meeting was arranged for the evening of Wednesday, March 12, the last day of the convention. The geologist arrived for the meeting dressed casually in bush clothes, but soon disarmed everyone in the room by his polite, soft-spoken manner — the usual deference he showed all Westerners of importance.

Hawkins was told that one of the concessions "did not look good," but that one of the two projects on the Upper Mahakam River was "very prospective." Naturally interested, he asked de Guzman if gold had been found and what results had been obtained from the work program carried out during the past year.

"He told me, 'yes, they had panned some gold from it,'" Hawkins said. "But he also said there was ground surrounding it that they would like to get, so not to say anything about it."

Hawkins was disappointed and pleased at the same time. A year had gone by since the projects were taken on, which meant the work being carried out should be far more advanced than the panning stage (an inexpensive, rudimentary technique used in the earliest stages of exploration, often before properties are acquired). He was no further ahead than when he started, with no reports or documentation of any kind and, even worse, no assay results from either sampling, trenching or drilling.

On the other hand, Hawkins was encouraged by de Guzman's comment that the concession was so "prospective" that it warranted the acquisition of more ground nearby. The meeting ended with de Guzman dishing out hope, his commodity of last resort, but little else.

Hawkins never got a formal report from de Guzman for any of the joint-ventured projects. "Not a word, nothing, not to this day." But his company, Tandem Resources, got another $65,000 cash-call from Bre-X for work supposedly done on the concessions, which really got Hawkins' dander up. "I said 'to hell with that — I'm not paying it.'"

Hawkins, a seasoned mining man with plenty of experience running exploration programs, knew full well that the cost of panning a few samples was generally no more than about US$20 for the pan, plus labor. And he had no intention of paying Bre-X $64,900 for the hour or two it must have taken de Guzman or an Indonesian helper to collect a few samples and swish the pan around several times — assuming it had been done at all.

On Thursday, March 13, in a decidedly less elegant part of

Toronto, de Guzman and Puspos were saying their goodbyes to exotic dancers Mandy and Candy (not their real names). The Filipino geologists, along with Bre-X confreres Jerome Alo and Jonathan Nassey, and another Indonesian from Busang named John who did not speak English well, had spent almost a week with the Toronto girls and three of their friends, relaxing and seeing the sights, including Niagara Falls.

Mandy had met de Guzman on Friday evening, March 7, at the nightclub where she worked. She was surprised when he sent flowers the next day and showed up again that evening, charming as ever. They spent almost a week together.

"I had no idea who he was, though he told me he was a famous geologist," she said. While de Guzman did not talk much about his business, he did confide that he was so poor after graduating from university as a geologist that he often slept in the streets. "I'm rich now," he told her. "I have everything I want. I'm happy."

During the visit to Niagara Falls, de Guzman complained repeatedly of heart pains, which Mandy thought might have been caused by his heavy drinking of the past few days. She jokingly suggested he see a lawyer and write a will, which prompted de Guzman to joke about the same thing.

De Guzman told Mandy that he planned to be back in Canada in two months, but she never heard from him again. The following week Candy received a phone call from Cesar that was difficult to understand because the Filipino geologist was crying uncontrollably. "Mike's dead," he sobbed. "Mike's dead."

The rocky road to opportunity

At the height of his brief career as a mining executive, David Walsh often told the story of how he bounced back from bankruptcy to become the head of a mining company with a bigger market capitalization than most of North America's senior gold producers.

The underlying theme was that great opportunities are out there, waiting for determined, visionary risk-takers like him to discover and exploit. It sounded great at the time, and more than a few reporters wondered whether some sort of genius might be lurking behind the bleary eyes of the chain-smoking, beer-bellied promoter they saw before them. People who knew Walsh better were more inclined to attribute his success to dumb, blind luck, while the really smart money turned up their noses and stuck to blue chips.

When Walsh first appeared on the mining scene in the early 1980s, there was nothing to distinguish him from thousands of other promoters with a story to tell and stock to sell. But he was ambitious and made it known that he expected something of himself over and above the ordinary.

Hawkins, who helped Walsh acquire some mineral properties for his first public company, Bresea Resources, described his long-time friend as "bull-dog determined," though perhaps more determined than capable. "I don't know how bright David is, but I would say he's street-smart. He's an aggressive sort of guy and a hard worker. There was nothing lazy about David, and I respected him for that."

Hawkins has no illusions about Walsh's knowledge of mining. "It's limited. He wouldn't know a mine if he fell over one. He's a promoter, a market guy."

A salesman first and foremost, Walsh has a boyish charm some people find disarming, but only if they get past his most obvious character flaw — a fondness for alcohol that sometimes brings out his demons. "David is quite likable," Hawkins explained, "though he has an Irish temper that can flare up from time to time."

Barry Tannock, Bre-X's first manager of investor relations, has a less charitable opinion about his former boss, which may have something to do with an unresolved dispute related to non-payment of a performance bonus. Tannock also believes Walsh shuffled him aside just as Bre-X began its meteoric rise, in order to make room for a crony, Stephen McAnulty.

No longer bitter about the forced career change, Tannock says the Bre-X blowup served only to reinforce his view that David Walsh is a man whose drive and ambition always greatly exceeded his talent and character. "I think he was beyond his depth once [Bre-X] took off. He was a very control-oriented sort of guy and I think it's hard for someone like that to delegate in areas they don't understand."

The early years

David Walsh was born on August 11, 1945, in Montreal, Quebec, which in its glory days housed the head offices of most of Canada's major corporations, banks and financial institutions. Despite harsh winters and hot summers, Montreal was the engine of Canada's postwar economic boom and the place to be for any aspiring executive who wanted to make money and enjoy life at the same time. With its fine dining and exciting night life, it was far more inviting and cosmopolitan than dour, puritanical Toronto, then derided by Quebecers for rolling up its sidewalks immediately after the supper hour.

David Walsh grew up in Montreal's Westmount district, an enclave of prosperous anglophones. The family was too Irish, too boisterous and too fond of alcohol to make it into the upper echelon of Westmount society; the town's upper crust expected the Irish to stay where they belonged, in Verdun or Point St. Charles.

Walsh was a poor student who failed one or two grades and

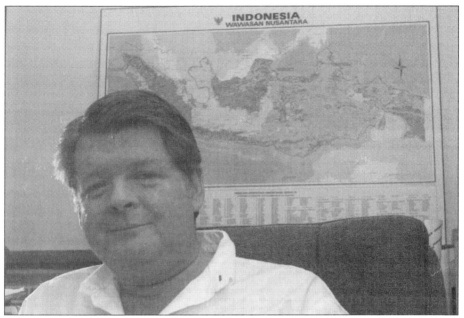

It all began here: David Walsh in his basement office in Calgary.

never finished high school. While still a teenager, he followed in the footsteps of his father and joined a brokerage firm in the city's financial district.

By the mid-1970s, Walsh had moved on to Midland Doherty (now Midland Walwyn Capital), where he became a vice-president of the institutional equity sales department. He met Jeannette Toukhmanian, a petite, attractive woman of Armenian descent who worked as a corporate secretary. Educated in Egypt, Toukhmanian was bright, multi-lingual and cosmopolitan. The couple married in Montreal, where they raised two sons, Brett and Sean. The early years of the marriage were rocky and, on at least one occasion, Jeannette initiated, and then abandoned, divorce proceedings.

As a young family man, Walsh had hopes of building a prosperous life in his home town, but these were soon dashed by forces beyond his control. He had some good years, when his commissions ran into six figures, but the overall trend was not good. The "Quiet Revolution" of the 1960s — a generally peaceful attempt to integrate francophones into Quebec's political life and business community — was being upstaged by youthful separatists who believed greater progress could be achieved by resorting to violence. In 1970, the kidnapping and murder of a Quebec cabinet minister and the kidnapping of a British diplomat shocked the anglophone community, and thousands pulled up stakes to move to Toronto, or points west, taking their money and business interests with them. The anglophone exodus continued into the 1980s, in reaction to restrictive language laws and a shrinking job market. While Walsh had some good years in the brokerage business in Montreal, the city's economy was clearly in decline, along with his client base and paycheque.

In 1982, Walsh packed up his young family and headed west to take on a post in Midland's Calgary office. Alberta had been enjoying boom times, thanks to a spike in oil prices, and Walsh was one of many who hoped to escape the recession that was then gripping Quebec and Ontario. But soon after his arrival, Alberta's boom times were brought to an abrupt end by then-prime minister Pierre Trudeau and his disastrously meddlesome National Energy Program. To make matters worse, interest rates were in the double digits and unemployment numbers were climbing, which meant fewer people had discretionary income to invest in the stock market.

Walsh soon found that it was not easy to drum up clients in a city where the national pastime was reviling easterners. But, through persistence, lots of schmoozing and a good-old-boy sales pitch, he managed to make enough contacts to keep him going, albeit not in the high-living style he had craved. After a frustrating and somewhat fruitless year, Walsh left the firm an unhappy man. He filed suit against Midland, alleging that his salary had been wrongfully cut in half to a mere $2,000 per month, a case later settled out of court.

After deciding that printing his own paper was a better idea than selling someone else's, Walsh decided to try his hand at running a public company. His first venture, Bresea Resources (named after sons Brett and Sean), was taken public on the Vancouver Stock Exchange in 1984. The junior exploration company began life with a gold property in the Sturgeon Lake area of Ontario, plus some oil and gas reserves. The initial board of directors consisted of Walsh, Ellen Dyell-Acton, William Timmins, Michael Duggan and Steve McAnulty, a former broker, then working as a self-employed investment consultant.

Timmins had, by far, the most mining experience, and not all of it pleasant. If Walsh wanted to get his career as a mining executive off to a solid start, he might have taken some time, pulled up a chair, and learned from Timmins how easy it is to get embroiled in a salting scandal.

Tapin Copper

The Tapin Copper salting scam was yesterday's news when William Timmins joined Bresea's board in 1984. But a decade earlier, the mystery of the missing core from Tapin's Oregon gold project was the talk of Vancouver's Howe Street.

At first, some of the suspicion was directed at Timmins, a consulting geologist who had been retained by Tapin to write a report on the gold property. As events unfolded, however, it became clear that Timmins had been set up by Tapin's president, a burly stock promoter named Russell Aronec.

Aronec and Tapin's corporate secretary, Reyard (Rey) Saadien, had secured the rights to a former gold producer in Baker County, Oregon, which they agreed to option to Tapin in return for shares and various exploration commitments. Saadien was a geologist-turned-broker, then employed with Tapin's underwriter, Canarim Investment.

Tapin took on the Oregon project mainly because it was virtually impossible to raise funds for mineral projects in British Columbia at the time. Dave Barrett and his socialist New Democratic Party had just been elected to govern the province, and many in the mining industry believed Barrett's newfound power had gone straight to his head. The left-leaning cabinet wasted no time putting the screws to the mining industry by introducing onerous royalties and other bizarre pieces of legislation. The industry responded by going elsewhere.

Timmins filed his report on the Oregon project on August 30, 1974. It was fairly skimpy, as the property had been idle since 1925, except for some intermittent "high-grading" (selective mining of only the richest ore). The report did list a number of old mines that had operated on a small scale from 1895 to 1910, but only the upper, free-milling ores were mined, as the processing methods of the day were not capable of treating the deeper, metallurgically complex sulphides.

Timmins recommended an exploration program, to be carried out in stages, consisting of geophysical surveys, mapping and sampling. Later that year, the first hole was drilled to test a geophysical anomaly believed to be a faulted extension of some old mine workings. The samples were taken by Tapin's geologist, D. Moule; Timmins was not on the property at the time.

Aronec then asked Timmins to incorporate the assay results — barn-burners by any standard — in his previous report, which was updated and provided to the company on November 27, 1974.

Tapin released the results a day later in a statement of material facts. While the first few intervals from the hole revealed modest grades ranging from 0.1 to 0.4 oz. of gold per ton, values from a depth of between 62 and 133 ft. were, in Timmins' words, "exceptionally high." Indeed, a few of these were spectacular: 5 ft. of 10.9 oz. gold per ton, 8 ft. of 6.5 oz., 4 ft. of 23.2 oz., and 4 ft. of 13.9 oz. gold.

After eliminating all assays greater than 8 oz. of gold, Timmins reported that the weighted assays over a core length of 70 ft. yielded an average of 1.97 oz. of gold and 0.45 oz. of silver per ton. He described the results as "extremely encouraging" (a bit of an understatement) and noted that they were "indicative of past values obtained in the North vein of the old workings." As might be expected, the reports caused excitement on Vancouver's Howe Street and generated a flurry of trading in Tapin shares.

The Northern Miner reported the drill results, but noted that core recovery was poor, with only sludge material available for assay in some sections. "Sludge assays are not regarded as a true indication of the metal content," the reporter cautioned.

The high-grade results proved too tempting for major mining companies to ignore, however, and a day or so after they were released, Toronto-based Camflo Mines (a predecessor to Barrick Gold) agreed to buy 100,000 shares of Tapin at $3 per share, which was considered big money at the time. Camflo also obtained the right of first refusal on any future financings and agreed not to sell, transfer or otherwise assign the shares for a period of six months.

Tapin, in turn, agreed to hold the funds in trust for 30 days and promised to rescind the share purchase if the representations contained in the November statement of material facts, or in the statement made by company officials, were found to be "substantially incorrect."

Fortunately for Camflo, the deal blew up before any money changed hands. As part of its "due diligence" (technical and economic evaluation), the senior company wanted to test the other half of the core from the first two holes drilled on the property. But before it could do so, Tapin reported that the core had been stolen en route to Vancouver. "We do have a suspect," Saadien told The Miner at the time, though he did not provide any details.

VSE officials immediately suspended Tapin Copper and began investigating trading in the company's shares. In order to check the previously reported results, holes 1 and 2 were redrilled on the same inclination and bearing, with the work supervised by consultants retained by Camflo and the VSE. But, before results from that work were in hand, it was learned that holes 3, 4, 5 and 6 showed only trace amounts of gold and silver. A week or so later, the check holes produced similar results.

Camflo informed Tapin that it had no intention of proceeding with the share purchase and filed a claim for damages "relating to the circumstances under which the agreement was negotiated."

In January 1975, irate shareholders sued Tapin Copper, naming

Aronec, Saadien and Timmins, among others. The writ, filed in the Supreme Court of British Columbia, alleged that the defendants "fraudulently misrepresented and willfully failed to disclose or, in the alternative, negligently failed to disclose material facts relating to the affairs and business of the company." Even worse, it was alleged that "foreign substances had been added to the cores prior to those cores being sent [by Tapin] for assay [and] the said foreign substances materially affected the abilities of General Testing Laboratories [the assayer] to assay fully and accurately the said cores."

Talk on the street was that the salter's handy standby — placer gold, panned or concentrated from a small stream bed gravel bar — had been purchased from local miners and introduced into the original samples before assaying.

Trading in Tapin shares remained suspended while the commercial fraud section of the Royal Canadian Mounted Police and the British Columbia Securities Commission continued their investigations. But no one was ever prosecuted and Tapin ended up settling most of the claims filed against it out of court.

Dr. Joseph Montgomery, a geologist who worked on the case for the Vancouver Stock Exchange, said Timmins was "unfortunately caught up in the mess" when he incorporated the drill results in the updated report he was asked to provide Tapin. "He was chastised by the Engineering Society for not checking the work and that kind of thing, but I know he had absolutely nothing to do with the salting." Neither did Saadien, he added. "He was a director, and that's one of the problems. You can be a director of a company and somebody out in the field does something and you get tarred with it."

Tapin tried to resume business under a new board, but financings proved impossible as new claims surfaced and the unsettled claims exceeded the company's assets. By the end of March, 1977, the company threw in the towel, declaring bankruptcy and requesting a suspension from trading.

The Tapin Copper salting scam ended as most did in those days — out of sight and under the carpet. Aronec hung around a few months and then faded into oblivion somewhere in the Caribbean, though no one knows exactly where. "All I remember is that the guy disappeared, leaving a girlfriend behind," said George Cross, editor of a Vancouver-based stock market newsletter that bears his name. "She was quite annoyed because she thought she was part of the whole adventure."

Saadien went on to establish a name for himself by promoting the early mining deals of the rising star on the Vancouver scene,

Robert Friedland. And Timmins continued working as a geologist, ending up, a decade later, on the board of David Walsh's Bresea Resources.

A seed is planted

In the early 1980s, the Canadian mining industry was, for the most part, focused on domestic projects, but Bresea would soon become an exception. In 1983, just after launching the company, Walsh and fellow director, Michael Duggan, headed off to Sydney, Australia, where one of Duggan's companies had oil and gas interests in the Arafura Sea. They ended up at the home of Peter Howe, a mining engineer who founded the Toronto-based consulting firm A.C.A. Howe International and who now presides over Diadem Resources. Howe was well-known in the Australian mining scene and was a major booster of the Australian-led exploration boom that was beginning to pick up steam in Indonesia.

"I didn't know Walsh then, but I knew Mike Duggan," said Howe. "They were looking for oil and gas properties, so I invited them to dinner at my house. John Felderhof was there and, for some reason, when John said he was going back to Indonesia, Walsh said 'I'll come with you.' So off he went to Indonesia with John Felderhof, just like that."

Felderhof, then managing director of A.C.A. Howe Australia, made an obvious impression on Walsh. A short while later, Bresea retained the firm to select certain mineral rights for evaluation in Kalimantan. The first was an alluvial gold prospect with possible hard-rock potential.

"Bresea is the first Canadian junior resource company to make a mineral exploration commitment in Indonesia," Bre-X boasted in its 1984 annual report, adding that an Australian company had agreed to participate as an equal partner. "Your company's involvement in Southeast Asia should prove exciting, given the potential of Indonesia, and sets the tone for future prospects on an international level."

While Indonesia was a popular exploration destination for Australian juniors, the country had little sex appeal for Canadian exploration companies. It did not take Walsh long to discover that alluvial (placer) projects were not viewed with much interest by mining analysts. It was too difficult to prove up resources and, unless tightly supervised, too easy for the gold to be stolen once operations got under way.

Most placer mines in Alaska and the Yukon Territory are small, mom-and-pop operations, but those with employees typically have armed security to prevent theft because the gold, which may include some tempting nuggets, is produced on-site using mechanical recovery systems. Analysts knew that if security was a minor problem in North America, it would be a major one in foreign countries. And no one could picture David Walsh riding shotgun over an Indonesian placer dredge, making sure everything was on the up-and-up.

Home-grown gold rush and a market crash

By the summer of 1985, the Indonesian project was overshadowed by an interesting and potentially more lucrative opportunity close to home. A gold discovery made in Quebec's Casa Berardi district by partners Inco Ltd. and Golden Knight Resources had sparked a huge staking rush. Hundreds of junior companies flocked to the region and scrambled to secure ground along the favorable geological structure known as the Casa Berardi Break. Latecomers made do with moose pasture.

Bresea quickly forgot about Indonesia and joined the rush to Casa Berardi, then Canada's hottest gold exploration area. The junior acquired 162 claims totalling 12,960 acres, covering geophysical anomalies believed to be prospective for deposits similar to those already found in the region.

The land package was acquired from Stan Hawkins and Peter Ferderber, the latter a well-known prospector from Val d'Or, Quebec. The introductions were made by Mike Duggan, who had done business with Hawkins in the past. It was a coming-home of sorts for Walsh and Duggan, both of whom were born and raised in Montreal.

The Casa Berardi gold rush prompted Walsh to form his second junior company, Ayrex Resources, which also obtained ground in the Casa Berardi camp. Bresea entered into a partnership with Ayrex, which pooled its claims with those owned by Bresea, thereby doubling the size of the land package. Each company held an equal interest in the joint venture.

Barry Tannock, Stan Hawkins' cousin, joined Ayrex as president, while Walsh took the post of chairman. The junior obtained its listing on the Alberta Stock Exchange in early 1986, which was a good time for a junior company to be alive in Canada. "Mike [Duggan] and I took half the issue," Hawkins said. "I did it just for a trade but, at the end of the year, I ended up with more stock than I started with."

David Walsh's two juniors were not handicapped by having mineral prospects that were still in the early stages of exploration. A good address in the Casa Berardi camp was worth far more than pie-in-the-sky in the jungles of a foreign land. Bresea was so encouraged by the good times in Canada that it opted not to budget funds for exploration in Indonesia in 1986, though it continued to monitor activity in the region.

"Our enviable land position in the Casa Berardi area ... and the work involved will keep [us] more than occupied during the course of the year," Walsh told shareholders.

Bresea even got some attention from mining analysts. Murray McInnis, who worked in the Vancouver office of Osler Inc., reviewed Bresea's exploration plans for 1986 and noted that 10 drill targets had been outlined. He wrote that Bresea was a "valid speculation for those interested in participating in the Casa Berardi play."

Things were finally looking up for David Walsh. Mineral exploration was booming, largely because of "flow-through financing," a government program that provided tax incentives to individuals investing in mineral exploration. It was one of the few times in Canadian mining history that the amount of money available for exploration greatly exceeded the number of quality properties. The winds of good fortune blew so strong for juniors that even the turkeys got off the ground.

In the fall of 1986, Bresea and Ayrex drilled 13 holes at their properties in the Casa Berardi camp. But, by year-end, they could report only minimal success.

Ayrex started looking for new projects and, later that year, signed an agreement to earn a 50% interest in a gold property held by Tandem Resources near Pickle Lake, Ontario. The Frond Lake project, as it was known, even had a small, near-surface resource of 300,000 tons grading 0.22 oz. of gold per ton.

Ayrex traded shares for the asset, though it failed to blossom into anything more substantial as work progressed. Later, when Walsh wanted to consolidate his stock, he made a deal with Hawkins to trade his Ayrex shares for those of Bresea. Hawkins acquired enough Ayrex shares in the process to take control of the junior. Bresea, meanwhile, took part in an exploration effort to find deposits containing platinum group elements in the Labrador Trough, again with little success.

In October 1987, a market crash killed off the flow-through-share-funded exploration boom. The bull market that had propelled the share prices of junior companies into the stratosphere crashed back to earth. Overnight, mining executives saw the market capitalization of their companies quartered, halved, or worse. It was a bloodbath that surprised even mining veterans. Hit hard by the market crash, and with only a few sniffs of gold to show for their Casa Berardi drill program, Walsh and Bresea were back to square one.

Goodbye, Howe Street — Hello, Montreal

Life was tough for all junior companies after the market crash in October 1987, and tougher still for those listed on the Vancouver Stock Exchange. Various promotional and spending excesses from the flow-through years were coming to light, and regulators were clamping down and making efforts to reverse the exchange's image as the scam capital of the world, an image it did not entirely deserve.

Vancouver-listed juniors seeking funds for exploration also felt they were at the mercy of Peter Brown's Canarim Investment, a brokerage firm that had a near-monopoly on underwritings and financings at the time. Mining executives often complained of Canarim's "my way or the highway" approach to doing business and, from several accounts, it appears David Walsh was one of them.

"He didn't like the attitude out west," said Stan Hawkins. "I know he was very upset about being in Vancouver at that time, because the guys out there were doing this and that and whatever to him. So he applied for a listing on Montreal."

Hawkins does not recall the circumstances that prompted Walsh's decision to withdraw from the Vancouver scene. "I just know he wasn't happy and felt that he wasn't getting the proper treatment."

Walsh applied to list Bresea in Montreal but was initially turned down. While still in his hometown, he called Hawkins and told him that the exchange would not list Bresea unless the company had a professional engineer, or someone with mining experience, on the board. "He asked if I would go on the board for him, and I said 'Sure,'" Hawkins said, adding that, by this point, his own junior company, Tandem, had been listed on Montreal for several years. "They knew me out there."

Bresea obtained its listing on the Montreal Exchange on November 30, 1987. Walsh promptly set about re-establishing ties with the Montreal brokerage community, where he still had some good connections. Shortly thereafter, Bresea got its shares listed on the over-the-counter market in the United States, thereby opening up a broader base of potential investors.

Bre-X and diamonds

David Walsh founded Bre-X Minerals, which he listed on the Alberta Exchange in July 1989. The initial board included Walsh and his wife, Jeannette, William Timmins and Montreal lawyer Joel King. The underwriter was Yorkton Securities.

The junior began operations by acquiring a 100% interest in two claim blocks in the Contwoyto-Back River area of Canada's Northwest Territories, some 80 miles from the producing Lupin gold mine operated by Echo Bay Mines. The properties were acquired with the help of Walsh's long-time friend, Mike Duggan.

After an initial public financing of $300,000, Bre-X began exploring the gold prospect. It also acquired another gold project in northwestern Quebec and flirted with the idea of taking on some old gold mines of dubious quality in Arizona. No results of any substance came from any of the projects, which soon withered on the vine. Memories of the 1987 market crash were still fresh, and investors had little interest in bottom-of-the-line juniors.

In Bre-X's 1990 annual report, Walsh complained of the lack of investor interest. "Instead of earning the checkered flag, 1990 turned out to be a checkered year," he wrote, after noting that, despite healthy gold prices, junior resource stocks were off by more than 30% that year. "This poor reception by investors is rather surprising."

Walsh rode out part of the industry slump by knocking back drinks at the Three Green Horns bar, along with other down-and-out promoters. The "poor reception by investors" also brought financial woes to the Walsh household. Times were so tough that Walsh helped himself to about $40,000 from the sale of shares mistakenly credited to his account by a broker at RBC Dominion. The firm realized its mistake, sued Walsh when he refused to return the money, and won its case. Walsh later told Brian Hutchinson of *Canadian Business* that his "priorities" in those days did not include "worrying about bank statements when you are putting out fires running a junior resource company."

Fortunately for Bre-X, and for many equally moribund juniors, a fiercely determined geologist named Charles Fipke made an important diamond discovery in the Lac de Gras region of the Northwest Territories. The discovery, made in 1991, resulted from a decade-long prospecting expedition in which Fipke traced trains of indicator minerals associated with diamondiferous kimberlites across half the western Territories. It was a remarkable accomplishment given Fipke's shoestring budget and the harsh working conditions, which, in any given day, could include being eaten alive by swarms of black flies and mosquitoes, run-ins with wolverines and barren-ground grizzlies, and sudden snow storms.

Fipke's discovery triggered a staking rush, one of the largest in Canada's history. By the time it was over, much of the territory north of Yellowknife was blanketed by claims.

The ever-ready Walsh joined the rush. He knew nothing about diamonds, but neither did most of the mining executives who dropped gold and base-metals projects to head north and join the search for precious stones. A few non-resource companies even got into the act, which led to jokes about what was really going on at claims acquired by a Vancouver-listed junior called Lifestyle Adjustable Beds.

Before long, everyone had found "circular bull's-eye anomalies," which they hoped were circular kimberlite pipes loaded with diamonds. But most of the anomalies proved to be duds, and the drills produced no kimberlite, let alone diamonds. But Fipke's Dia Met Minerals found enough kimberlites with diamonds to keep excitement alive, as well as a deep-pocketed partner in Australia's BHP Minerals. Before long, other majors, including diamond giant De Beers Consolidated Mines, began looking to pick up ground held by the junior companies.

At first, Bre-X looked as though it might be one of the lucky ones. Not long after getting into the diamond scene, Walsh announced that his company had formed a joint venture with Kennecott Canada, a subsidiary of RTZ, one of the world's largest mining groups. In March 1993, Bre-X's consulting geologist, Kevin Waddell, told the company that "indicator minerals have been recovered on and near the Bre-X property, which suggests source areas for the discovery of kimberlite pipes nearby."

It was a badly needed reprieve for Bre-X, but only a brief one. Kennecott carried out a work program, but results were not all that encouraging. The major maintained the option with Bre-X, but its attention was being diverted to claims closer to the Dia Met discovery.

Barry Tannock said Bre-X's diamond story eventually "petered out," which left Walsh scrambling to find a new story. "He knew he needed something and was thinking and looking around, and then he remembered John Felderhof. He had been impressed by him, and thought gold sounded pretty good, so he tracked him down on the phone and arranged a meeting."

Chapter Two:
THE SEEDS OF DISCONTENT

All work is as seed sown;
it grows and spreads, and sows itself anew.
Thomas Carlyle

Third white man up the Fly River

Two different men must be at war inside John Bernard Felderhof — the man he was in Canada and the man he became in Southeast Asia. For there is no other way to reconcile the dichotomous accounts of those who knew only one or the other. But these same accounts show that both were driven by the desire to achieve, to be noticed, to leave a mark on the world.

This determination could be inherent, or it could stem from the fact that John Felderhof was one of twelve children born to parents who had high expectations for their offspring. Then again, it could have its roots in the Second World War, which swept across Holland, where Felderhof was born on July 28, 1940 — a war that interrupted his childhood and stole his parent's time and attention.

In 1954, the Felderhof family immigrated to Nova Scotia, where John's father, a doctor, set up practice. The family first lived in an old farmhouse in a rural area outside Belmont, a small crossroads near Truro. Later, they settled in Pictou County, which remains the family seat today.

John Felderhof graduated from Dalhousie University in Halifax in 1962 with a bachelor of science degree in economic and structural geology. His university friends say he was a solid student, more average than brilliant. He was likable, and girls found him attractive. And he had little trouble finding summer work, owing to his energetic, gung-ho attitude.

"John impressed people because he loved geology and loved

being out in the field," said William Burton, a Maritimer who studied geology at Dalhousie with John's twin brothers, William and Herman. William became a mining stock promoter; Herman later became a lawyer and the lead prosecutor in the Westray trial, which focused on a mine disaster in Nova Scotia where, in May 1992, twenty-six miners were killed by an underground explosion. "They came from a good family and had a good upbringing," Burton said of the Felderhof clan. "Most of them became professionals — doctors and lawyers and the like — and did well for themselves."

In April 1963, after graduating, Felderhof was hired as an open-pit engineer by Iron Ore Company of Canada (which was later headed by Brian Mulroney, before he became Canada's 18th prime minister). Several other Dalhousie graduates joined him at the isolated site in Schefferville, Quebec, where they conspired to keep each other entertained to ward off cabin fever. "It was like being at war," said one. "We formed strong friendships. Our common bond was that we all hated the company."

Felderhof enjoyed his work more than most, but wanderlust soon took hold of the young geologist. In the summer of 1964, he headed off to Zambia, where he worked as a mine geologist. While in Africa, he met and married Denise, a South African girl. In the summer of 1967, he decided to move on yet again. He joined Kennecott Copper and started work as an exploration geologist in the remote rain forests of Papua New Guinea.

John Felderhof has often said he was "the third white man up the Fly River" of Papua New Guinea, right behind two missionaries. The story has the ring of truth, for only missionaries and prospectors are foolhardy enough to venture into the unknown to advance their respective quests for souls and gold.

Whether third or fifth is inconsequential, for Felderhof was one of the first Caucasians to follow the Fly River to its headwaters in the rugged and remote Star Mountains, a few miles from the Indonesian border. It was here that he first felt the rush of excitement that overcomes geologists when they are hot on the trail of a mineral find. And it was here that he tasted success by helping discover the huge Ok Tedi copper deposit.

An official account of the discovery, written by Robert Bamford and published in a 1972 issue of *Economic Geology* (the scholarly journal that is the bible of applied geology), describes how Felderhof and fellow geologist Douglas Fishburn traced a train of mineralized boulders to the discovery outcrop in early 1968. But several recent books fail to mention Felderhof at all, which surprised Gerry Rayner, a Canadian geologist who managed the initial exploration program for Kennecott.

"John worked for me and was definitely one of the people involved in the discovery," Rayner said. "He was an excellent geologist and I would certainly stand for his character, though I have barely seen him since."

Getting near Mt. Fubilan (as Ok Tedi was originally known) was a feat in itself. The trip entailed a 575-mile-long boat ride from the mouth of the Fly River to Kiunga, followed by an additional 65 miles by fixed-wing aircraft and helicopter to the project site. The exploration team, a hardy group of bush rats, lived at a base camp in the jungle.

"We [Kennecott] went in to do stream-sediment sampling on a lease we had taken up and basically found the deposit from float (mineralized boulders) in the river," Rayner explained. "We were seeing enough magnetite and copper-bearing float downstream to know that we had a significant deposit up there somewhere."

Rayner said Felderhof was one of two geologists running that phase of the exploration program. The other was Fishburn. The two-man team traced the float 14 miles up river to the discovery site, where elevations ranged from 5,000 to 7,000 ft. Exploring in the region was no picnic, he added. "The weather was so bad in that part of world that there were no air photos and, consequently, no topographic maps. That was our main handicap."

Another was the relentless, heavy rain.

"Four hundred inches every year," Rayner moaned. "Any time you didn't get an inch of rain for a few days you started to worry because you knew you had to catch up [the next day]."

The initial fieldwork focused on testing rich mineralization in skarns on the lower flanks of Mt. Fubilan. Skarn, a rock formed when granitic magma reacts with carbonate rocks, often occurs on the flanks of large porphyry-copper deposits. Porphyry denotes any igneous rock that contains distinct crystals imbedded in a much finer-grained groundmass.

Dr. Robert Jones, then a senior geologist with Kennecott, said clouds always hung over the higher parts of the mountain, concealing its secrets.

"Then one day they lifted, revealing a giant red thumbprint with no trees on it, up the mountain," Jones said.

What the exploration team saw was a giant kill zone — an area where the mineralization was so rich it poisoned the vegetation, stunting or killing it — covering the main body of the Ok Tedi deposit.

It was an exciting moment, Rayner recalled. "The first three people who actually landed on an exposure [of the deposit] were Felderhof, Fishburn and a field assistant."

The prospecting excitement continued into 1969, when the first

Huts on muddy hillsides near the Mt. Muro mine in Kalimantan.

core hole drilled into the main deposit hit high-grade copper mineralization. But despite this impressive start, the project experienced various problems on the road to production. Some of these were technical (for example, someone forgot to have the cores assayed for gold and, consequently, no one knew the deposit had a gold-rich cap); others had to do with external events that came into play involving both Kennecott and the government of Papua New Guinea.

Kennecott's initial field program at Ok Tedi lasted two years and involved 100,000 ft. of drilling. This work proved up 137 million tons grading 0.88% copper, plus 0.02 oz. of gold per ton — respectable figures by any measure.

Felderhof left the project in April 1970. His name was almost forgotten when Charles Fipke (the man who went on to discover diamonds in Canada's North) worked at Ok Tedi a year or so later. "I don't remember his name ever coming up," Fipke said. "We were told Fishburn had made the find."

Peter Howe, now president of Diadem Resources, says Felderhof was presented a medal by Kennecott for his role in the discovery. William Burton, while not part of the discovery team, later worked with Fishburn and heard a firsthand account of the find. "Doug [Fishburn] would say John was as instrumental as he was," he said.

Felderhof caught malaria and otherwise paid his dues in the jungles of New Guinea. But he emerged as the co-discoverer of the Ok Tedi copper deposit, one of the most significant finds of its day. Standing atop the deposit at Mt. Fubilan was his finest moment. From that mountaintop, it would be downhill all the way.

Life Down Under

As a married man with children, John Felderhof grew tired of living in the jungle and left Kennecott shortly after Ok Tedi was discovered. He moved to Australia and, in April 1972, joined a small group of geologists hired to explore for uranium in the northeastern state of Queensland. The exploration team, which included Canadian geologist Randy Turner, shared the top floor of an old hotel in Cooktown, a village near Cairns best known as the godforsaken place where Capt. James Cook ran aground with the ship *Endeavour* in 1770.

Each day, the geologists were split into two-man parties and dropped off in the dense forest by a helicopter dubbed "Easy Rider," and then picked up at day's end.

"We all had nicknames," Turner recalled. "John's was the 'Jolly Green Giant,' because he wore green shirts all the time and was hard to see in the bush. He would call the pilot down with a walkie-talkie, yelling 'ho-ho-ho' with his thick Dutch accent. He was a bit of a string bean at the time because of the malaria he'd picked up in New Guinea."

Geologists working in jungle camps are vulnerable to malaria, which is transmitted to humans by female *Anopheles* mosquitoes, which bite between dawn and dusk. The disease is characterized by fever and flu-like symptoms but is rarely fatal if treated promptly. Anti-malarial medications are commonly used, but do not prevent all infections. There are side effects too, which one geologist jokingly likened to having premenstrual syndrome. "It makes me bitchy and all emotional, if you know what I mean." This was one geologist who found the cure worse than the disease, and preferred to rely on bug repellent rather than use any of the nasty drugs that brought out the worst of his feminine side.

While in Australia, Felderhof was still experiencing occasional relapses of malaria, but these did not appear to affect his work. "John was high-strung, almost hyperactive," Turner said. "But he was technically skilled, a quick study and very hard-working."

At night, the geologists would relax in the local pub. Felderhof chain-smoked and, on occasion, indulged in his favorite meal of steak tartare topped with a raw egg. But he ignored all warnings to avoid alcohol — advice given to most malaria patients as the disease sometimes weakens the liver.

One evening, Turner found a glum-looking Felderhof drinking heavily in the bar. The men had just returned from a prospecting expedition where they had spotted an interesting-looking stained outcrop that appeared prospective for copper.

"John was saying things like, 'I found that thing today,' and 'they are not going to take it away from me this time,'" Turner said. "I didn't know what the fuss was about because it was just a showing. But he started to cry, and the more he drank, the more he cried. He was upset about Ok Tedi."

Felderhof told Turner that he had spotted the first discovery at Ok Tedi, only to have Fishburn's role played up more than his. He blamed the bigwigs at Kennecott for being sentimental and putting the limelight on Fishburn because his former colleague had been the sole survivor of a helicopter accident that killed several Kennecott geologists.

"In John's mind, Ok Tedi was his find," Turner said. "He was bitter that he had to share the credit."

Felderhof and Turner went their separate ways when the uranium exploration project came to an end. Felderhof joined his family in the small town of Atherton. He had little luck finding work and, for a spell, drove a taxicab to earn a living. It was honest labor, but a depressing turn of events for a proud man who, only a few years earlier, had co-discovered one of the largest copper deposits in the world.

Soon afterwards, Felderhof packed up his family and returned to Canada. In 1974, he found exploration-related work by signing on for a temporary assignment with Peter Howe's consulting firm in Toronto.

"I hired him for a summer job in New Brunswick," Howe said. "I don't know how the subject came up, but we also discussed the possibility that if we liked each other, he could open an office [for us] in Johannesburg."

Felderhof proved to be a "very good geologist," Howe adds, which led to the decision to open an office in South Africa as promised. Felderhof's wife, Denise, was sent on ahead to set up house, but it was to be a short stint. In 1979, Howe transferred John Felderhof to Australia and hired John's brother, William, to take over the office in Johannesburg.

John probably did not know it at the time, but he would soon be back in the jungle, fighting off snakes, hostile locals and malaria.

Historic footprints

A geologist is part scientist and part adventurer, which explains why so many spend most of their careers far from home. A geologist is a historian too, for much of his work is aimed at testing, with modern methods, areas previously explored for gold, silver and other valuable metals and minerals.

The first foreign geologists to venture into Indonesia simply followed in the footsteps of the native explorers who preceded them. Fortunately, there were plenty of footprints to trace, as gold and silver had been worked there for more than a thousand years by the native population, as well as by Chinese and Indian immigrants. Production came mostly from small alluvial operations, and from vein systems which outcropped on surface.

The Chinese, in particular, mined and traded gold from Borneo as far back as the fourth century. The trade became so lucrative that, in the seventeenth century, a Chinese emperor sent out a general to unite the Chinese workers into groups (or "Kongsies"), originally to improve efficiency, but also for mutual protection against Malay chieftains and the local Dayak tribesmen.

Over time, three great Kongsies developed and began to dominate local peoples. In 1850, the Dutch government decided to break them down, and did so in less than five years. British and Dutch firms attempted to fill the void left by the Chinese, but few were successful in the inhospitable Borneo climate. While the primary gold deposits remained elusive, the search for other mineral wealth did result in some tin and diamond production dating back to the eighteenth century.

The foundation of Indonesia's present-day mining industry was laid by the Dutch, who carried out extensive exploration and development between the 1890s and 1930s. During this period, Indonesia, then known as the Dutch East Indies, became the world's second-largest producer of tin, as well as an exporter of small amounts of gold, silver, nickel, bauxite and coal.

Some geological mapping was carried out by the Dutch, but the initial maps were large-scale and patchy. More detailed data were compiled between 1935 and 1939 — most of it gleaned by Dr. R.W. Van Bemmelen and included in his book, *The Geology of Indonesia*, published in 1949.

The ravages of the Second World War and the post-war independence movement left the mining industry in a shambles.

Achmed Sukarno (1901-1970), the nation's first president after independence, was both left-wing and anti-imperialist. He fancied himself a socialist revolutionary and showed little interest in the economy, except as a tool for his political ends. Debt and inflation soared. Most foreign enterprises were nationalized during the period between 1957 and 1960, and, by 1966, production for most minerals had fallen to below pre-war levels.

The Sukarno era came to an end in early October 1965, when

Major General Suharto (born 1921) assumed control of the army and launched a *coup d'état*. Real and suspected communists were hunted down and, more often than not, killed. Civilian vigilantes and religious extremists used the occasion to wreak some murderous havoc of their own. The fiercely territorial Dayaks also got into the act, by driving the already persecuted Chinese from rural areas.

Suharto wrested political control from Sukarno in early 1966. A year later he was named acting president. After he was officially sworn in in 1968, Suharto launched his "New Order" government, which focused on national unity, economic growth and political stability.

Consolidating power was not easy, as Indonesia is made up of more than 13,000 islands (only half of which are inhabited) stretching more than 5,000 km from east to west. The present-day population of about 190 million is racially and religiously diverse. Suharto's solution to national unity was simple, and similar to that used by the last czars of Russia: He would be a strict but benevolent father to those who behaved; anyone who fell out of line would be dealt with harshly. This paternalistic policy was effective in the early years of the Suharto regime, when the population was rural, poor and uneducated; it has proved woefully outdated and inadequate in today's modern, industrial society.

Immediately after seizing power, Suharto and a small group of technocrats carried out sweeping changes to the nation's economy, including a foreign capital investment law and a revision of the Mining Law in 1967 so as to allow foreign investment.

The first wave of foreign companies was primarily interested in mineral prospects and districts identified by the Dutch. The government at first put some of the better projects out to tender. Later, huge tracts of ground were opened up for exploration under the contract of work (CoW) system, which was based on the model used for contracts with oil companies.

Since Indonesia issued its first contract of work in 1967, the government has periodically revised the general terms of the contract without altering the terms of the existing ones. Each revision, or "generation," has slightly different terms. Contracts of work are therefore often identified by generation as a guide to the provisions under which they operate.

"I think it is a brilliant concept," said Peter Howe, one of the first Westerners to venture into the country after the system was developed. "The basic theory was that the mineral resources belonged to the Indonesian people but that foreigners could come in, explore for and mine the minerals. What you did was sign a contract that laid out for you all the terms, including taxes, rents, royalties and so on. Unlike many other countries, where things change every few years, in Indonesia everything was spelled out for you."

In the early days of the CoW system, foreign companies understood that they had to divest their holdings over time in order to offer increased ownership to Indonesian partners and local investors. This policy helped ease nationalist hard-liners who resented foreign ownership of domestic resources.

"You had to offer 10 or 15 per cent, and in the next five years you had to divest 51 per cent," Howe explained. "It wasn't a gift. It had to be paid for either at book value or on the stock market. And it was supposed to be bought by private individuals and not the government, though not many individuals had that kind of money in those days. And there wasn't much of a stock market then either."

Michael Novotny, an Australian prospector who arrived in Indonesia before Howe, said the earliest generations of CoWs were relatively unattractive. "No one was interested. But by going in early, I learned the language, got to know the Indonesian people and came to understand their pragmatism."

Enter Freeport

Another pioneer in Indonesia was Freeport Sulphur, predecessor of Freeport-McMoRan Inc., the American resource company that, much later, would be the undoing of David Walsh and John Felderhof. That story begins in the mountains of Irian Jaya and neighboring Papua New Guinea, where, many millions of years ago, the Pacific and Australian tectonic plates collided, leaving behind prime hunting ground for huge deposits of copper and gold.

The first mining men to venture into this diabolically inaccessible region came face-to-face with the Stone Age — fierce, primitive Melanesian (not Asiatic) societies in which headhunting and cannibalism were practised, where territorial and tribal rivalries were intense, where women went topless and men sported the "koteka" penis gourd. Even today, many geologists are hesitant to explore the coastal rainforests of New Guinea where the most virulent forms of malaria are found, including the dreaded cerebral variety, which is often fatal. Malaria is less of a risk in the highlands, yet the locals there are inclined to be even more hostile to foreign intruders.

In 1936, a Dutch geologist-mountaineer named Jacques Dozy made his way to the snow-covered mountains of New Guinea (as Irian Jaya was then known) and discovered the copper deposit known as Ertsberg, which, loosely translated, means "ore mountain." The orebody formed a spectacular outcrop in glaciated terrain at an altitude of 3,600 metres (11,800 ft.).

Dozy reported on his trip in 1939, and included a brief reference to the Ertsberg showing, noting its high copper content and traces of gold. But the report's contents were overshadowed by the outbreak of the Second World War. The document sat unnoticed until 1950, when a geologist came across it during a literature search for nickel in Irian Jaya. As the story goes, the geologist was not particularly interested in Ertsberg but took the routine precaution of applying for an exploration concession.

A few weeks later, excerpts of the report found their way into the hands of Forbes Wilson, manager of nickel exploration for Freeport Sulphur, who was immediately intrigued. Wilson, accompanied by several others, mounted an expedition to sample Ertsberg, and about 30 years later wrote a fascinating account of the adventure under the title *The Conquest of Copper Mountain.*

Results of the investigations surpassed all expectations, showing Ertsberg to be the world's largest above-ground outcrop of copper ore. Wilson recommended that Freeport immediately carry out further studies of the deposit, but technical and political obstacles rendered this impossible. Seven years passed before a detailed evaluation was finally launched.

By 1969, a helicopter-supported drilling program had outlined 33 million tonnes grading 2.5% copper and 0.75 gram gold per tonne, and a preliminary feasibility study had been completed at a cost of US$7.5 million.

Construction of an open-pit mine — named Gunung Biji, the Indonesian name for Ertsberg — was built in 1970, and production followed two years later.

More exploration drilling in 1975 led to the discovery of a second major deposit, named Ertsberg East, about a kilometre east of the original discovery. The area had been identified as a promising prospect during the 1960 expedition, when the presence of a malachite-stained limestone cliff was noted. (Malachite is a greenish form of oxidized copper that some children have been known to "create" by soaking copper pennies in water and allowing them to rust.)

Over the next few years, a drilling program outlined the deposit and led to the discovery of two new deposits below Ertsberg East, and a third, situated a short distance to the south.

Production at Ertsberg East began in 1980. Then came Grasberg, an even more exciting discovery a few kilometres from the original Ertsberg mine. The area had been noticed by Dozy, who named it "Grass Mountain," after recording a "rather smooth, grass-covered mountain, which forms a striking morphological element amidst the limestone mountains."

Dozy's report contained important clues about the presence of copper-bearing mineralization at Grasberg. But when Freeport sent geologists to investigate the occurrence in the mid-1970s, the copper values proved disappointing. The outcrop samples did yield significant traces of gold, but, as prices for the metal were low at the time, mining companies paid little attention. And given that several new deposits at Ertsberg were known to have higher copper grades and more favorable locations, Grasberg was placed on the back burner.

In the mid-1980s, when gold prices soared and the precious metal became a commodity worth pursuing, the outcrops at Grasberg were re-examined by Freeport's geologists. On the basis of the new data, drilling was carried out to test the near-surface gold potential. The first hole, drilled in early 1988, intersected a truly impressive 600 metres averaging 1.05% copper and 1.49 grams of gold per tonne. It was immediately recognized as a bonanza discovery and, within two years, production was under way.

Today, Grasberg has immense reserves and spectacular exploration potential. But, unlike Busang, Grasberg's reserves and resources took many years and many millions of dollars to define and develop.

The 1980s gold rush

The 1980s gold rush into Indonesia had its origin in the mid-1970s, when the Kelian gold deposit was discovered in the foothills of the central Kalimantan Mountains, just 3 km south of the equator. The project was explored and developed by the Australian mining giant CRA (now joined with RTZ in the Rio Tinto colossus).

As is the case with most gold deposits in Indonesia, Kelian was actually "discovered" much earlier — in 1947, to be precise, by local Dayaks. More than 1,000 people mined alluvial gold there until about 1963. A second invasion of up to 10,000 artisanal miners occurred in the late 1970s after the primary source of the gold was identified by means of stream-sediment sampling. The stream sediments contained traces of gold and associated minerals which the exploration team traced back to the lode source.

The first phase of exploration at Kelian, which took place between 1976 and 1979, was generally disappointing. Scout drilling yielded grades in the range of only 2 grams per tonne, which is a marginal grade for any open-pit operation when gold prices are weak.

Exploration was halted, though it resumed a year or two later, fuelled by a rise in gold prices and a re-interpretation of the geology. Grades were still in the range of 2 grams, but a sizable resource in the order of 20 to 30 million tonnes was outlined and a CoW was applied for. Kelian was a promising-looking gold deposit, but not yet a mine, when junior companies began flocking to Kalimantan in hopes of making similar discoveries.

The Godfather, Peter Howe

Mt. Muro was one of several exploration projects managed by A.C.A. Howe on behalf of a joint venture between Australian juniors Jason Mining and Pelsart Resources. Unfortunately, Jason lost its stake in Mt. Muro, along with its other gold finds, for reasons that included bad business decisions and the 1987 market crash. Jason also failed miserably as an operator, losing millions on alluvial operations in Kalimantan and Sumatra. But this was not uncommon, as few juniors survive the perils associated with making the transition from exploration to production. More often than not, the senior partners ended up with the gold while the juniors got the shaft.

Working in Indonesia was a coming home of sorts for Peter Howe, who was born and spent his childhood years there with his English father, who worked as a tea merchant, and his Australian mother. At the age of six, Peter was shipped off to England for his elementary schooling. His middle-school years were spent in Australia, and then it was back to England where he attended the Royal School of Mines (part of the University of London).

Howe graduated as a mining engineer in 1949 at the age of 20. His first mining stint was in Southern Rhodesia, where he spent about four years. There, he developed the aura (which he retains today) of the quintessential Englishman who goes out in the midday sun. He then went on to manage a few gold mines in Saudi Arabia before coming to Canada. He formed his consulting firm in 1960, which was then a one-man show based in Toronto. He incorporated the firm a few years later and, by 1969, was doing well enough to open an office in Sydney, Australia. There, he and Tony Gray, a lawyer, co-founded a company called Pancontinental Mining. Says Howe: "One of our big successes was the Jabiluka I uranium deposit, which Howe International found for Pancontinental, with the work financed by Getty Oil."

Unfortunately, for all concerned, the first ore reserves at Jabiluka were announced in 1972 — the same year that the Labour government under the autocratic Edward Gough Whitlam came into power and banned uranium mining. "We closed up shop until they were kicked out," Howe said. "Once they were gone, I moved my family up and reopened the office."

Until this point, Howe's involvement with Indonesia had been limited to a visit to Irian Jaya in 1970 for the purpose of looking at

Mining Consultant Peter Howe was a major booster of the Australian-led exploration boom in Indonesia in the early 1980s.

some properties for one of his Canadian clients, Chemalloy. By the time he returned to reopen his Sydney office in 1978, the properties had been farmed out to a local company, Jimberlana Minerals.

Asked to become involved in that project, Howe saw potential for even more business in Indonesia, which led to a decision to open an office in Jakarta.

"We hired local people from Irian Jaya to work on the project," he said. "The geologist we hired to run it was Jonathan Nassey. That's how he came into the picture."

Nassey was brought up in Indonesia by missionaries, who sent him to a Baptist University in the United States. His resumé does not name the institution from which he obtained his Bachelor of Science degree in 1973 and his subsequent Masters degree, but it does note that he obtained a doctorate in geology in 1988 from the University of Beverly Hills' School of Engineering, a now defunct diploma mill.

Nassey began his early career with Peter Howe and, just before joining Bre-X Minerals, worked for Inco at its huge nickel-mining complex on the island of Sulawesi. During the course of his career, he travelled around Southeast Asia and visited Freeport's Grasberg-Ertsberg operation, the Kelian gold mine, as well as mines owned by Benguet Corp. in the Philippines. Nassey's familiarity with his native country was a valuable asset to Howe as he set up shop in Jakarta. But Howe himself was a quick study and obtained one of the few third-generation CoW agreements ever signed by the government. As a result, he made important contacts in the mines ministry.

"People starting bringing properties to our office," Howe said. "As a consequence of this, I met [Australian prospector] Mike Novotny, who had acquired a number of properties in Indonesia, mostly in Kalimantan."

Novotny told Howe that he needed financing and, perhaps, a joint-venture partner for some properties held by Pelsart, a company then owned by flamboyant Australian entrepreneur Kevin Parry. The day-to-day business was carried out by Novotny, as Parry had other business and personal interests that vied for his time and money. "Mike pretty much ran Pelsart in those days," Howe recalled.

With things heating up in Indonesia, Howe decided to enlist the help of John Felderhof, who was known to have considerable skills as a field geologist. If his star employee had misgivings about returning to the jungle in the early 1980s, Howe was not aware of them.

"John tramped the bush with Mike Novotny, looking at all these properties and selected six of twelve that looked good," Howe said. "A joint venture was set up between our client, Jason Mining, and Pelsart."

At the time, Jason was in the process of acquiring a public listing. Its chairman, Robin Carey, was a retired lawyer; Peter Howe, who by this point had become better known as a promoter than an engineer, became managing director; Felderhof was chief geologist.

Jason was floated on the Brisbane Stock Exchange in the summer of 1984 on a portfolio of Australian and Indonesian gold prospects, assets put together by A.C.A. Howe International. A total of 16 million shares was offered at 20¢ each. But markets were weak and the public subscribed to only 14.1 million shares.

"We [Jason] raised about $3 million as a result of that [offering] and explored those properties with Pelsart," Howe said.

The properties were acquired from Indonesian landowners and prospectors, who stayed on as local partners. During this period, Howe and Felderhof met Haji Syakerani, a politically connected businessman, who later became one of Bre-X's Indonesian partners at Busang.

The field work was shared by both companies. The key players on Jason's team were Felderhof and geologist Michael Bird, while Novotny and geologist Laurie Whitehouse represented Pelsart.

The foursome made up an interesting cast of characters.

Bird was an Australian who had been in Indonesia since 1965. He had previously worked for Kennecott in Australia. "He didn't exactly fit the company mold," said Dr. Robert Jones, a former colleague. "He was a bit of a will-o'-the-wisp who went native for a while before straightening himself out."

Bird learned the language and appeared to prefer the company of locals to that of Westerners. Prior to the Jason-Pelsart partner-

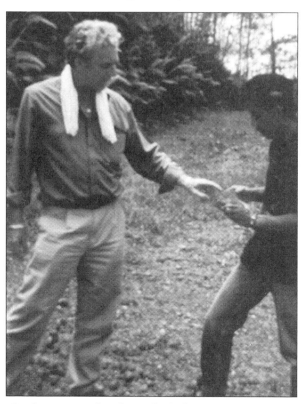

Geologist Michael Bird (left), an early colleague of John Felderhof in Indonesia and a bush mate of Michael de Guzman.

ship, he and Novotny had worked together in Australia for Tropic Endeavor, a somewhat promotional exploration venture.Whitehouse had also worked for Kennecott, spending a few years at the Ok Tedi project that Felderhof helped discover.

According to a number of his colleagues, Novotny has royal blood. The "Czech prince" (a deposed one, of course) found his way to Australia from Eastern Europe after the Second World War. He was the oldest of the group, multi-lingual, cultured and a great raconteur.

Novotny has high praise for Felderhof's skills as a field geologist, with one caveat: "He was a poor administrator — I made this criticism of him a long time ago."

Up to this point, mineral exploration in Indonesia had an unremarkable history. But the efforts of Jason and Pelsart attracted other Australian juniors and, before long, a frantic scramble for ground by local and foreign companies took place. By 1986, thirty-four CoWs had been signed, followed by a further sixty in 1987. Most of this ground was secured by juniors, signalling a major change in government policy. Until that time, previous contracts had been awarded almost exclusively to large international companies. The CoW system also was changed during this period. The new contracts were standardized, thus eliminating protracted negotiations, and companies were free to select the location and size of CoW areas, rather than having to apply for predetermined blocks of a specific size.

The Indonesian gold boom caused quite a stir Down Under and, before long, Australian newspapers were interviewing mining executives whose bullish sentiments raised expectations that new discoveries were to be had simply for the taking. The reality was much different, as the jungle vegetation masked outcrop and made exploration difficult and costly.

Nor was it easy to get around Kalimantan in those days. The road systems were poorly developed, though timber companies operating from the banks of the larger rivers were opening up the interior by building roads through the virgin jungle.

This network of timber-roads, combined with river systems, made it possible to conduct exploration by trail bikes, four-wheel-drive vehicles, speedboats and motorized sampans. To trek by foot to the more remote sites, a sturdy pair of boots was required. "It was the timber roads that led to the initial discovery of Mt. Muro, Muyup and Kasongan projects," Felderhof noted in a 1987 report.

Mt. Muro, by far the best of the lot, was optioned to Pennzoil, an oil company. "They spent something like $26 million drilling this thing, and Jason couldn't keep up with the expenditures, so we got diluted out," Howe explained. "Eventually, Pennzoil decided to leave Indonesia and sold its interest to Aurora, which operates the Mt. Muro mine today."

Howe says Felderhof deserves credit for the Mt. Muro discovery. "But I think Mike [Novotny] should get equal credit, because he identified the thing originally, while John was the one who said 'Let's go for it.' John was in charge of our office and in charge of exploration."

Another Felderhof find was Muyup, a gold project (now owned by Rio Tinto) which is believed to be an extension of the Kelian gold mine. In 1987 the project was being drilled by Jascan Resources (or Jason Canada, as it was then known). Jascan was headed by John Felderhof's brother, William, who worked with fellow Dalhousie graduate William Burton.

Both companies were promoted by T.C. Coombs of London, a speculative brokerage firm that raised funds for the Indonesian exploration boom, as well as for Jascan's North American properties. Jascan was eventually acquired by a North American company in a deal that provided shareholders with a respectable return on their investment.

Peter Howe credits John Felderhof with the discovery of the Mirah gold deposit in south-central Kalimantan, a project operated by Pelsart from its office in Jakarta.

"That one was found based on interpretation of airborne surveys and John's theory of fractures intersecting what came to be known as the gold belt of Kalimantan," he said. "It was about this time that Michael de Guzman was hired. He was a pleasant enough guy, though I never knew him well. But John had a high regard for his capabilities, and I relied on John's judgment that he was a good geologist." De Guzman also worked at Pelsart's Amphalit alluvial project, which is still producing placer gold today.

Pelsart eventually sold its interest in Mirah to a Chinese-Indonesian group, which took over Pelsart's role and became Jason's partner. "At this point, our client Jason was diluted out with a small interest," Howe said. "The Chinese group eventually acquired control of Pelsart from Kevin Parry, and they've been developing Mirah ever since. It has something in the order of a million ounces, though it is still not in production."

Felderhof had identified the Busang project as a prospective area, and a CoW application was made. But this effort came to naught as Jason was almost washed up at this point. The CoW was eventually acquired, but by an Australian junior other than Jason.

Howe said Novotny and Felderhof made other discoveries which were later acquired by Canadian juniors exploring in Kalimantan, and he believes these may shape up to be significant projects in the years ahead.

"Novotny identified a lot of them, but he was a draughtsman, not a geologist. John was the brains, the technological mind behind the development of these discoveries. He was the geologist, whereas Mike was the entrepreneurial mind who found the properties mainly because Indonesians were panning for gold in the area."

All the fuss about who discovered what and when is much ado about nothing, according to a number of geologists active in the country. One of them sniffed, "If you call going in where local miners are digging 'making a discovery,' I guess it's true, those guys did find mines."

Market crash blues

Peter Howe had been around the mining business long enough to know when the party is over. He returned to Canada, where an exploration boom, fuelled by flow-through financings, was in full force, well before the 1987 market crash brought activity in Indonesia to an abrupt end.

"By 1987, everyone had pulled out, and I don't think much happened after that," Howe said.

Maybe not for Howe. But John Felderhof complained to several friends that he was left holding the bag when Jason foundered and lost all his hard-won discoveries in Indonesia. He had suffered several more bouts of malaria, which gave rise to his oft-repeated claim that he'd had the disease "more often than most people have sex." Howe, meanwhile, had returned to Canada a wealthy man.

The Indonesian government, reacting to fears that foreign companies controlled some of the best mineral rights in the country, imposed a moratorium on new CoW applications in late 1987. The act was moot, as it was already impossible to raise money for exploration in the country.

The market crash of 1987 flattened most juniors, but the few dozen companies exploring in Indonesia were hit the hardest, recalls John Menzies, an Australian geologist who now heads up a Canadian junior. "The money literally disappeared. The ability of those small companies to explore in that part of the world evaporated and they all withdrew."

Australia also tightened up the rules of the game for junior companies. Contrary to published reports, it was not the promotional activities of Jason and Pelsart that triggered the first demands for new reporting standards for Australian-listed companies. Kevin Parry's downfall no doubt helped matters along, once shareholders learned their money had been used to pay for yachts and other extravagances.

"Kevin Parry may have contributed to it by his comments that Indonesia would become the world's second-largest gold producer," said geologist Theo van Leeuwen, a director of the Indonesian Mining Association. "But the Cambridge Group was — what's the right word — more promotional. They had the most ground and didn't find anything."

The call for reforms Down Under began in the early 1970s, after two high-flying juniors named Poseidon and Kathleen crashed and burned, bringing down several brokerage firms in the process. It was a huge scandal at the time as one of the juniors had calculated a uranium "deposit" with only a few samples and a pass of the scintillometer. It is said the grade was so high that company executives glowed in the dark. This industry crisis is well-documented in Trevor Sykes' book, *The Money Miners*. Ironically, representatives from the Canadian mining industry were engaged to help the Aussies clean up their act. In 1971, the Australasian Institute of Mining and Metallurgy established a committee to make recommendations on listing requirements for public mining companies, and, between 1972 and 1988, several reports with recommendations were issued. Nothing much was done until after the 1987 market crash, which provided the impetus for the guidelines to be incorporated into stock exchange listing rules. Since 1989, they have been expanded and upgraded further still.

While in Indonesia, Felderhof and his second wife, Ingrid, had their first child together. The baby was named John, even though Felderhof already had a son with that name from his earlier marriage. Some of Felderhof's friends were surprised by all this, while others were not. "Ego is the only reason for doing something like that," said a former colleague.

Friends say Felderhof's first marriage ended largely because of his absences and because the long-suffering Denise was too mild-mannered to exert much influence over her strong-willed husband. Ingrid, an Australian of Dutch descent, was vibrant and every inch her husband's equal in personality and will.

The couple met on a boat cruise in the Philippines. Felderhof was there on business and because his wife had sent him off to decide what he wanted to do about their failing marriage. Ingrid was there with her husband in a last-ditch effort to reconcile their rocky union. John made friends with the couple.

They met again, minus Ingrid's husband, after their respective marriages had fallen apart. Felderhof later told friends that Ingrid had called him first, but only she knows the real story. Men's versions of such events are not usually trustworthy.

"She was the best thing that ever happened to John," said Felderhof's former bush mate, Mike Novotny. "She had a good brain, and when things got tight she would get little businesses going, such as selling earrings, to help sustain the family. She is a very industrious person."

Ingrid's skill at managing household finances stood her in good stead as her husband's fortunes declined. While many of the geologists and prospectors from Pelsart and Jason "dabbled" in the stock market during the 1980s gold rush (including Felderhof who made, and then lost, a small fortune), none of them, with the exception of Peter Howe, was known to have made huge amounts of money. That would come much later in their respective careers, thanks largely to Bre-X.

Karpa Springs

Australian gold projects rarely make the front pages of *The Northern Miner*, but Karpa Springs enjoyed that distinction in July 1990 when Toronto-based Noranda announced it had bought into the exciting new discovery. And, with drill results that included 125 ft. averaging 0.65 oz. of gold per ton close to surface, who wouldn't get excited?

The initial discovery had been made by a team of Australian prospectors: brothers Robert and Dean Ireland and their partner, Clark Easterday. Mike Novotny heard of the fabulous results and became interested. "The prospectors told me they wanted to sell it for $6 million, but I didn't have that kind of money," he said.

Intrigued, Novotny sent his old friend Laurie Whitehouse to

examine the property. Whitehouse's geological report was enthusiastic, to say the least. Novotny agreed to take on the project and,
with partners Bill Galbraith and Geoff Stokes, formed a syndicate
called Icarus.

After the positive report was written, Australian junior Perilya
Mines called Novotny to express its interest in Karpa Springs.
"They told me, 'You beat us to it,' and asked if they could still par-
ticipate," Novotny recalled.

At the time, Perilya was acting as Noranda's exploration arm in
Australia. The major had kept Perilya alive after the 1987 market
crash by providing seed money for exploration. "They [Perilya]
would basically shake the bushes for us and serve as our arms and
legs in the exploration field," said Clarence Logan, Noranda's international exploration manager at the time.

Novotny agreed to sell the property for $10 million, $6 million of
which was allocated to the prospectors. The junior agreed, on the
condition that it be permitted to redrill the property to confirm the
results. In a bizarre twist, the prospectors were allowed on the
property when the six-hole drill program took place, though
Novotny says two Perilya geologists were there along with his people. "I was in charge of the program," he said. "Laurie was in
charge of the samples and splitting of the drill cuttings. But we
took all the necessary precautions."

The samples "ran," returning impressive gold grades. The discovery triggered a wave of euphoria, and comparisons were made
with the Hemlo gold deposits in northern Ontario. "You could see
the free gold," Novotny said.

Noranda agreed to acquire up to 70% of Perilya in a deal worth
$15 million, to be paid in stages. A toehold 30% interest was
acquired for $6 million, which Perilya, in turn, was to pay to the
prospectors through Novotny's syndicate.

When the deal was announced, Logan warned that "some caution must be read into the initial assay results until diamond
drilling could confirm the grades," as he had noted a problem with
coarse, visible gold from the drill holes that caused "nugget effect"
during assaying. (Nugget effect is the tendency for gold to be
unevenly distributed in a sample.)

Duly warned, Perilya performed some random checks on the
samples. The results did not mesh with those previously reported,
which made the company nervous. "There were all kinds of plausible explanations," Novotny said. "But the Perilya people said, 'we
want to see the rejects.'"

The prospectors balked and said they had completed their end
of the deal and demanded their $6 million before they would turn
over the keys to the warehouse where the rejects — crushed sam-

ple material in excess of what is needed for the assay process — were stored. The prospectors held the key to one lock while Novotny held the other. After the money was paid, the doors were opened. "There was nothing in the warehouse," Novotny said.

A few weeks later, a front-page story in *The Northern Miner* revealed that follow-up drilling had returned no gold and that the original samples had been salted — that is, gold had been introduced into them, resulting in phoney assays. The Canadian mining industry was aghast, and much fuss was made about the wild and woolly ways of the Australian miners. While some sympathy was expressed for Noranda, many said the company "was over 21" and should have known better than to buy a horse without checking its teeth and taking it for a run. An investigation was launched and the three prospectors were found guilty of fraud and served jail sentences. Noranda recovered most, but not all, of its money. A Noranda spokesman said "no smoking gun" could be found to link Novotny or Whitehouse directly to the fraud, though their lack of due diligence (technical and economic evaluation) and poor supervision of the drill program tarred their reputations in the Australian mining community. In the minds of many, Novotny's Icarus had flown too close to the sun and singed its wings.

The Karpa Springs scam was not terribly sophisticated, but major mining companies learned one important lesson from it: Do not, under any circumstances, pay a cent for a mineral property without conducting due diligence on the site.

The Minindo mess

In the early 1990s, when his former partner, Michael Novotny, was extricating himself from the Karpa Springs scandal, John Felderhof ran into serious problems of his own.

With work tough to find, and the raising of capital for exploration more difficult than ever in Australia, Felderhof headed back to Jakarta, where he teamed up with a colorful French-Canadian, Armand Beaudoin. How and why Beaudoin came to Indonesia is unclear, but the prospector-turned-property-dealer had been in the country about a decade prior to his meeting up with Felderhof. He was married to an Indonesian woman and had established some connections in the country's business community.

With sidekick Michael de Guzman brought in as chief geologist, Felderhof, Beaudoin and some high-profile Indonesians launched a new exploration vehicle known as PT Minindo Perkasasemesta.

Most of the properties were acquired from the Cambridge Group, an Australian company of dubious reputation that had folded in 1987 after the market crash. The Cambridge Group was related to the Independent Resources Group run by Malcolm "Jockey" Johnson, a colorful rogue who, before his empire imploded, dabbled in mining and oil-and-gas deals of questionable quality. Cambridge's Indonesian partner was Jusuf Merukh, a prominent businessman who retained his minority interest in the Contracts of Work after Minindo took over control.

The idea of creating an Indonesian-listed junior company to explore domestic properties found favor in high places, and the company was underwritten by a local bank and floated on the Indonesian stock exchange. Suharto's brother-in-law was on the board of directors, along with a military intelligence officer and a close relative of the mines minister.

Despite the high-profile board, Minindo went nowhere fast. It was under-subscribed, and serious problems emerged when it was found that the company had filed false reports to regulatory authorities.

Part of the problem for Felderhof, then general manager of Minindo, was that companies listed in Indonesia had to prove they could produce profits. Ostensibly, these were to come from a small, alluvial dredging operation in Sumatra, previously held by the Cambridge Group and now one of the main assets of Minindo. While the books showed that the project was making big profits, it was actually producing huge losses. Once Minindo's books were found to have been cooked, the underwriter was sanctioned, forced to buy back the shares, and take a huge loss on the deal. The stock was eventually de-listed.

"It was quite a big scam in Indonesia," said one foreign geologist working in the country at the time. An Indonesian mining executive said he noticed, in the prospectus, many glaring errors that he assumed everyone else would have noticed as well.

Indonesians hesitate to discuss the fiasco even today. "The First Lady's brother was in on this one," they whisper, as though Suharto's wife were somehow able to hear beyond the grave.

John Felderhof's name was tarnished by the whole episode and, to add insult to injury, he had not been paid in months. Since coming to Indonesia, he had been up and down like a yo-yo, and geology was starting to look as if it had been a bad career choice. De Guzman, or his Filipino assistant, geologist Cesar Puspos, had not been paid either. Armand Beaudoin's name was muddied too, and some say that, for a period after the Minindo blowup, a sign was posted in the mines ministry to the effect that he was "not to be served."

Felderhof moved back to Australia for a period, where he was helped out by his former bush mate, Mike Novotny. Before long, however, he was back in Indonesia, waiting, along with everyone else, for something to happen.

Chapter Three:
BRE-X AND BORNEO

*For years one does business with a man, and if his credit is
good and his merchandise sound, one clicks the abacus and sets
aside the doubts one feels on looking into his eyes.*
Whampoa, a Chinese merchant in Singapore, speaking of
a Borneo pirate in G.M. Fraser's *Flashman's Lady*

First pass over Busang

While the Busang prospect in East Kalimantan did not receive
much attention during the heyday of the Australian-led
exploration boom, it was prodded and poked by a fair number of
geologists long before Bre-X arrived on the scene in 1993.

John Felderhof identified the area as a gold target for Jason
Mining in 1986 but did not explore the Muara Atan prospect, as it
was then known. Geologist Jonathan Nassey became intrigued
after following the footsteps of local miners working the drainages
of what later became the Central zone for alluvial gold. By this
time, Nassey had joined Westralian Resource Projects, an
Australian-listed company headed by Warren Beckwith.

In 1987, before any serious work was carried out to test the
Muara Atan prospect, Nassey was dismissed by Westralian for
"unethical behavior." Colleagues say the dismissal was prompted
by nothing more serious than Nassey's propensity to dabble in outside business, namely wheeling-and-dealing mineral properties for
parties other than his employer.

While Nassey was on his way out, Stephen Walters was on his
way in, though he had no way of knowing this when he showed up
for a job interview at Warren Beckwith's mansion outside London.
The 28-year-old British geologist was hoping to land a job in
Australia but was told nothing was available there at the moment.

Would he consider an offer to work in Indonesia with another company under Beckwith's control?

Walters accepted and went to work for PT Westralian Atan Minerals, colloquially known as PT WAM. "Busang was the first thing I worked on here when I arrived from England in 1987," he said. "We did the basic, first-pass sampling and geological mapping in the area of the Central zone."

At the time, Beckwith's Westralian Resource Projects controlled an 80% interest in PT WAM, with two Indonesian companies, PT Krueng Gasui and PT Sungai Atan Perdana, each holding 10%. The kingpins behind the two domestic companies were Indonesian businessman Jusuf Merukh, local logging operator Haji Syakerani and Syakerani's son, Ahmad Yani Syakerani.

In late 1987, PT WAM signed a fourth-generation contract of work (CoW) for Muara Atan, which included the Central zone. Under a schedule in the contract, new shares of PT WAM had to be offered to the Indonesian government, to domestically controlled companies, or to private Indonesian citizens, moving the balance of ownership steadily toward Indonesian interests. By the end of 1997 (the tenth year of the contract), 51% of PT WAM would have to be domestically owned.

But 1997 was a long way away when Walters and his logistical field officer, Douglas Pickard, began their program from a field camp on the Atan River. Their efforts were focused on an area with some veins that resembled the mineralization at the Kelian gold deposit in Kalimantan, and which contained base-metal values, along with gold and silver.

"But it was very small, only a couple of hundred metres by a hundred metres sort of thing," Walters said. "What we saw was geologically interesting, and if there were a few kilometres of it, there might well be a mine. But what was there was restricted in areal extent, and I think Montague Gold [another Beckwith company, which later farmed into the project] found that out when it did its work program."

After a brief hiatus, during which Walters moved on to other projects, Westralian decided to continue exploring the Muara Atan CoW and several others in Kalimantan using a consulting firm rather than its own team of geologists. An Australian outfit headed by Murray Rogers was selected for the work program. The project geologist was John Levings, who reported to Rogers and to Graeme Chuck, an Australian who became Westralian's exploration manager in January 1988.

Two months later, Chuck and Levings travelled to Balikpapan, on the southeastern coast of Borneo, where Westralian had a small base for its projects. Muara Atan lay deep in the jungles of

Kalimantan; to reach it, the geologists had to take a 12-hour speed-boat ride up the Mahakam and Kelinjau Rivers, followed by four or five more hours by canoe to Westralian's camp on the Atan River.

Chuck and Levings examined the CoW and, after zeroing in on area where some locals were mining alluvial gold, decided that the likely source was a small hill of andesite porphyry. (Andesite is a volcanic rock containing little or no quartz and composed of feldspar and one or more mafic minerals; the term "porphyry" generally refers to any igneous rock that contains distinct crystals imbedded in a much finer groundmass.) The porphyry looked like a magmatic dome that might have formed beneath a volcano; geologists familiar with vein-type gold deposits know that gold mineralization is often found in the area around small sub-volcanic domes. The geologists inspected the porphyry and nearby alluvial workings; together the favorable host rock and the gold mineralization in the overburden invited broad comparisons with the geological environment that hosted the Kelian gold deposit, to the southwest. Chuck and Levings decided that Westralian's program should focus on the "Busang prospect," as it was called from then on, together with a regional exploration program.

"We put up a standard camp at Busang using local materials and started work," said Chuck. The initial mapping and sampling returned encouraging assays, ranging from 4 grams of gold per tonne to a high of 27.3 grams, both from outcrops of bedrock and from "float" (boulders in the unmineralized material overlying a deposit). The highest grades were those encountered in the Central zone. A few of the samples were collected in an area later controlled by Magnum Minerals (the area that eventually became Bre-X's Southeast zone), but these returned gold values much lower than in the Westralian area.

Next they cut a grid of north-south lines through the jungle over the main target zone. The lines, spaced 30 metres apart, allowed field men to collect soil samples every 20 metres along each line. By analyzing the samples for gold and plotting the concentrations on a map, Chuck and Levings were able to define a series of gold-enriched zones which formed a pattern of bands running east-northeast.

In the latter part of 1988, they hired a bulldozer and dug trenches across these gold anomalies. Three of the trenches showed exciting numbers — widths of 6 to 12 metres and gold grades of 10 to 15 grams per tonne. But most of the results were prosaic — grades of 1 to 2 grams per tonne and widths rarely greater than 2 metres. Still, it was a decent start to the project, and Chuck said so in his report, calling the results "very encouraging."

The results were reported by Westralian in its 1988 annual report; they were also reported by Montague Gold, which was

The original camp at Busang set up by Westralian Resource Projects, where John Felderhof began work at Busang.

farming into the Muara Atan CoW by taking over Westralian's funding obligations.

Before the year was out, Montague had begun promoting the Busang project based on the encouraging trenching results. By early 1989, Busang had become Montague's prime exploration project, and the company approved a budget of US$600,000 for a program in which 19 holes would be drilled to test the area below the most promising trench results. Levings supervised the program, and Montague let the work out to one of Indonesia's leading drill contractors. In all, Montague drilled 1,488 metres.

Graeme Chuck and Murray Rogers visited the project several times as work progressed, bringing along, on one occasion, a representative from Homestake Mining who was evaluating the project for a possible joint venture. The Homestake man went home unimpressed and opted not to participate.

When the cores came out of the ground, the style of mineralization was just the same as Stephen Walters had described a few years earlier. All but two of the 19 holes hit gold mineralization, usually over intersections less than 3 metres long and carrying grades of around 1 to 3 grams per tonne. Grades and widths in that league did not measure up to the high expectations the trenching program and Montague's promotional efforts had generated. The

Early drill site at Busang in the days when Bre-X's Jakarta office began exploring the property.

best result — 5 metres grading 4.29 grams of gold in hole 1 — was good news, but most of the other intersections were narrow and the intersections did not line up on a coherent structure. "They were quite short and not particularly high grade," Chuck said. "Basically, in three dimensions, we couldn't join them up and make any sort of resource at all."

To continue work at Busang, Montague and Westralian solicited major companies in the hope of forming a partnership. Had the grades been better, Montague might have made a case for Busang as a prospect with potential for underground mining; had the veins been wider, they might have been able to sell it as a potential open-pit operation. But several companies visited the site, and none was sufficiently interested to make an offer. At the end of 1989, the project was put on hold.

By now, Montague's exploration efforts had earned it a 50% stake in the Muara Atan CoW. Westralian still had 30%, and Krueng and Sungai, whose interests could not be diluted under the terms of the CoW, retained their 10% interests. It is a feature of the CoW system that land holdings must be steadily relinquished as exploration progresses; Muara Atan had been reduced in size from the original 84,586 hectares to 57,571 hectares. Under

Indonesian law, a further relinquishment of at least 15,728 hectares would be required at, or before, the end of 1990.

Indonesian fire sale

The early 1990s were years the Australian mining community would rather forget. Investors had not forgotten the huge losses of the 1987 market crash or forgiven the promotional excesses of the junior mining companies, particularly those working in Indonesia. The mood was so sour that many would rather smoke dollar bills than invest in grassroots exploration.

Busang sat dormant for a few years until efforts to sell it were initiated by a colorful Scottish entrepreneur named William McLucas. Ask anyone in Australia or Britain about McLucas — "Willie" to his friends — and the answer is always the same: rogue U.K. financier to the mining industry. The description is apt, given that he was one of only a handful of Europeans who were both willing and able to raise capital for junior mining companies exploring in Indonesia during the 1980s.

While raising speculative capital for mineral exploration is commonplace in Canada and (to a lesser extent) Australia, it has been extraordinarily difficult everywhere else in the world, particularly at the institutional level. The difficulty stems from the high risks involved. In Europe, speculative funds for exploration typically came from big-money retail investors who were lured into the game by the potential for big gains.

McLucas was the head of Waverley Asset Management, a mutual fund that had invested in the Australian-led exploration boom in Indonesia during the 1980s. The fund was a subsidiary of Waverley Mining Finance, an investment company. By all accounts, Waverley preferred to get involved in mining deals at the early stage, often when "seed capital" is being raised to finance the initial setup and operating costs. Many of the juniors in which Waverley took an interest were promoted by T.C. Coombs, the London-based firm that had underwritten Jason, Jascan and other companies exploring in Indonesia.

It was through William McLucas and Waverley Mining Finance that John Felderhof and his former boss, Peter Howe, first became involved in Busang, in the early 1990s. Both men were aware of the project in the mid-1980s, when it was first identified as a gold target by Jason Mining, but the market crash put an end to their efforts to secure the ground.

"McLucas had made money on Jason and on some other Australian companies he had invested in and, therefore, had got to know me," Howe explained. "He asked me to go on his board [Waverley] and, somewhere along the way — I guess about 1990 or '91 — he decided to take over Westralian, which was the main shareholder of Montague."

How McLucas acquired control of Westralian and Montague is not clear, but one thing is certain; both companies were in the doldrums and so were easy pickings for any bargain-hunter hoping either to revive the companies or dispose of their assets. The takeover of Westralian gave McLucas a 49% stake in Montague and control of a gold mine in Australia, as well as interests in various properties in Indonesia, including Busang.

Howe went on to explain that McLucas was investing in projects in Alaska and elsewhere, and, for this reason, decided to get out of Indonesia and divest himself of the properties he had acquired there. "He'd met John Felderhof, so he asked John to find a buyer for the properties."

The offer was a godsend for Felderhof, who had just emerged from the Minindo mess bruised and bloodied, not to mention unemployed and unpaid. And yet, despite his involvement in the stock scandal, Felderhof had retained a certain cachet in the Indonesian mining community for his skills as a field geologist and for his work at Ok Tedi. Even today, some Indonesians refer to him as "the founding father of mining in Papua New Guinea." Moreover, he had kept an ear to the ground and established contacts in Indonesia, Australia and Canada.

Howe added: "John found a buyer for the property in Irian Jaya, a company called Dominion Mining, which I think paid something like $600,000 for it. He found a buyer for the Sumatra one too, but couldn't find a buyer for Busang, until David Walsh came along."

So Busang sat, unwanted, until late 1992 when John Felderhof — acting with the full knowledge of the vendor — decided to send in a geologist to find something worth selling at Busang. The man he chose was Michael Antonio T. de Guzman.

Used and abused at Benguet

Michael de Guzman developed an extraordinary ability to transform waste rock into ore with a mere stroke of the pen, or a wave of his arm. This he did, with considerable audacity, in late 1992 — his work being the cornerstone of an effort to package the Busang property for sale to a foreign company.

De Guzman did not start his career with this dubious talent, and that it existed at all came as a shock to Birl Worley, his American-born mentor and former boss at Benguet Corporation in the Philippines.

Worley was an institution at Benguet when the Filipino geologist joined the large mining company in 1977 straight out of Adamson University in Manila with a bachelor of science degree in geology. Benguet had its choice of graduates from the top universities in the country and rarely, if ever, recruited from Adamson.

"Mike walked into the number-two man's office one day, impressed him, and he sent him out to me and said, 'hey, this guy looks like he's worthwhile,'" Worley recalled. "That's how we got Mike. Never regretted it."

The task of training de Guzman fell to Worley, Benguet's vice-president of exploration, who was impressed with his trainee's native geological ability, as well as his personal integrity and honesty. The latter qualities were important as the company was having no shortage of problems with dishonest employees and petty corruption through the ranks to middle management.

De Guzman's initial duties involved locating bore sites for water wells and ground stability determinations at Benguet's Acupan gold mine, situated in the mountains near Baguio, close to Manila. These were not particularly exciting tasks, nor were they much related to exploration geology, but de Guzman did everything required of him with enthusiasm, and this impressed his superiors.

In 1979, after obtaining a master's degree in geology, he returned to Benguet, this time as an assistant geologist trainee. The first three months of his internship were spent sampling and mapping surface and underground mine areas. He learned more about sampling and grade control in the next three months and then moved into the mine's assay laboratories. There, de Guzman spent three months becoming familiar with fire-assaying, the chemical tests performed on samples to determine the amount of valuable minerals in them. He studied mineralogy and metallurgical processes. The last three months of his first year at Benguet were spent as an apprentice diamond driller and production mine geologist.

Worley said de Guzman was a quick study. "He was taught to be forward, because when I first went to the Philippines, I found the people would nod when you explained what you wanted and then go off in confusion."

Worley explained that this response is common in developing nations where employees have few rights in the workplace. It takes time and considerable effort to convince workers that they are allowed to disagree, and to ask questions if they do not understand what is required of them to complete the task at hand. "I never had this problem with Mike. He was as aggressive as he could possibly be. He wanted to work in geology and he wanted to be the world's best geologist. That, to him, was riches."

By 1980, de Guzman was in charge of grade-control activities at the Acupan mine. He studied the structural geology of its ore-shoot patterns, delineated orebodies and made projections of the shoot patterns for mine development. He outlined the areas to be mined and the limits of the ore in active production areas, and supervised the crews taking samples for grade control and metallurgical testing.

While all this is routine work for most geologists, working at Acupan posed physical challenges other mines did not. The working places were narrow and temperatures underground were hellish.

In late 1982, de Guzman moved to Baguio City where he began managing Benguet's underground gold operations. He held this post until March 1987, when he was promoted to the position of chief geologist for all underground operations. During this period, he managed the geological functions of eight producing gold mines. He co-ordinated research projects, both in-house and with government agencies and foreign institutions.

"He had exceptional talent," Worley said. "He was a keen observer and could see things that most other geologists could not. He had a marvellous mind and saw things that even I failed to see, and I thought I was probably one of the best observers and recorders that God put on the face of the earth." Worley's self-confidence is no idle conceit; he learned his craft from the legendary Reno Sales at the geology department of Anaconda Copper, long known as the unchartered graduate school of mine geology.

Worley encouraged de Guzman to take a number of company training programs, including a Dale Carnegie course, which helped him develop the skill and self-confidence to speak in public and make company presentations.

But Worley did have one problem with de Guzman that no training program or amount of lecturing could solve. "He was a womanizer, and I warned him about it several times. Now, I know this goes on all over and I can't reform the world, but Mike was important to me. I told him, Mike, this can't go on. You have a family."

Worley's feelings were personal. De Guzman had named his oldest son Birl in his honor — "the only Filipino in the country with a Danish name," joked Worley. The American geologist also felt sympathy for de Guzman's wife, Teresa, a simple, shy woman who had lived in rough mining camps to be near her husband during the early days of his career.

In his later years at Benguet, Worley worried about de Guzman's treatment at the hands of Benguet's middle managers. Since joining the company in 1960, Worley had made repeated efforts to introduce reforms. He had a broad base of experience to draw from, as he had previously worked for several American mining companies. He also had worked for the United States government — first with the Navy, where he was assigned to compile hydrographic charts, and then with the Army, where he was assigned to the Far East Command as a general intelligence specialist.

Worley left Benguet in 1984 as part of an effort to "Philippinize" the company and turn over management to nationals. But he was asked to return in 1987 to help revive the company's flagging fortunes. Upon his return, he found that de Guzman had been abused for not playing ball with corrupt middle managers involved in a gold-theft ring.

De Guzman's performance reviews would get lost or sit on someone's desk for months on end. And despite his ability to find pockets of good-paying ore in the company's mines, little effort was made to give him raises or bonuses.

Worley had warned Benguet to step up supervision of its underground mines, particularly those that produced high-grade gold. But this was not done, and Worley says the void was "rapidly exploited by an organization dedicated to gold theft from the mines and mills."

De Guzman's hard work and remarkable ability to find pockets of good-paying ore were constantly negated by corrupt managers who falsified his numbers and then exploited the ore for their personal gain. Feeling he had been used and abused for too long, de Guzman left Benguet in August of 1987 an unhappy man. The newly returned Worley made efforts to convince his star employee to stay and interceded on his behalf with the company's chief executive. "He was offered a very good deal, but Mike declined as he frankly stated that he could not work in Benguet given the terrible dishonesty of those above him," Worley said. "He would rather take a gamble on the unknown in Indonesia."

Down a slippery slope

By the fall of 1987, de Guzman was at work on the Mirah hard rock gold project in Kalimantan, which was one of the projects being explored by the partnership of Jason and Pelsart. It was here that he first met bush-mates John Felderhof, Mike Bird and Mike Novotny.

Working in the jungles of Borneo was a breath of fresh air from the hierarchical and regimented corporate environment at Benguet. De Guzman threw himself into the work with his usual enthusiasm and quickly impressed his co-workers with his skills as a field geologist. He particularly admired Mike Bird and, years later, often described his co-worker at Mirah as "my geological guru."

Though not a geologist himself, Novotny had high praise for de Guzman's abilities. "He was systematic and did good, solid work. He was invaluable, and his recording and reporting were excellent."

Later, de Guzman worked at a number of other hard rock and alluvial gold projects in Kalimantan, but the market crash of 1987 was the beginning of the end for Pelsart and Jason, and de Guzman suffered alongside them.

The hard times began taking their toll. De Guzman had not made his big discovery, nor had he taken the world by storm with his geological prowess. Without the supervision imposed on him by a large corporation and professional managers such as Birl Worley, the quality of his work began to slip. De Guzman was a good geologist and observer, but he was methodical and used to structure and order. Innovative, conceptual thinking was not his forte.

Too much of his attention was directed at pursuing and wooing women, which, by all accounts, was something he did well, with more charm than money.

After de Guzman was released from the disintegrating Pelsart-Jason partnership (or fired for petty embezzlement, depending on who tells the story), he returned to the Philippines. He found work as a geologist for Longos Gold Mines, but that position did not last more than a few months, so he tried his hand at consulting.

Birl Worley was back in the Philippines during this period, advising his old company on how it might revive its troubled operations. Corruption still ruled at Benguet. One of the mines, the Kelly, could have provided all the gold needed to make Benguet profitable. But Worley said that, instead, it was "a complete shameful mess," and charged that its records had been deliberately falsified. He also recommended moving to bulk mining so as to discourage the gold thefts, which depended on access to high-grade ore in select, narrow veins.

Worley ran into de Guzman during this period and asked him to return to Benguet as chief geologist. "He said, 'No, the same people are there that were doing everything that I objected to before, and I still can't work in such a dishonest atmosphere.' He not only said that; he put it in writing."

De Guzman went back to Indonesia to work on a coal project in Kalimantan, but that also proved to be a short stint. Mike Bird then made enquiries on de Guzman's behalf and, in the early 1990s, introduced him to the management of PT Hunamas Putra Interbuana. De Guzman was hired on at the private Indonesian company and asked his new employer to take on Cesar Puspos, a young Benguet geologist who had followed de Guzman to Indonesia. They agreed, and the two Filipino geologists started work on the company's gold project in Java, as well as on various projects elsewhere in the country. The position lasted only a year, as the mining industry was in the doldrums and money for exploration was tough to raise.

But de Guzman's boss, Takala Hutasoit, had nothing but praise for his former employee. "He was a workaholic and sometimes too optimistic about the resources, but he was honest. I had no problems with Mike. When we didn't have any money for exploration he would go out, make presentations and try hard to get us a partner."

John Nainggolan, Hutasoit's partner, said he was surprised at times by de Guzman's confidence in making eyeball projections about the resource potential of mineral properties. "Most people say, if you want to find a resource, you have to drill it," he explained. "But sometimes Mike would say: 'You don't have to drill it — I can calculate the resources.'"

The advice was ignored, and the property was worked and drilled in the usual manner, Nainggolan pointed out. "Mike had a revolutionary point of view. He was not conventional. But some of his projections were right, and we often found the resources where he said they were."

De Guzman also urged his employers to begin production on a limited scale in order to raise funds to keep exploration going. "But, unfortunately, his dream did not come true," Hutasoit said. "And because we didn't have a new partner, or budgets for exploration, he moved on. He left when John Felderhof recruited him to join Minindo."

After Minindo collapsed, de Guzman was in dire financial straits, along with Cesar Puspos and John Felderhof. At times, they relied on the kindness of friends to make ends meet. But had times been better, Hutasoit says, all three would have easily found work. "I've met many geologists from that time, but only a few could stay in the jungle for three weeks, sometimes a month at a time. Those guys could do that. They were not spoiled geologists. They worked hard and were believers."

At the end of 1992, Felderhof and de Guzman had little going except their combined effort to package Busang for sale. The two agreed that de Guzman would go to the site for a "field verification study," which he carried out from November 27 through to December 7. He spent a total of four days on site; the rest of the time was spent in transit or on visits to offices of the Indonesian Ministry of Mines to consult property files.

In early December, de Guzman wrote a report on his visit to the Muara Atan CoW, which he provided to David Hedderwick and Wayne Kernaghan of Montague Gold (and Waverley), with copies to Felderhof and to Jonathan Nassey, who somehow or other had become involved in the effort.

De Guzman's field notes make interesting reading. He repeatedly emphasized that the property's "surface impressions confirm favorable features related to gold mineralization." He also pointed out that the Muara Atan CoW had potential that went beyond the Busang prospect. "This is only one of at least three hypabyssal plug-related mineralized zones situated in a maar-diatreme geologic environment," he wrote. Translated into plain English, the report suggested that there were two more subvolcanic intrusions like the Busang porphyry, all of which were situated around a crudely elliptical fault structure.

De Guzman recommended some field work, which he said was "necessary to upgrade the viability" of the CoW in preparation for a joint venture or farm-out to other parties. A budget of US$40,000 was proposed for a program of mapping, sampling and trenching. He also recommended that a Winkie drill — a lightweight, portable diamond drill machine — be brought in to drill "at least four holes of 80 metres depth" for an additional cost of US$10,000.

Next, de Guzman took six "verification samples" near areas previously drilled, all of which ran for gold. In one, he noted the presence of "fine grains of visible gold."

The report then took a sudden turn into fantasyland. First, de Guzman stated that the "comparative mining operation" is Benguet's producing Acupan mine, without providing any grounds for such a comparison.

Next, he calculated a resource estimate for the Busang prospect of 20 million tonnes with a gold content of more than 2 grams, minable from surface to a depth of 50 metres. He assigned this resource a "minability confidence factor" of 40%.

He then boldly estimated an underground minable resource (which included 50% of the surface minable resource) of 60 million tons with a gold content exceeding 3.5 grams per tonne to a depth of 150 metres. This resource was assigned a minability confidence factor of 20%.

It was pure smoke and mirrors, and everyone must have known it. The results of Montague's past drilling were still in the company's files, along with rejection letters from the half-dozen or so mining groups that had walked the ground and looked at the results of past work.

John Levings and Graeme Chuck had not been able to cobble together any sort of resource from 18 drill holes, but de Guzman was able to come up with fantastic numbers based on their past work and his six hand-picked samples.

The recommendation to do more field work was not heeded and would come back to haunt McLucas. The proverbial sow's ear was transformed into a silk purse, and the Busang property was ready for sale. But John Felderhof knew it would be almost impossible to sell the property to an Australian company. The majors had already kicked the rocks and walked away, while most of the juniors did not have two nickels to rub together.

Enter Bre-X

In March 1993, David Walsh picked up the phone, tracked down John Felderhof and said he wanted to come to Indonesia to look at mineral properties for his latest junior company, Bre-X Minerals.

Walsh later told others, including Peter Howe, that it all started with a "dream". Walsh's nocturnal reverie told him he could recoup his fortune by going back to Indonesia, so he called the only person he knew there, John Felderhof.

"I never heard that," chuckled Barry Tannock, Bre-X's first manager of investor relations. "The company needed a new story. It was as simple as that."

Walsh was told that because the Australians had packed up and gone home after the market crash, some good properties were available. Several sources say Walsh agreed to pay Felderhof $10,000 for the month or so it would take to beat the bushes and find properties for him to review in Jakarta. Whether this ever happened is questionable, as Walsh was not exactly rolling in dough at the time. He did manage to scrape together the necessary money to make the trip to Indonesia, thanks to credit-card advances and a loan to Bre-X from Bresea Resources (Walsh's first publicly listed company), which still had a few dollars in its till.

After allowing Felderhof some time to compile a property portfolio, Walsh flew to Jakarta for his eagerly awaited meeting with a man he was then describing as "the best geologist in the business." He was accompanied by his son Sean, newly graduated from high school, and geologist Kevin Waddell, who was to review the properties Felderhof had assembled. Waddell had first met Walsh in 1986, through Mike Duggan (a director on the board of Bresea), when Bresea and one of Duggan's companies were exploring for gold in the Northwest Territories. Later, during the diamond exploration boom, he did some consulting work for Bre-X.

The trip to Indonesia was a "this-is-it sort of deal," Waddell said, adding that Walsh's bankruptcy proceedings were already in progress when they flew to Jakarta via Hong Kong. "He had to find something. I was at his house on at least one occasion when the bailiff came. He was under severe financial duress."

The group arrived on April 24 and met Felderhof that evening at the Sari Pan Pacific, a posh hotel in Jakarta. They also met Mike Bird in the hotel lobby, the only member of A.C.A. Howe's Jakarta office to have found permanent employment since the exploration team disbanded after the market crash. At the time, Bird was managing the Tewah alluvial project in Kalimantan for Suharto's half-brother, Probosutedjo. He spoke Bahasa, the national language, and had integrated well into local society (helped, no doubt, by his marriage to the daughter of an army general).

"It was quite funny, actually," said Peter Howe, who heard a recap of the dinner meeting from friend Bird. "They were expecting a rich promoter and in walked David Walsh. They were quite shocked to find out that he actually had to borrow money for his fare to get there."

Waddell said a few Indonesians were present for the dinner at the Sari, though he was not sure why. Also present was a prosperous-looking businessman named Adam Tobin. "He had a lot of different businesses and was supposedly very influential," he said. "We were told he was negotiating with the government for cellular phone rights in Indonesia. We also were told that he was connected to the government somehow or another. I got the impression he was a partner on some of the properties."

Peter Howe said Tobin had been involved in various mineral properties during the 1980s. "He had been one of our partners. Later, when John was broke, he stayed with Tobin. I think John felt an obligation to get Adam's properties placed with people."

Waddell said Tobin hosted the dinner, which was a catered affair in one of the hotel's private banquet rooms. "It was a ritzy affair, with several courses. I remember sushi was involved. I had been told that it was rude not to eat everything put in front of you in Indonesia, but I had to apologize. I don't do raw fish."

Waddell said some of the dinner conversation focused on North American stock markets. Tobin was "a keen listener," Waddell said, and was particularly interested in how stock markets worked in that part of the world. "Adam was fairly quiet — total observation, uncanny observation, like looking through souls. Bird didn't say much and stayed in the background, but he was keen on what was going on."

Waddell did not meet either Michael de Guzman or Jonathan Nassey at the dinner, though he said Walsh later had several private meetings with Felderhof, in which one or the other might have been present.

"David met privately with John, and I think Adam, a few times in the three or four days that we were in Jakarta. I'm sure that is where the discussions got a little more nitty-gritty. I wasn't asked to attend. My job was to review the various properties Felderhof had put in the portfolio."

Felderhof gave Walsh and Waddell a copy of de Guzman's resume, saying he intended to hire the Filipino geologist, who was then completing a short-term work assignment. "Michael de Guzman was not involved whatsoever and I don't think I met Jonathan Nassey either," Waddell said. "Umar Olii was John's man at that time."

Olii, a geologist and the nephew of a former mines official, had worked with Felderhof and Peter Howe in the past. The Indonesian squired Waddell around town to look at data on various properties.

"He was very up-front and seemed like a good guy," Waddell said. "John [Felderhof] seemed a bit too on edge, pushy, for my tastes. He was on hard times then too."

Waddell read a geological report on the Busang project written by John Felderhof, which included results of Montague's drill program. While he thought the project looked "interesting," he was surprised that the report contained only numbers, with no assay sheets as appendices to verify that they were true as stated. "I thought, maybe they do things differently here," he said. Waddell was allowed to make copies of the reports for all the other projects under review, except Busang.

Walsh and his group left Jakarta on April 28. "It was a short trip, though we did get to see the city a bit. When I went out with Umar one afternoon, all these little girls were following us down the street. I was a real novelty. I guess they don't have too many green-eyed, six-foot-four guys in Indonesia."

According to Peter Howe, Felderhof then phoned McLucas and told him that he had a buyer for Busang. David Hedderwick of Waverley Finance and David Walsh negotiated the deal, which granted Bre-X an option to buy 80% of the outstanding shares of PT Westralian Atan Minerals for US$80,000, at an exercise price of US$100.

The option entitled Bre-X to an 80% interest on a 57,571-hectare CoW in the Busang region, held by PT WAM. Assuming de Guzman's most conservative estimate of 1.3 million oz. of gold, Bre-X was getting an 80% share (or a million ounces in the ground) at 8¢ an ounce. A gold prospect with real potential for millions of ounces would sell for a lot more than US$80,100, even in those days; for example, junior gold companies often have stock market valuations in the US$50-per-oz. range. There was no mistaking it: McLucas had not put much stock in de Guzman's bullish resource projections.

The low price might have reflected the fact that Muara Atan was an old CoW. De Guzman had noted this in his late 1992 memo to Felderhof and Waverley, which contained his bullish resource calculation. "Realization of this potential is dependent upon the rate and scope of exploration activities; considering a limited one-year remaining period of exploration as per CoW agreement provision." Almost six months of the exploration period had already gone by.

Felderhof, meanwhile, was angling for a longer-term position than selling Indonesian properties no one much wanted. David Walsh was no Kevin Parry with millions to burn on yachts and wild-cat drilling, but he was the proverbial bird in the hand worth more than two in the bush. Bre-X would need someone with local experience to explore the property — and who better than the people who knew Busang best?

After some discussion, it was agreed that Felderhof would become Bre-X's Indonesian manager. Barry Tannock does not recall how the deal was structured, or how it came about. "I'm not sure how they persuaded each other, but they cut some sort of deal."

Felderhof then hired de Guzman as chief geologist. Also joining Bre-X's Indonesian team were Jonathan Nassey as senior geologist and Cesar Puspos as geologist and project manager.

Walsh went back to Canada with an Indonesian property and an exploration team, but not much else. He still had to raise money to explore the property, which was not an easy task as the market was still as weak on his return as it was when he left.

Pounding the pavement

"Ten years of patience involved while following events in Indonesia appears to be ready to bear fruit," David Walsh told Bre-X shareholders in late April of 1993. "It would take an enormous amount of time and money for others to set up and achieve our level of properties and expertise."

Walsh also told shareholders that it was important to have an Indonesian partner to conduct business in the country. "Mr. Adam Tobin, a prominent businessman in Jakarta, has agreed to be our domestic partner. This association will greatly assist in dealing with the government and acquiring mineral properties."

Whatever Tobin did, he must have done quickly, because Bre-X never mentioned his name again. "I thought they were going to give him options and all the rest of it," Waddell said. "What happened there, I have no idea, but it is intriguing." Olii, meanwhile, bowed out of the venture because of a personality conflict with de Guzman.

In May 1993, Bre-X Minerals announced it had entered the Pacific "Rim of Fire," as a potential gold and base-metal miner. The Rim of Fire is the boundary of the Pacific tectonic plate, the sheet of oceanic crust that forms the floor of the Pacific Ocean. It stretches through New Zealand, Fiji, the Solomon Islands, Papua New Guinea, Indonesia and the Philippines, colliding with the Asian and Indo-Australian continental plates. The collisions give rise to volcanic and seismic activity, throwing the switch on the processes of ore formation.

Bre-X's announcement also stated that Felderhof had agreed to head Bre-X's Indonesian exploration efforts as general manager. The company referred to him as "the man credited as co-discover of the large Ok Tedi gold mine in Papua New Guinea [and] the discovery of four mineral properties, of which one is in production, two scheduled to go into production and one at the feasibility stage."

Walsh and Felderhof parroted de Guzman's report of November 1992, which stated that the geological potential of this target was 20 million tonnes grading greater than 2 grams of gold per tonne, or one million recoverable ounces minable to a depth of 50 metres using surface methods. They did not mention that a confidence factor of 40% had been attributed to the deposit; nor did they release the results of the holes from the 1989 program upon which the calculation was based.

Brian Fagan, author of *Asian World Stock Report*, pointed out, some time later, that such a news report would attract immediate attention. "But, in early 1993, Indonesia was an unknown entity."

Having made that easy leap into the one-million-ounce category without any challenge, Walsh and Felderhof took another giant step and became "potential miners."

Their back-of-the-envelope study estimated that the company's net annual after-tax cash flow would be US$10 million, based on mining and processing costs of US$155 per oz., a US$25-million capital cost, and an annual production capacity of 2 million tonnes.

All this, without so much as a metre of new drilling.

Within weeks of the announcement, Walsh and Felderhof were making the rounds in Vancouver and other Canadian cities in order to raise the necessary funds for the Indonesian acquisition.

Walsh and Felderhof dropped by the Vancouver office of The Northern Miner, where the former was already known as a player in the Northwest Territories diamond rush. "We're working the press," Walsh joked. "It's part of the job to work the press."

Walsh was cordial and sober, and introduced Felderhof as a "a man of experience in Indonesia." And Felderhof looked the part. He launched into his "maar-diatreme" geological theory and compared Busang to the Kelian gold mine in Kalimantan and the Acupan gold mine in the Philippines. Neither mine was well-known in Canada and it was an interesting discourse. Felderhof also mentioned his role in the discovery of Ok Tedi, a famous deposit well-known in Canadian mining circles. He seemed credible, though a little rough around the edges, like he had been in the jungle too long.

In the summer of 1993, Bre-X opened its office in Jakarta. By this point, the company had acquired another project, on one of the Sangihe Islands in North Sulawesi. The deal was given the nod by one newsletter writer, who noted that it "strengthened" Bre-X's Indonesian focus and provided investors with "a better shot at success."

Behind the scenes, though, Bre-X was still scrambling for money. Tannock said enough was raised by July 1993 to pay Montague $80,000 for the Busang acquisition. But he is not certain whether the shares of PT WAM were ever received in return for those funds. That was Felderhof's area of responsibility.

In September of that year, Bre-X announced the acquisition of a third Indonesian project, this time on the island of Sumatra. At the time, the company's shares were trading at about 45¢. The stock never fell below this price again, though it was to remain below $2 for almost another year.

Felderhof, meanwhile, had put on his promoter's hat. That autumn he wrote an article, published in *The Bull & Bear* tout sheet, which ostensibly was about Indonesia's mineral potential. A closer reading reveals that it was really a puff piece on Bre-X in which he was asked to "choose" a senior producer and a junior company active in Indonesia. In an ironic twist, Felderhof selected Freeport-McMoRan Copper & Gold for the "more conservative" investor and recommended Bre-X for the "more growth-oriented" investor.

A few desperate men and a salt shaker

John Felderhof, Michael de Guzman and Cesar Puspos had much at stake when the first rig began turning at the Busang property in October 1994. Everyone knew David Walsh was operating on a shoestring and that there was no potful of money to be squandered on wildcat drilling. To play it safe, the drill was set up in an area known to contain at least some gold mineralization — the Central zone, previously drilled by Montague.

Bre-X later reported that the first hole hit "weak mineralization," which usually means anomalous, or slightly higher than trace, values. The second hole also was a dud.

After the third hole was pulled, one or more persons on site decided to add gold to the core to keep the project going and the

Drillers working on the Busang gold project in early 1994.

paycheques coming. It was a humble beginning for what was to become the world's largest, most daring and the best engineered salting scam. The salting might have had another rationale, however. The Muara Atan CoW was aging fast. The CoW could only be kept alive if it was moved to the feasibility stage from exploration. A resource had to be proved up on the Central zone, or the CoW would have to be relinquished.

Results from the first three holes at Busang were not released until December 12. Why the samples took this long to assay is not known. Perhaps there were problems with reproducibility of results (good labs regularly split samples and assay the duplicate as an internal check). Perhaps the lab was simply busy. Or perhaps the samples took an unusually long time to get to the lab.

Hole 3 was impressive, by any standard, though not consistent with the results previously obtained by Westralian. The drill hole cut three mineralized zones, one of which was 40 metres long. Subsequent reports show the third hole was crudely salted. Some man-made copper-gold shavings were found in one portion, while placer gold had been added to another.

The risks of early detection were enormously high at this point. The salting methodology had to be refined. It was about this time that the metallurgical skills of Jerome Alo were brought to bear on Busang.

Normally, exploration projects do not have metallurgists working on site. But Alo had special skills that were badly needed at this juncture. He had previously worked in the mill at Benguet, where Guzman knew him.

In mid-January of 1994, Cesar Puspos returned to the jungle to begin upgrading the field camp in preparation for more drilling. According to Puspos's internal company report, which covered the period up to April 1, 1994, Alo was on site before drilling began. Soon, the camp housed Puspos, Alo, a surveying crew, two samplers, an eight-man drill crew, and sundry camp help.

Puspos busied himself with core logging and with some reconnaissance mapping around the Central zone of mineralization. In a foreshadowing of things to come, he took some rock samples near the southeastern corner of the property, where he reported "very impressive assays."

His drill holes, BRH 4 through 9, all had encountered mineralization, as had hole BRH-2A, a re-drilling of the second hole in the program. Hole 4 encountered a single intersection measuring 6 metres long and grading 10.8 grams of gold per tonne. Hole 7 caught 5 metres grading 16 grams per tonne. BRH-8 intersected 26 metres grading 12.9 grams, and BRH-9 found 21 metres that averaged 8.1 grams. The Central zone was on its way, with a little help from its friends.

There were signs, even then, that the project staff was unusually interested in the sampling and assaying side of the project. An internal memo from de Guzman to Felderhof, dated March 19, 1994, was copied to Puspos and Alo. It dealt with the preparation and analysis of check samples that held coarse gold. De Guzman was concerned about the reproducibility of the assays.

Exploration companies rarely assay their own samples in the field; analytical equipment is too expensive to buy for every project and too temperamental to perform well in remote locations. Bre-X was no exception; de Guzman and Puspos had been sending samples to PT Indo Assayutama Nusa, a commercial assay laboratory in Balikpapan widely known as Indo Assay. Labs attract business by offering good prices and fast turnaround of samples; they keep it by providing reliable analyses. Run by an Australian expatriate, John Irvin, Indo Assay had built a solid reputation with mining firms operating in Indonesia.

De Guzman, apparently wishing to ensure that the assays he was getting from Indo Assay were accurate, selected "14 coarse-gold-bearing drill core samples" from the bags of coarsely crushed rock and finely ground rock pulp that Indo Assay had returned to

Busang. From each bag, he split off 200 grams of coarse material and 100 grams of pulp, and sent the samples to another commercial lab, PT Geoservices in Jakarta, for analysis.

The results came back from Geoservices, and de Guzman drew up a table with one column showing the grades Indo Assay had reported, and two adjacent columns with the grades Geoservices had reported on the duplicates. Geoservices showed slightly higher gold assays than Indo Assay, possibly because the samples it received had been homogenized more thoroughly during handling.

There were too few samples to render these "check assays" conclusive, but de Guzman, who evidently knew just enough sampling theory to jump to conclusions, felt a modification to the sampling procedure was going to be needed. Jerry Alo would complete a study of the sample preparation procedure and recommend a way to achieve reproducible results.

Send money

Bre-X's first newsletter convert was Les Reid of the *Mining Desk*, published by Regency Capital in Phoenix, Arizona. A colorful figure, Reid makes liberal use of superlatives to describe the people behind the companies he recommends to his followers. "Bre-X is led by a dynamic personality, one who is capable and determined," he wrote. "And Bre-X has engaged the man who is the best-qualified person, perhaps in the entire world, as its general manager in Indonesia."

Reid began following Bre-X in May 1993, shortly after Walsh's visit to Indonesia. "[He] shared our vision", Walsh told shareholders. "He authored an initial research report followed by numerous updates."

Another early backer was investment newsletter writer Jay Taylor, who makes a habit of following projects where the "gold" is believed to occur in such complex forms that the mineralization cannot be detected by conventional assaying techniques. Taylor's blind faith in such projects has led him to revile *The Northern Miner*'s skepticism as "closed-minded," and worse.

But the going is never easy in the early days and, by most accounts, David Walsh was "doing what he had to do" to keep the drills turning at Busang. With a few assay results in hand, he began to get nibbles of interest from retail investors closer to home.

Patrick Sheridan Jr., who runs a small Toronto-based junior company, agreed to help Walsh after being apprised of the Busang project when the Bre-X stock was still below 75¢. "The first time I spoke with him [Walsh], he had already drilled a few holes,"

Sheridan recalled. "By the time we looked at it, there was enough there to get us interested to a degree."

Sheridan said Walsh raised some money by exercising options held by directors, officers and employees. This was not an uncommon practice for junior companies during times when markets were bad, though it was never very popular, as insiders do not enjoy giving up their options. "Walsh would offer us X number of shares at X price, usually at a small discount to the market," he explained. "The money would go into the till; at least that's what we were told. We were left with free trading stock and so everyone was happy."

Sheridan said Walsh asked him whether or not he should have core from Busang assayed in Canada, rather than in Indonesia. "I told him that as long as the lab was reputable, it was OK to do it there; otherwise the turnaround time might be slow."

Sheridan and his brother were involved in two such transactions, all below a dollar per share, for a total consideration of less than $150,000. Their profits were modest, however, as they got out early. "We sold our stock because we felt that they would eventually miss on subsequent holes, as all good mines do. But of course they never did."

Walsh did some fundraising of this sort in Calgary, though word soon got around that Walsh's wife, Jeannette, did not take kindly to having her options sold to raise money for exploration. On at least one occasion, David sold Jeannette's options without her permission, though he paid the price in the form of a public tongue-lashing and was the butt of gossip on Calgary's restaurant row for some time afterward.

Stanley Hawkins, president of Tandem Resources, also gave Walsh a hand and introduced him to the Toronto mining community. In late 1993, while in Toronto to see brokers, Walsh and Felderhof dropped by Tandem's Christmas party. "It was the first time I had met Felderhof," said Hawkins. "He seemed OK then, though I didn't get to talk with him much. Later, as the Bre-X story developed, I found him arrogant."

Barry Tannock, Hawkins' cousin and Bre-X's first manager of investor relations, found Felderhof not much more capable than Walsh when it came to legal matters and details of the property agreements. "I could have done it, and I think I half-volunteered a few times," Tannock said. "But their reaction was to say: 'stick to the computers and investor relations.'" Both Walsh and Felderhof were "protective" of their turf and had no interest in bringing in talent from outside. "Felderhof, in particular, struck me as a very control-oriented sort of guy, very hands-on."

While Walsh worked the market side of the business and raised the money, his boss showed little or no interest in either geology or

Teck Corp. geologist James Oliver examines a trench at Busang.

office administration, which are the nuts and bolts of running an exploration company. "He never got involved in that," said Tannock. "He either didn't understand it or didn't like it, though if there was money involved, he would get down to the nitty-gritty." As Felderhof settled into Bre-X's Jakarta office, the areas of responsibility between him and Walsh became sharply divided. "All the time I was there, basically the only interaction between Calgary and Jakarta was that David would send money to Felderhof — and it was never enough — and Felderhof would send back some results."

Majors take notice

Dr. Paul Kavanagh, head of exploration for Barrick Gold, read an article about Busang in the *The Northern Miner* of August 9, 1993. He called David Walsh for details and went to visit the property.

"It was an interesting story," he later told The Miner. "I was impressed with what these guys could do if they had a little money."

As head of exploration for one of the world's largest gold miners, Kavanagh had to keep his eagle eye trained on any project that appeared to have potential to deliver more than one million ounces of gold. The million-ounce principle is common among top-rank gold companies; projects that did not add a million ounces to the reserve base were cut loose regardless of their rate of return. Busang was in the right neighborhood and had the right geology to meet that criterion.

Discussions between Barrick and Bre-X were launched after Kavanagh's site visit. Walsh was looking for a $500,000 private placement at 41¢ per share, roughly equivalent to 14% of the company, but Barrick was in no hurry to bite. Kavanagh was near retirement; his replacement, Alex Davidson, was less than enthusiastic about Busang and more interested in Cerro Corona, a Peruvian property near a gold mine operated by rival Newmont Gold.

At first, it appeared that the deal might go through. The market got excited that a major was talking with Bre-X and bid the shares up to over $1. Several weeks later, Walsh announced that the deal was off and that "no further discussions are contemplated." The circumstances surrounding the deal's collapse vary depending on who is telling the tale, but Walsh clearly believed he was purposely being strung along until he ran out of cash so that Barrick could pick up the project for a song.

"David was pissed off," Tannock said. "But I think Alex [Davidson] wasn't very excited about it one way or another because it was a no-win situation for him. If it turned out to be a good deal, it was Kavanagh's, and if it was a bummer, Alex would be left holding the bag.

"It's speculation on my part, because yes, they were going to make an offer, and then maybe not. When I finally saw the offer in writing, which was in January 1994, it was just awful. It didn't make sense."

As a benchmark, Tannock compared the offer to one he knew Barrick had made with a junior of similar size operating in South America. "The deal Barrick made with them was one helluva lot better than what they were talking about doing with Bre-X. There was no comparison, and I can only conclude that the Busang offer was Alex Davidson's way of finessing out of the thing."

David Walsh, meanwhile, was already shopping the deal to other parties. "I know David and John had been up to Vancouver to see Teck — in December of that year I think — but Teck was not interested," Tannock said. "I remember talking to one of the Teck fellows at the Prospectors [convention] in March [of 1994], and he was pooh-poohing it. He was less than impressed, and said David seemed very nervous and was sweating and that sort of thing. I said, 'well, maybe he had the flu,' and talked to somebody else."

Just to be on the safe side, Teck sent Wayne Spilsbury to Indonesia to check out the Busang project. Spilsbury, who managed the company's exploration effort in Southeast Asia from an office in Singapore, was accompanied on the trip by another Teck geologist, James Oliver.

"When we looked at it, only Mike, Cesar and John were on the property," Spilsbury said. "They had a crew of Indonesians there, but it was a small camp at the time, with only one drill going on the Central zone."

Spilsbury was given an oral presentation on the geology, complete with Felderhof's maar-diatreme theory, before being taken to see the Central zone. The story, in his view, was not unreasonable.

"There was a dacite plug there [a circular mass of volcanic rock, in this case consisting of a fine-grained to glassy quartz-bearing andesite] and, as I remember, around the rind of this plug — which was punched into graphitic sediments — there was a stockwork of veining. One of the things that bothered us was that it was silica-poor and mostly carbonate veining, but in it there was a little bit of sulphides, chalcopyrite and sphalerite. That sort of fit the model we figured we would see from Kelian [the gold mine in central Kalimantan].

"Plus, the assays they were getting at the time were not all that different from what Montague Gold had got in the past, except that Montague had drilled perpendicular to the contact. John had turned the drill rig around ninety degrees and, as far as I could see, was drilling parallel to the contact and was getting some of these stockwork veins for long intervals. Basically, he was drilling down dip [along, rather than across, the geological structure], which, I thought, explained the longer runs."

Spilsbury walked up the north side of the hill at Busang and did see at least one reasonably sized quartz vein, up to a metre wide and about 50 metres long in the sediments. "We sampled that and got some gold. The setting didn't look bad, but, at the same time, it didn't look that strong, so we declined to make them an offer."

At the time, Bre-X was fishing for a $3-million private placement and sweetened the pot by offering to become Teck's "strategic partner" in Indonesia. Walsh told companies that the decision to fund exploration through equity deals only was made after "consultation" with John Felderhof, his general manager in Indonesia. But, if all went well, Teck could earn a property interest in Busang some time down the road. Teck still did not bite.

Felderhof tried to argue the case by telling Teck he was "not concerned" about the lack of quartz at Busang. He said mineralization on the whole is not silica-hosted, which is why the previous owners failed to intersect significant grades and widths. Felderhof's persuasion didn't work.

Other companies checked the rocks at Busang and moved on,

including Newmont Mining, which had several advanced projects in the country. Another tire-kicker was Placer Dome, a large gold producer based in Vancouver, B.C., with offices in Sydney, Australia. Lawrie Reinertson, then the head of subsidiary Placer Pacific, was skeptical about both the project and the people. At that time, Placer could have bought 50% of Bre-X's equity for a mere three to five million dollars, but, for various reasons, the deal went nowhere.

One reason was that a Placer field geologist, on visiting Busang, found it strange and a bit suspicious that Felderhof had a metallurgist, Jerry Alo, working at the property.

The rogue "metallurgist"

Birl Worley, Michael de Guzman's former boss at Benguet Mining, had returned to the United States long before Bre-X Minerals began reporting its initial exploration success at the Busang project. He had high regard for de Guzman's work and professional ethics and, therefore, no reason to doubt the quality of work being carried out on the Indonesian property.

Worley was not aware, however, that Jerry Alo, another former employee of Benguet, was the metallurgist at Busang. Had he known this at the time, his confidence may have been shaken for reasons other than the fact that Alo does not have the credentials of a metallurgist.

"He worked in the mill at Benguet, but we invited him to leave," Worley said. "I didn't want him around. He was too close to the people who were being dishonest, and he also knew how to goof up samples."

Benguet's problem had become so serious that, in some months, gold theft exceeded 15,000 oz. — more than the corporation was recovering. And, as Worley often reminded his bosses, these were highly profitable ounces, as the thieves did not have to pay any overhead for their nefarious activities. "We [the corporation] pay all those costs."

Worley knew that drastic action had to be taken to solve the problem as the gold-theft ring had used part of its huge profits to purchase powerful allies, both within and outside the organization. He grew tired of whitewash after whitewash and, eventually, the matter was brought to the attention of the country's military police.

In addition to the gold theft in its own mines, Benguet was having problems with some of the contract milling that was being done in its processing plant, which served other companies. "One of the contract mines was getting tremendous grades that it didn't have in its reserves. The mine was getting bonanza ore — we did tests and it was running about 64 oz. per tonne — but nothing near this [grade] was going into the mill."

Worley said the samples were being "fouled up" and the 64-oz. ore was being credited with grades of below 1 oz., which meant certain insiders were profiting from the difference. The conspirators were substituting low figures in the assay sheets: their scheme was a sort of salting in reverse.

"Alo was inside the mill and he was making the figures up, so I got rid of him. Some of the people were very, very angry, but I knew the ones who were angry were the ones who were dishonest. After the deed was done — and I took a lot of flak for it — others came up and said; 'we didn't trust him.'"

Some time later, Worley was introduced to a project on the island of Mindanao. The property was ostensibly owned by a Jesuit priest who wanted to sell it to Benguet. After reviewing the information, Worley thought the results were "impossible," and asked who had done the sampling and assaying.

"We hired a guy named Jerry Alo to do it," the hopeful vendor replied.

Worley had his own people sample the prospect using tamper-proof bags. "None of the samples showed up properly."

One baby step

Ted Carter, an engineer and self-described stock market speculator, met David Walsh at the Three Green Horns bar in Calgary's restaurant row, not long after the portly stock promoter launched Bresea Resources in the early to mid-1980s.

"I had finished my lunch and was sitting there, and [Walsh] was sitting around the corner looking glum, so I struck up a conversation," Carter recalled. "He started talking to me about problems on the Vancouver Stock Exchange with Bresea and how he was going to move to Montreal and be done with those jerks."

Carter listened but was not sufficiently interested to buy shares in Bresea. "My relationship with David was purely social at that time," he said. "He was a friendly guy; I liked him and enjoyed his company."

Later, Carter befriended Barry Tannock and took an interest in Ayrex Resources (the second junior company formed by Walsh, which held ground in Quebec's Casa Berardi camp), buying in at 20¢ and getting out at 70¢. He also dabbled in Bre-X when the company held properties north of Yellowknife in the Northwest

Territories, and was searching for a lookalike to Echo Bay Mines' Lupin deposit, also in the Territories. He'd been in the stock again when the company was looking for diamonds. When the diamond story fizzled, Carter believed that Bre-X would make the same damp noise.

In July 1992, Carter launched his investment newsletter, *Carter's Choice*, which today is considered one of the best of its type in North America. It was no year to start a business of this nature; in 1992 the industry was in the midst of a slump, and finding junior companies with sufficient upside potential to produce returns for investors was no easy task.

In September 1993, Carter received a call from Barry Tannock asking him to come over to David Walsh's basement and hear details of Bre-X's foray into Indonesia. Having paid little attention to the company in the past year, he was surprised to hear that it was alive and well and trading above 50¢.

Carter met with Felderhof and was impressed with his competence and experience. "Of course, Bre-X was really pushing his involvement in the Ok Tedi mine, but I thought maybe David has a shot here, because if anybody is going to know this area it would be a guy like Felderhof, who had been down there for years. I thought David might have done it this time; he finally might be on to something."

The newsletter writer looked at Bre-X's early exploration results and was even more impressed. "What I liked about it was near-surface, open-pittable mineralization, starting at zero, which meant you go in with bulldozers and start mining the stuff. They were optimistic they could find two or three million ounces in the Central zone."

Carter believed that if Felderhof delivered on his projection, Bre-X had the potential to climb to $10 from 59¢. "I told my subscribers that every now and then, a deal [such as Bre-X] comes along that is too compelling to ignore." He and his subscribers began buying at the 59¢ level, rode it up to $1.20, took profits and bought back in when the stock fell to 90¢. "We played around like this until the stock reached the $2 range, but the story just kept getting better."

Kavanagh comes aboard

March 24, 1994, was a banner day for Bre-X Minerals. Dr. Paul Kavanagh, the former head of exploration at Barrick Gold, joined the board of the Calgary junior, causing the entire Canadian mining fraternity to sit up and take notice. He brought with him an aura of respectability the junior badly needed.

Everyone in the mining industry knew Paul. Paul made a point of knowing everyone that mattered in the mining industry. Tall, distinguished and always impeccably dressed, Kavanagh is a supporter of the arts, and the quintessential Princeton man. He also is complex, opinionated, sometimes abrupt and more emotional than one might expect of a scientist. A proud man, he takes the smallest of slights to heart.

By his own account, Kavanagh departed from Barrick on terms that were not entirely amicable. He respected most of the technical team but made no secret of his dislike for some of the top executives. Nor was he terribly keen on his replacement, Alex Davidson. "A massive sulphide man," he would say, adding that he wanted Barrick to hire David Watkins, a Canadian geologist he felt had more gold experience.

Kavanagh's decision to join Bre-X raised eyebrows when it was announced, but the results of six holes released less than a month later made him look a genius. One hole, starting at surface, returned 26 metres averaging 12 grams of gold per tonne. Bre-X also hinted that two new target areas, southwest and southeast of the Central zone, had been identified and would be tested shortly by drilling. By this point, the boys at Westralian and Montague must have wondered what they did wrong.

Ted Carter said he became even more interested in Bre-X when Kavanagh joined the board of directors. "Now I'm really convinced these guys are on to something. Otherwise, why would Paul Kavanagh — who by this time, with all his Barrick options, would not need money — dink around with a company like this and risk ruining his good name?"

In early May 1994, Bre-X announced its first financing from a respected investment dealer. Loewen Ondaatje, McCutcheon (LOM) raised a total of $4.5 million by selling 300,000 units (one share plus a half-warrant at $1.75).

It was an important milestone for Bre-X and a measure of the cachet Paul Kavanagh brought to the company. Doors that once slammed in David Walsh's face opened, as if by magic, as the former head of Barrick Gold's exploration team made the rounds of brokerage firms across Canada.

As the story goes, John Felderhof also hit it off with LOM analyst Robert van Doorn, a fellow Dutchman. In late July 1994, Van Doorn put out a "buy" recommendation on Bre-X, which he described as a "small hunter in elephant country" (the phrase refers to large ore deposits, not to pachyderms). Bre-X shares were trading at $2.10 and Van Doorn's one-year target price was a modest $4, though this would be achieved much sooner.

The results of work programs at Busang were duly reviewed, and the analyst noted that an open-pit resource was shaping up with potential for one or two million ounces of gold. The report also included an exhibit of drill results, starting with hole 2A and including holes 3, 4, 4A, 7, 8, 9, 11 and 12.

The report contained an interesting footnote on preliminary metallurgical tests. A bottle-roll test, in which the sample, finely ground, is shaken with a cyanide solution that dissolves the gold, gave a 79% recovery after 24 hours. It was an unusual result, suggesting that the gold was coarse-grained and that the cyanide solution was taking a longer time than normal to dissolve the grains.

The evidence for salting is strong even at this stage of the project. Not only had the cyanide leach tests worked slowly, suggesting coarse gold, but, from drill hole 3 onward, there was a sudden increase in the grade and length of mineralized intersections. This was strikingly evident in hole 2A, drilled in early 1994 as a "twin" of hole 2, which had been drilled in November 1993. Whereas the earlier hole had cut two intersections, each a metre in length, grading 1.1 and 1.8 grams of gold per tonne, the later one returned 6 metres grading 8 grams and 12 metres grading 7.4 grams per tonne.

De Guzman's hand-written progress report to Felderhof on April 11 was full of excitement. "Hole 3A finished yesterday, STOPPED IN VERY FAVORABLE MINERALIZATION", he printed. "This should be the main zone of mineralization!! at BRH-3A. Overall, this intercept is the tip of the iceberg, which fully justifies the stage two deep-drilling program."

It was also some time in the last half of 1994 that someone on the project directed Indo Assay to start using a cyanide leach analysis routinely on the core samples. Perhaps this instruction came out of Jerry Alo's sample preparation study; or maybe the order came from Puspos, de Guzman, or Felderhof, all of whom were authorized to give instructions to the lab. The new method, very similar to the metallurgical bottle-roll test, used a sodium cyanide solution to leach the gold from the sample pulp. Indo Assay analyzed a 750-gram mass of sample, far more than the 50 grams it had been analyzing by fire assay.

Gold is often unevenly distributed in a piece of rock, and a larger quantity of material has a better chance of having its fair share of the gold in any core sample. So the immediate result of the switch to cyanide leach was an improvement in the reproducibility of analyses. It wasn't that the lab was suddenly doing a better job, just that two 750-gram samples from the same bag of core were more likely to carry identical concentrations of gold than were two 50-gram samples.

Probably around the same time, the project staff decided to ship the entire core, rather than a split core, for analysis. This was unconventional; normally the core is sawn or blade-split down its length, with half sent for analysis and the other half retained for later examination and, sometimes, re-assaying. It helps with later core logging, because there is some rock from previous drill holes to look at; and it helps to prove assays are correct, because it is always possible to send the other half to check earlier results. But Bre-X, defying accepted practice, kept only a 10-centimetre length of core as a "library" specimen.

Market attention

Dorothy Atkinson, senior mining analyst at Pacific International Securities in Vancouver, B.C., issued a "strong buy recommendation" for Bre-X at $2.40 on August 30, along with her target price of $4 within one year. Her bullish view appeared modest when, less than a month later, Bre-X reported that it had drilled 31 holes at Busang and that 22 of them had intersected "significant widths of gold mineralization."

Felderhof also expressed confidence that "an open-pittable resource ranging between 30 and 60 million tonnes at an average grade better than 3 grams [gold per tonne] can be attained at Busang." Newsletter writer Brian Fagan noted that this 6-million-oz. figure would make the project "the biggest gold mine in Indonesia." Fagan overlooked Grasberg and Ertsberg — perhaps it was nostalgia for the brief post-colonial period when the Dutch still ruled West Irian.

The drills continued spinning through to the end of 1994, when the stock was just below $3, and into early 1995. Bre-X scaled another credibility hurdle in February of that year when it announced its first independent resource calculation for the Central zone. Consulting geologist Roger Pooley estimated that the deposit hosted a total of 10.3 million tonnes grading 2.9 grams per tonne, roughly equivalent to one million contained ounces. All the analysts who had projected that Bre-X would achieve this target breathed a sigh of relief. The good news was topped off with some impressive drill results, including a 20-metre interval grading 6.9 grams gold and 22 metres of 9.37 grams.

As the good results continued to flow from the Busang property, Kavanagh brought along the impressive assay numbers to his meetings with Bay Street analysts. In mid-1994, he sold John Embry on the merits of Busang. It was a coup, as Embry managed mutual funds for the Royal Bank of Canada and was not known as a fan of

Bre-X or its management until Kavanagh came on board. Not long afterwards, Kavanagh made a positive impression with the fund manager at TD Asset Management, a division of Toronto Dominion Bank.

South of the border, Kavanagh achieved another coup by having the high-profile Scudder Funds take down some shares of Bre-X. Fund manager Douglas Donald was a Princeton graduate, so the men met at the university's club and enjoyed a pleasant lunch. Kavanagh returned home not knowing whether he had made a convert or not. It turned out he had, thanks to the old school tie, though Donald is reported to have been a conservative investor satisfied with a modest gain; he got out while the getting was good.

Despite all this attention in North America, Bre-X's exploration success at Busang was barely noticed in the Indonesian mining community. Takala Hutasoit, de Guzman's former boss in Indonesia, heard about the discovery while on a business trip to Vancouver in 1995.

"Someone was telling me that Bre-X stock had run from $2 to $10 and that the geologist was Mike de Guzman. Mike had told us, many times, that it was his dream to find a mine in Indonesia, and to have his name registered in the books and known around the world. I thought: Mike's dream is coming true, he found something."

Chapter Four:
THE SOUTHEAST ZONE DISCOVERY

As long as there's no find, the noble brotherhood will last, but when the piles of gold begin to grow, that's when the trouble starts. I know what gold does to men's souls.
An old prospector passes along some wisdom in B. Traven's
The Treasure of the Sierra Madre.

Taking a back seat to Voisey's Bay

When Bre-X Minerals reported the discovery of a new gold zone at the Busang property in early 1995, the event was overshadowed by the remarkable progress made by Diamond Fields Resources at its Voisey's Bay nickel-copper-cobalt discovery in Labrador.

Diamond Fields, a partnership between American stock-promoter Robert Friedland and diamond entrepreneur Jean-Raymond Boulle, hired two Newfoundland prospectors to look for evidence of diamond deposits in the rocky, windswept terrain of Eastern Canada. What they found instead was a spectacular gossan, or rust-stained showing, that concealed a valuable nickel-copper-cobalt deposit near Voisey's Bay.

Had the men brought along geological maps, they might have decided to fly on and try their luck elsewhere. Government geologists had sampled the showing, but no significant values were returned and the target was mapped as a pyritic gossan. This meant that common pyrite, or fool's gold, was thought to cause the staining, rather than sulphides of economic interest.

The two prospectors, Albert Chislett and Chris Verbiski, landed on the gossan, collected their own samples and sent them for assaying. Because they had collected fresh rock, rather than the weathered, leached surface samples collected by others, the Chislett and Verbiski samples were found to contain highly encouraging values of copper and nickel.

It was a classic boot-and-hammer prospecting success story. "We sat on that gossan and imagined where the mine and mill would go," Chislett told *The Northern Miner* during a subsequent visit to the site.

While Chislett and Verbiski knew they were onto something important, they had a tough time convincing Diamond Fields that the showing warranted a work program. After some debate, the two prospectors were given a shoestring budget to explore the prospect during the 1995 season.

As soon as weather conditions allowed, Chislett and Verbiski were back at work and ready to drill. The initial holes were impressive and caught the immediate attention of two Vancouver-based majors, Teck Corp. and Cominco Ltd. "Norm Keevil [president and chief executive officer of Teck] and Bob Hallbauer [former president of Cominco; now deceased] were in my office talking a deal that night," Friedland recalled. "But I looked at Norm and asked him, 'With these kind of results, what would you do?'"

Friedland knew Keevil's answer had to be "keep drilling," which he did. At the same time, though, he allowed the two majors to buy a small slice of the Voisey's Bay pie. By being first in the door, Teck and Cominco were able to purchase 12 million shares of Diamond Fields at a cost of $108 million, which, at the time, some people thought was a foolhardy risk.

Though Voisey's Bay was found in late 1994, it was not taken seriously by the Canadian mining establishment until March of the following year, when spectacular core from the property was put on public display at the annual convention of the Prospectors and Developers Association of Canada. Until that point — when mining executives and analysts got to the core of the matter and saw for themselves that Voisey's Bay was real — Diamond Fields was perceived as little more than the latest smoke-and-mirrors promotion of Robert Friedland.

At the time, Friedland was struggling to distance himself from a failed Venezuelan gold play. He also was under fire for his role in the ill-fated Summitville gold mine in Colorado's San Juan mountains. The open-pit, heap-leach mine was an environmental and financial disaster, but Friedland ended up taking the fall for more than just his company's part in the fiasco. The property had been previously mined several times, with the first operations dating back to the turn of the century. Despite his considerable skills at oratory, Friedland was not able to convince the Environmental Protection Agency (nor the press) that other parties had contributed to the problems at Summitville, until a court case in 1995 substantiated his position.

Toronto's Bay Street was hesitant to buy into the Voisey's Bay story because of the "Friedland factor." Analysts were skeptical, and one even suggested the core might have been salted. While that is relatively easy to do with gold, it is much more difficult with base metals, where the sulphides are often visible to the naked eye. In the case of Voisey's Bay, not only were the sulphides coarse-grained and easily detected, the core itself looked as though someone had drilled through an engine block. When mining analysts visited the site and brought back samples, the pieces of core set off metal detectors in airports.

The ongoing drill program generated spectacular results. Friedland brought in the world's top nickel experts, who substantiated the find, and Bay Street, finally convinced, dived in. A vigorous bidding war erupted between Inco Ltd. and Falconbridge Ltd., Canada's top nickel producers. Inco won the day in a multi-billion-dollar buyout, and Teck and Cominco saw their investment in Diamond Fields climb to $461 million.

Friedland, now christened "Saint Robert of Labrador," was a hero again, notwithstanding snide remarks that he had merely been in the right place at the right time. Mining executives were envious. "Friedland couldn't be that lucky," one moaned. "He must have sold his soul to the devil."

The success of Voisey's Bay taught Bay Street two important lessons — first, that mineral projects should stand on their technical merits (rather than on the personal or professional merits of their owners) and, second, that the biggest and best returns come to those who get in the door early.

John Felderhof and David Walsh watched events at Voisey's Bay with extreme interest, particularly Diamond Fields' transaction with Teck and Cominco. The equity deal gave Diamond Fields a credibility boost and enough cash to continue work on its own. It was then able to increase the value of the property and boost the price eventually paid by the suitor with the deepest pockets. Felderhof made no secret that he liked the deal and wanted a similar one for Bre-X. He was not happy that the Southeast zone had to take a back seat to Voisey's Bay, though, and his irritation at being upstaged sparked the industry observation that Felderhof had developed "a chronic case of deposit envy."

The stars line up

Timing is everything in the mining business. The launch of Bre-X Minerals as a vehicle for Indonesian exploration came on the heels of two major discoveries made by junior companies — diamonds in Canada's North and the Voisey's Bay nickel-copper-cobalt project in Labrador.

Brokerage firms, fund managers and investors had made millions of dollars on these plays, which only whetted their appetites for the healthy returns junior companies could deliver in a bull market. By this point, the pool of investment capital in North America had grown to immense proportions, largely because of an aging population. The baby-boomers collectively had socked away millions of dollars in retirement savings plans and pension funds. The professionals managing these huge pools of capital were looking for returns far greater than those provided by some of the more traditional investment vehicles. Real estate was in the doldrums and interest rates, at least in Canada, were at historic lows. Junior companies delivered far better returns and it soon became all too easy to forget that where there is potential for high reward, there is corresponding high risk.

Felderhof and Walsh tapped into this overheated market by offering a project they claimed had potential for "millions of ounces." The claim was not unreasonable, as Southeast Asia was home to several mammoth deposits, including Freeport-McMoRan Copper & Gold's Grasberg mine and Placer Dome's Porgera deposit. Major producers such as Barrick Gold and Placer Dome were hungry for ounces and were prepared to pay top dollar for them. After all, both companies were producing huge amounts of gold each year, and in order to grow and stay ahead of the game, they had to more than just replenish those mined ounces.

Had Busang came along a decade earlier, Walsh and Felderhof probably would have had little success breaking into the conservative, blue-chip world of Bay Street. But Voisey's Bay opened a door, and behind that door was a group of mining analysts, pumped up and waiting for "the next big one" which they vowed not to miss.

The analysts had learned not to judge a book by its cover. Voisey's Bay was discovered by two down-to-earth Newfoundland prospectors who, before their big strike, probably would have been unable to raise two cents on Bay Street. Vancouver-based stock promoter Murray Pezim was known more for his womanizing and show-biz grandstanding than for his big gold strikes at Hemlo, Ontario, and at Eskay Creek in northern British Columbia. And Charles Fipke was passed off as a eccentric geologist who had been out in the bush too long before he made his big diamond find. All these players got their start using funds raised on the speculative Vancouver Stock Exchange.

If some analysts had a problem with Walsh and his fondness for beer before noon (and plenty did), they would look to Felderhof,

Bre-X Geologist Michael de Guzman on the Busang property.

who would step up to bat and show off his first-hand knowledge of the geology of Southeast Asia. The underlying message was that while he might never make the cover of *Gentlemen's Quarterly*, here, at least, was a man who wore his jungle-scars as a badge of honor. And, as the old saying goes, gold deposits are not found on Bay Street by men wearing Gucci loafers.

Those who found Felderhof rough around the edges and arrogant took comfort in the presence of Paul Kavanagh, a man of integrity and a known quantity on Bay Street and Wall Street.

Check and checkmate

Michael de Guzman was as competitive as any other geologist when it came to wanting his name credited with a major find, and yet, at Busang, he showed no sign of resentment when glory for the discovery of the Southeast zone was showered on his superior, John Felderhof. Indeed, he generously insisted that his young protégé, Cesar Puspos, deserved much of the credit for the geological detective work that led to the discovery of the new zone.

Puspos and de Guzman had worked together at Benguet Corp. "I hired Cesar," said Birl Worley. "He did well, from the time he was right out of school. He has a face that nobody would love and a name that everybody made fun of, but Cesar has a very good brain.

He was honest and he was a professional."

Puspos followed de Guzman to Indonesia, where they worked together on several projects. He also worked briefly for Stephen Walters, the English geologist who had been one of the first to explore the Busang prospect. Later, he married Walters' secretary.

Said Walters: "Cesar was an excellent geologist, technically, when he worked for me in Sulawesi [the island in central Indonesia formerly known as Celebes]. I was sorry when, in 1991, I had to let him go due to cutbacks at the project I was working on."

Puspos and Walters lost contact until they met by chance at a supermarket in Balikpapan and stopped to chat. "Cesar was pretty depressed because things were still not going too well [with Bre-X]," Walters recalled. "Money was still tight, and they weren't being paid that well, though they were being given a lot of share options."

The fortunes of Cesar Puspos had improved considerably by 1995, when the Southeast zone discovery transformed the Busang project into something quite extraordinary. De Guzman's original site visit in late 1992 had already established that the area's potential went beyond the Central zone. John Felderhof launched efforts to cover new targets in early 1994, and positive results were obtained from scout drilling and samples collected by Puspos that year.

De Guzman gave mining analysts a more exciting recount of the Southeast zone discovery, which differed somewhat from the riveting story told to newspaper reporters about "brainstorming" in the middle of the night until all the pieces of the puzzle fell together.

The "Eureka" version was too hokey for analysts, who were told the discovery resulted from a surface exploration program carried out early in 1995, simultaneous with drilling of the Central zone. The stage had been set by de Guzman, who found an exposure in a creek bed where locals had supposedly panned for gold. The presence of sulphides and bleached fragments of altered rock in the creekbed suggested that Busang's potential went well beyond the known Central zone, prompting de Guzman to flag the outcrop.

Puspos later revisited the site while supervising the surface program. He found de Guzman's marker, on which he scribbled "checkmate," reflecting their mutual interest in chess. The area later proved to be near the discovery outcrop for the Southeast zone.

Not long afterwards, another exposure of similar-looking rock was found in a road cut. Puspos noticed that the mineralized exposure was different from the Central zone in several ways. The rocks contained more sulphides (suggesting a more active mineralizing system) and were more broken up and fractured (suggesting the rocks were better prepared to receive and trap gold). He measured the orientations of the fractures with a compass and clinometer (an instrument for determining angles of inclination or slope) and found that they were different from those at the Central zone. He surmised that Bre-X had been drilling obliquely to the fractures, rather than straight through them. "What turned the key was Cesar's fracture analysis, which is one of the first lessons learned in school," de Guzman explained.

Suddenly, the geological potential of Busang had transformed into something monstrous. The structures that played host to the new "discovery" were mapped and traced over 5.4 km of strike length, dwarfing the Central zone. (Strike is the direction or bearing of a geological structure in the horizontal plane.)

Excitement was in the air. According to a recount of events by Felderhof and de Guzman, David Walsh and other directors were brought to the site and shown the new developments.

Mining analysts were told that Walsh was "so elated" by the new discovery that he paid little heed to the jungle heat and hiked a considerable distance down a steep, slippery hill to look at the rock fragments in the creekbed.

"We were a bit worried he would have a heart attack," quipped de Guzman, with a sly smile.

There were no hoots of disbelief, though a few jokes were made after the story was told. The analysts had just hiked to the creekbed themselves, sinking knee-deep in red mud several times along the way. One wondered aloud how on earth the portly Walsh managed to hike down this particular trail without spilling his beer.

While de Guzman entertained the analysts with his tall tales, Puspos would smile sheepishly and nod when appropriate. He was a man of few words and always seemed ill at ease when his boss rattled on about the big breakthrough at Busang. He was there in body but never in spirit. At the time, people thought he was a shy person, uncomfortable in the limelight.

As the drilling progressed and returned positive results, de Guzman also lavished praise on Walsh and Bre-X management for "being open to new concepts." That support, he later told analysts, "added momentum to our efforts."

The share price gained momentum when, on April 12, 1995, Bre-X released news of the first two holes drilled at the northern end of the Southeast zone. Hole 52 hit 196 metres grading 3 grams gold per tonne, while hole 55 hit 129 metres of "significant mineralization," though the assay results themselves were "still pending."

The beauty of the Southeast zone, Bre-X told analysts, was that it was held 90% by Bre-X, compared with only 80% of the Central Zone area.

Through foreign subsidiaries, Bre-X had entered into a joint-

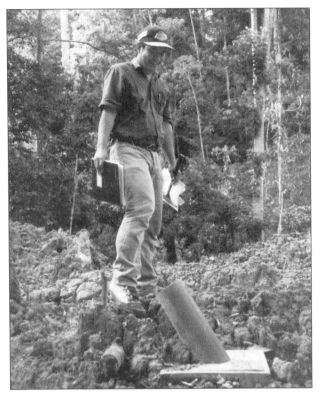

Bre-X geologist Cesar Puspos examines the drill collar of the discovery hole at Busang's Southeast Zone.

venture agreement with PT Askatindo Karya Mineral, owned by the Syakerani family, who also held an ownership position in PT Westralian Atan Minerals (PT WAM).

Bre-X would hold a 90% participating interest in a contract of work (CoW) application referred to as Busang II, while Syakerani would hold the remainder. The CoW was for 45,221 hectares and it covered the area that became the Southeast zone.

Jusuf Merukh, Bre-X's other local partner in PT WAM (which held the Central zone, also known as Busang I), was not invited to participate in the new CoW. Nor was he asked to participate in Busang III, a CoW application covering 127,448 hectares held by a joint-venture agreement with PT Amsya Lyna, another company owned by the Syakeranis.

Alarm bells should have rung, but did not. Normally partners in a joint-venture have a fiduciary duty to share information and the benefits of that information to acquire adjoining ground near a mineral discovery. The principle is a cornerstone of mining law in countries with common-law systems, such as Canada. Indonesian mining law elevated the principle to a strict requirement of its CoW system, though few knew this at the time. Nor did anyone realize that when Bre-X cut out Jusuf Merukh, the company had sown the seeds of its own demise.

Both CoW applications were "agreed to in principle" by the Indonesian government, and a preliminary licence to explore, called a SIPP, was issued for a one-year term on each property. This meant the permit to explore Busang II would expire on July 20, 1996, whereas the permit for the Busang III CoW would expire in mid-December of that year.

Work on the Central zone was still being carried on under PT WAM's Muara Atan CoW, which, by then, had been reduced to 15,062 hectares, as required under Indonesian law. By this point, Bre-X reported that PT WAM had filed for, and received, an extension from the government so that it could carry out a feasibility study.

Bring on the boiler room

Newsletter writer Ted Carter noticed the change in tone, and a few others did too.

With the discovery of the Southeast zone, David Walsh and John Felderhof no longer had the air of desperate men at the mercy of exploration results from the Busang project. They had become prophets. They began telling investors what the Southeast zone would deliver and, more often than not, they were right. Mother Nature had been put in her place.

"They started talking about how this thing [the Southeast zone] could be really big," Carter recalled. "Before this I had not considered the company extremely promotional."

Still interested, Carter tracked the progress of drilling, hole by hole. Then he noticed something strange. A series of holes reported as being from the new Southeast zone were, it seemed, actually from the Central zone. "When I got the results, I called David and said, 'That's not the Southeast zone — that's the southern edge of the Central zone.' He just chuckled and said, 'Yeah, probably.'"

Carter was mollified when the few holes were eventually attributed to the Central zone. But tracking results soon become more difficult as the drilling became more widely spaced. "They started going hell-bent for leather down the Southeast zone, going in quantum leaps, trying to define strike. They were not consistent in their fence lines [survey lines cut through the bush on a grid pattern, which serve as a guide for exploration] — especially later on, after I was long gone."

As 1995 progressed, Carter watched in amazement as Felderhof and Walsh pulled out all the stops to promote the Southeast zone discovery.

"The tone had changed," he said. "These guys were starting to talk 30 million oz., [and they] had never talked like that before. In the early days they were cautious, even about the Central zone having 2 to 3 million oz. Yet now, glibly rolling off the ends of their tongues were numbers like 20 million, 30 million oz. I sold all my stock in the fall of 1995 at 28 bucks, and I was one happy camper, even though it subsequently went over 50 bucks."

About this time, Carter was asked by a reporter from *The Calgary Sun* for his opinion on Bre-X. He gave the reporter his frank assessment, including what he believed were the positive and negative aspects of the story.

"The real negative was my comment that, based on the results released to date by the company, the stock is way ahead of itself," Carter recalled.

The next day, Bre-X stock dropped from $54 to $36. "David attributed that to me and, for a while, I became *persona non grata*," Carter added. "I was even taken off their fax list [for news releases]."

Eventually, other people interceded and convinced Walsh that the reporter had played up Carter's comment in order to put a negative spin on the story. Walsh conceded that, yes, reporters were nasty people not above doing that sort of thing. Fences were mended.

"It shows one thing about David," Carter said. "He is a very loyal friend, but he demands the same kind of loyalty from the people he deals with. If he feels you have treated him unfairly, he takes that to heart and is very resentful. He is sensitive to being betrayed."

Carter continued to monitor Bre-X's progress, but, from that point forward, could never justify buying the stock again. After the fall of 1995, he never mentioned Bre-X in his newsletter (until the spring of 1997). "I never put out any of their news releases. As far as I was concerned, it was a dead issue for myself and my subscribers. Everybody had the chance to make their money, and what they did afterwards was up to their own greed or whatever."

Carter was quite content with the gains he made riding Bre-X stock from 59¢ to $28. "It was a helluva score for me. I didn't need to run these risks on a company that I always thought was running 50% more than what its reported results merited."

The Southeast zone re-discovered

Ted Carter was right about more than the wisdom of taking Bre-X profits early. The first holes drilled on the new Southeast zone discovery turned out not to be the "discovery" holes after all.

Hole BRH-55, ostensibly the second hole to test the new zone, simply went off the radar screen and no results were reported. Perhaps the person who visually estimated the 129 metres of "significant mineralization" was not fully competent in the art, or perhaps Carter's scrutiny prompted a review of Cesar Puspos's

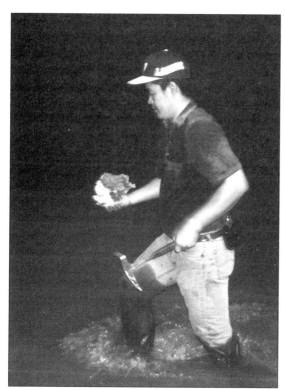

Michael de Guzman's right-hand man in the Indonesian bush was fellow Filipino Cesar Puspos, project manager at Busang.

"fracture analysis."

Despite this slight mix-up, Bre-X, in May, was busy drilling the Southeast zone with two rigs. The program was to entail 64 holes, drilled at 250-metre spacings along a series of lines cut across the strike of the zone. The new holes were all labelled "SSE," to differentiate them from the "BRH"-numbered holes previously drilled on the Central zone.

On June 20, Bre-X issued a press release stating that "visual analysis of four completed holes indicates considerably more mineralization than originally anticipated." At the same time, it reported that consulting geologist Roger Pooley had updated his resource calculation for the Central zone to 31 million tonnes grading 2.62 grams of gold, or 2.3 million contained ounces.

Walsh (or possibly his alter ego, Felderhof) then did some mental calculations, and shareholders were told that Bre-X was "confident" that resources in the Central zone would be "about 3 million ounces" once the assay results of nine more holes were in hand. Walsh took the exercise one step further and incorporated someone's "eyeball assays" from the Southeast zone. "Based on extremely encouraging data to date from assays and visual results, Bre-X continues to be confident that six to eight million ounces of gold, in various resource categories, will be achieved by November," he wrote.

It was a good thing Bre-X was not listed on the Vancouver Stock Exchange, where "eyeball assays" are frowned upon and where resource projections based on them are vigorously discouraged. It was a brave statement for Walsh to make, considering the vagaries

Drill roads winding through the dense forests of Busang.

of exploration and the fact that Mother Nature rarely gives up her riches easily, and never on demand.

But she did exactly that when results were released from the first hole drilled to test the Southeast zone discovery. The hole returned a number of mineralized intersections; 3 metres of 3.98 grams of gold, 10 metres of 2.23 grams, 4 metres of 3.37 grams and a mind-blowing 212-metre interval grading 3 grams.

When mining analysts visited the property the following summer, Cesar Puspos stood atop his famous discovery hole, number BSSE-1, and posed for photographs, grinning sheepishly all the while.

The second hole, BSSE-2, had even higher grades; 24 metres grading 6.38 grams and 112 metres of 6.5 grams. Move over, Voisey's Bay.

Bay Street jumps in

Until the spring of 1995, Bre-X's budding reputation as an Indonesian trail-blazer had won few converts on Toronto's Bay Street. That changed in May 1995, when a financing involving LOM, Nesbitt Burns, Scotia McLeod and McLean McCarthy placed a total of 1.3 million shares at $3.75. Bre-X management placed 650,000 at the same price, for total proceeds of $7.5 million.

"National brokerage houses do not finance junior companies

without doing a lot of due diligence," noted Brian Fagan of *Asian World Stock Report*. "This stamp of approval is a signal that what Bre-X has been saying all along has a lot of merit to it."

The Bay Street houses were rewarded for their leap of faith when results from the Southeast zone began pouring in. By June 20, the stock hit $6. By the middle of July, it reached $12. Everyone was happy and no one was arguing with success.

In the early days, despite the stock's solid performance, not all investment firms were sold on Busang. One small blue-chip Toronto firm, wanting to understand what the fuss was all about, called Walsh and Felderhof and set up a meeting. The principals were surprised when the top men from Bre-X waltzed in with nothing — no printed information of any kind — and started talking about the wonders of Busang. The blue-chip boys asked questions; so many that Felderhof became annoyed, reached in his pocket and pulled out a grubby piece of paper, unfolded it and said: "Here's the map." Suffice it to say, those wallets remained shut.

In Indonesia, things were not much better. Felderhof, de Guzman and Jonathan Nassey gave one of the first presentations on Busang to the mining community in Jakarta. Someone present described the event as "hokey" and "embarrassing" and "full of nonsense about maar-diatremes, grabens, skarns and every possible geological theory in the world."

But many others began buying into the story, which, at the very least, was good for local geologists and mining businesses. As the good results continued to gush forth from Busang, any skepticism began to be dismissed as sour grapes.

Teck goes bottom-fishing

John Morganti is a classically trained mining geologist of the old school, though he is still young enough to become excited when major discoveries are made. As the head of gold exploration for Teck, the Vancouver-based major that had checked out the Busang property during the earliest stages of drilling, he wanted to see the property's geology for himself.

"Wayne [Spilsbury] and another geologist [James Oliver] had looked at it before I joined Teck but didn't see a major structure," he recalled. "In September of 1995, the project started popping up on the screen in a big way and we developed the feeling that it may be a major discovery."

It was no idle speculation. The company had seen the results of some satellite imagery which showed that cutting through the property was a major fault line in the rock. As every geologist knows, gold deposits often form along faults, particularly in areas where the main fault intersects a number of smaller faults that cross it at an angle.

That autumn, Teck wrote Bre-X to express its interest and asked if the junior was interested in making a deal. "We even wrote up a general offer, which had a back-in agreement allowing us to earn an interest in the property," said Morganti.

The Teck geologist informed Bre-X that the offer was subject to due diligence, which would include redrilling some holes, as he had heard the junior was keeping only a small portion, rather than half, of its core.

"That was part of my training," he said. "It was drummed into me that when you don't have core, you have to redrill. That rule came about because of the Tapin Copper scandal [where the core went missing]."

Morganti had assembled a team to carry out the due-diligence program. Yet it was a waste of time, as Teck's offer was handily rejected. Walsh wrote to the company, telling it that Bre-X management had decided to postpone any negotiations regarding joint-venture possibilities until the spring of 1996. Teck also was informed that Bre-X did not intend to release technical data, other than what was released to the public, to potential suitors.

By then, Bre-X management had decided not to allow mining companies to visit the site until the Southeast zone drill program was completed, sometime in the spring of 1996.

Teck began kicking around the idea of buying Bre-X shares, a strategy that had proved a resounding success with Diamond Fields Resources, founder of the Voisey's Bay nickel deposit in Labrador. "I didn't push to buy the shares, and we didn't," Morganti said. "It would have been a bit dangerous, as there is usually a lock-up period that prevents the sale of the shares for a certain period. Plus, this was gold, which always has hype attached to it. Base metals, you can see. Plus, you can't do due diligence on shares, and they wouldn't allow me on the property."

Rocket ride to $50

October is traditionally a lacklustre month for stock markets, but this was not true for Bre-X in 1995, when the company began producing returns that quickly made it the darling of many of Canada's top brokerage firms.

The Bre-X train was picking up speed, and passengers were piling aboard.

The excitement began on October 2, when Bre-X reported results from seven more holes drilled on the developing Southeast zone. Two missed, but the remaining five produced some impressive numbers. The stock was trading at about $18.

Later in the month, Bre-X reported a new resource calculation for the Central zone. This calculation was done by PT Kilborn Pakar Rekayasa, the Indonesian unit of the Kilborn consulting and engineering firm. Kilborn, well-established in the Canadian mining industry and known for everything from resource calculations to complete mine project management, gave Bre-X a level of credibility with investors that a lone operator like Roger Pooley could never have provided. The news was encouraging — more than 2.75 million ounces contained in 35 million tonnes grading 2.44 grams per tonne — but was completely overshadowed by results from three "stepout holes" (drilled to intersect a mineralized structure along horizontal strike or at a down-dip angle) in the Southeast zone.

Holes 61 and 64, which contained 301 metres grading 4.42 grams gold and 137 metres grading 5.71 grams, respectively, caught everyone's attention. Although there were huge gaps in the pattern of drilling, the market began to visualize a multi-million-ounce deposit.

"The Central zone pales in comparison to the potential of the Southeast," stressed Felderhof, "and the Busang project, in its entirety, has the potential of becoming one of the world's great gold orebodies."

Bre-X was trading at about $29 when the announcement was made, but a road show put on by Bre-X quickly pushed it higher. Felderhof was called to Canada to take part in the marketing effort. On his way to Vancouver, he stopped over in Singapore, where he spent the evening with Wayne Spilsbury, manager of Teck's exploration efforts in Southeast Asia. After a few drinks, some shop talk and a geological discussion on the maar-diatreme model, Felderhof leaned over and told Spilsbury, "Buy some stock. It's money in the bank, Wayne. You can't miss." Spilsbury laughed: "John, I've never bought a penny stock for $28."

It would indeed have been money in the bank, for Felderhof left Singapore with more than his crystal ball. The company was about to release the results of several new holes that confirmed the huge size-potential of the Southeast zone. Busang was beginning to look like that thing every promoter says his property has potential for: "a world-class discovery."

The initial stop was First Marathon Securities' office in Vancouver, where Felderhof and Paul Kavanagh made their pitch to the firm's top brass. Word on the street was that the story was so good that the First Marathon team was running in and out of the room to place its buy orders. By the end of the road show, Bre-X's

Leftovers: A box of library core from drilling at the Busang project.

share price was up over $50.

Spilsbury heard the news a while later in Singapore and thought to himself that John Felderhof had become "quite the prophet."

By early November, however, Bre-X began slipping from its high of $59. New drill results were taking longer than expected to be released and investors were interpreting the delays to mean bad news. The price fell $1.78 one day and $2.75 the next. The trend did not look good, and the-ever vigilant David Walsh took action.

"While [we] have never stated in prior releases a specific date when releases will be announced, it appears investors anticipated results to be released at an earlier date than November 20th," he wrote. "However a logistical problem regarding the dispatch of the drill core to the assay laboratory has caused a minor delay."

He did not elaborate on what the "logistical problem" was, and the results were released on the date Walsh promised.

By early December, Bre-X had still not regained the ground, but nothing was shaking under Walsh's feet either. Everyone expected a rally in the New Year, including Yorkton Securities, which put out a buy recommendation, along with a six-month target price of US$75 for Bre-X.

First Marathon made its first property visit to Busang in late 1995 and came back impressed. "Geological site staff are quite knowledgeable and capable, and are managing the exploration program efficiently and professionally," the firm reported.

First Marathon later hosted a luncheon at Toronto's Royal York Hotel where Paul Kavanagh and John Felderhof updated investors and fund managers on the Southeast zone.

Felderhof's wife, Ingrid, looking more plain than glamorous, was in attendance. She said little and seemed content to remain in the background.

The turnout for the luncheon was relatively modest, though heads turned when mutual-fund manager Veronika Hirsch walked in and took a seat. Hirsch was known as one of Bay Street's most astute traders, having been among the first to buy into Diamond Fields' Voisey's Bay find, and her interest in Bre-X was the subject of much speculation. No one liked eating her dust.

Stan Hawkins also attended, and later ran into Peter Howe, who appeared to be surprised how good Busang was looking. "Peter kept saying, 'Gosh, we could have had that thing,'"

David Walsh was as pleased as punch that Bre-X was finally getting attention from the larger brokerage firms. The only pea in his shoe was that many were ignoring his other baby, the first-born Bresea, which then held 24% of Bre-X. The pea would become a stone in the months ahead.

Little white lie

Michael de Guzman's star was on the rise, and news of his success at Busang soon found its way to some of his former colleagues at Benguet. While most were happy for his success, a few took exception to the fact that Bre-X, in its promotional material and annual report, was touting de Guzman as a "co-discoverer" of the Dizon gold mine in the Philippines.

Birl Worley was surprised to hear that his former trainee had included the claim in his list of accomplishments. "It's not true," he said. "The prospect was found in 1936."

Worley said the project was identified by the Japanese, who did some work on the property before the Second World War. Another Japanese firm took it on in the 1960s, and yet another did some work in the 1970s before abandoning it altogether.

Worley had Benguet pick up the Dizon project when it became available, as the company was working nearby and knew the geology was attractive. "Other people were involved, not Mike," he added. "It happened before Mike even graduated as a geologist."

Worley and several others who knew the real story considered writing a letter of complaint to Bre-X, stating that de Guzman's claim was not true. At the same time, everyone knew that geologists often exaggerate their accomplishments, claiming credit as "a co-discoverer" when their role really was splitting core or some such peripheral activity at the project site.

Worley decided not to make an issue out of de Guzman's claims when a professional report on Benguet's Acupan mine appeared. The report, written by several Australian geologists, made liberal use of de Guzman's geological work, as well as some of Worley's —

without giving either of them credit. "I said, 'OK, if these Ph.Ds can get away with [being disingenuous], let Mike go,'" Worley said. "But I advised Mike of the situation and reminded him that he had quit Benguet because of [others'] dishonesty."

The Canadians are coming

The impressive assay results from the Southeast zone did more than excite mining analysts. Junior companies hoping to emulate Bre-X's success began flocking to Indonesia to get orang-utan pasture near Busang or, failing that, somewhere in the general neighborhood.

Many found that Indonesia is not a place where a Canadian stock promoter can expect to step off a plane, check into a hotel, and tie up a sound property deal between afternoon martinis. Getting around the country is difficult, and connections are required not only to acquire good properties but to ensure that everything is as represented. Every David Walsh wannabe who arrived in Jakarta hoped to find his own Felderhof so as to avoid being led down the garden path by unscrupulous wheeler-dealers.

After all, stories had already circulated in Canada about the mining executive who decided to save time by having his chief geologist examine half the properties while he saw the rest. Imagine their surprise when they met on the same property, each with a separate "vendor" in tow. An argument ensued about who was the rightful owner, but the damage was done; the potential purchasers were too suspicious to be sold even a cold beer.

By the time most of the juniors had arrived in Indonesia, the best ground had already been tied up by a couple of enterprising speculators. Newly arrived companies had a choice of doing business with either Michael Novotny or Armand Beaudoin, two prospectors-turned-property-dealers.

Novotny had pulled together a fairly decent portfolio of properties, most of which consisted of ground relinquished over the years by Australian-based Pelsart Resources, which he had helped manage years earlier, and various other companies. He brought in Laurie Whitehouse as a partner and began making deals with Canadian juniors. Both men had worked with Felderhof and de Guzman in the 1980s exploration boom and knew where some of the better gold prospects near Busang were situated.

Novotny said he came to Toronto in March 1994, "six months behind John [Felderhof]," looking to vend his properties to Canadian juniors for cash, shares or a combination of both. But, as far back as late 1993, he began making calls to line up prospective parties in North America.

Beaudoin had made a remarkable comeback since the Minindo fiasco of the early 1990s. He had also tied up large blocks of ground and begun dealing properties to several Canadian juniors.

The Indonesian government started to worry that it was in for a replay of the 1980s exploration boom — this time with Canadians instead of Australians. The main concern was that huge tracts of ground would be tied by junior companies that might not be able to raise exploration funds should an industry downturn come along. By the time 1996 rolled around, the government had tightened the rules by requiring companies to place "seriousness bonds."

Meanwhile, Bre-X Minerals, the company that started the land rush, was having a few land problems of its own. There were two unsettling facts contained in the junior's 1995 annual report, tucked away in the notes to consolidated financial statements.

At the end of 1995, Bre-X had not satisfied all obligations or received approval to mine any properties in Indonesia. The new CoW applications had not yet been approved and, in the area covering the Central Zone, PT WAM was operating under extensions to the provisions of its original CoW.

Bre-X also had yet to receive formal approval for the share transfer of PT Westralian Atan Minerals. That no one asked why is surprising, considering that Bre-X was supposed to have acquired 80% of PT WAM in 1993 for $80,100. It would have been a simple matter for John Felderhof, as Bre-X's agent in Jakarta, to register the change of ownership in PT WAM as required by Indonesian law. But, for whatever reason, he did not carry out this simple task before Bre-X began its drilling program. Only Felderhof knows why.

Red flags

As the drilling at Busang progressed, Bre-X reported that the mineralization was "predominantly sulphides," which dashed hopes that the near-surface deposit would be mostly oxidized (weathered and rusted), thereby making it cheaper and easier to extract the gold.

It was the first real clue that something was amiss. In tropical environments, heat and high rainfall work on sulphide minerals, which react with oxygen to form oxides. Mineral deposits in the tropics are typically oxidized from the surface to considerable depths. This was certainly the case at the nearby Kelian mine.

In mid-December of 1995, Bre-X reported results from metallurgical testwork that indicated the preferred option for ore processing would be a conventional carbon-in-leach circuit, coupled with a gravity recovery circuit. In other words, the gold ore would be dissolved in cyanide; then, the gold would be recovered directly from pregnant cyanide solutions by absorbing the metal on to granules of activated carbon. Analysts concluded that a mill costing millions to build would be required. The good news was that some of the gold could be mechanically separated from the host rock by simple, low-cost mechanical means.

The next red flag unfurled when Bre-X reported "preliminary results" from Kilborn's prefeasibility study, which was scheduled for release in early 1996. The study initially contemplated a 500,000-tonne-per-year mining operation, which would seem piddly and woefully undersized in the coming year.

The preliminary results showed that a gravity circuit could recover a large percentage — a remarkable 86% — of the gold. Furthermore, Bre-X noted, the study showed that the 33-hour period for leach recoveries of 93% could be "substantially reduced" by adding activated carbon. (The reason for adding activated carbon is not clear. It is used in cyanidation plants to draw the dissolved gold back out of solution, and if ores contain carbon, or carbon-rich organic matter, it has a similar effect in leach tanks, where it decreases recovery by robbing the cyanide solution of gold.) In hindsight, Bre-X's proposals for gold recovery should have raised more suspicion than they did. The long leach time showed that the mineralization being tested was far more coarse-grained that the gold observed in the original samples from de Guzman's 1992 site visit. Also, the leach time was far longer than what normally would be expected.

Not only that; the rate of recovery from a simple gravity circuit was higher than anyone would have dreamt possible from the deposit type. Few gold mines in the world are able to recover more than half their gold using simple gravity. The more typical extraction rate is in the range of 25% to 40%.

To anyone who questioned these findings — and only a few did — Felderhof pointed out that the Southeast zone was a different animal than the Central zone and that Busang was "one of a kind in the world." He might even have added another of his trademark sayings: "We can't be giving away all our secrets."

Chapter Five:
A YEAR OF GOLD AND GLORY

The world is a perpetual caricature of itself;
at every moment it is the mockery and the contradiction
of what it is pretending to be.
George Santayana

The 'ounce' factory

Lady Luck parked her notorious fickleness and lavished uncon-
ditional love on Bre-X Minerals, or so it seemed in early 1996 as
a new exploration season got under way at the Busang property.

Mother Nature, the other bane of a geologist's existence, had
been tamed till she purred. She always complied when John
Felderhof and Michael de Guzman expected her to do this or that
by such-and-such a time.

David Walsh had abandoned his basement office and mailbox at
the Market Mall in Calgary and climbed up in the world, literally.
His new digs were a square, rather ordinary Calgary building made
majestic with the words Bre-X Minerals emblazoned across the
façade. If that didn't inspire the rapidly expanding investor relations team showing up for work every morning, nothing would. Even
Barrick Gold and Placer Dome, the two largest gold companies in
Canada, didn't have buildings named after them, though they did-
n't have futon stores and barbecue shacks as neighbors either.

Bre-X's stellar performance was heady news for the Alberta
Stock Exchange, which long ago had resigned itself to taking a
back seat to all other Canadian exchanges. But 1995 was a stellar
year, thanks to Bre-X, its most active listing. Trading value on the
exchange that year was a whopping $3.4 billion, more than double
that of the previous year.

When the share price shot up by nearly $30 during Bre-X's high-

*There goes the neighborhood: Bre-X Minerals Ltd. opens up shop at 119
14th Street N.W., Calgary, Alberta.*

---

profile road show in October 1995, exchange officials were amazed
but enjoyed the ride. It was an exciting and busy time, even if Bre-
X officials were planning to take their business to a more established, senior exchange in a few months.

By mid-January, Bre-X had resumed drilling the Southeast zone
on fence lines 250 metres apart, using two rigs per line. The holes
along the fence lines were spaced 50 metres apart, and angled at
60° downward.

This was enormously wide-spaced drilling compared with the 50-
metre line spacing used by drill crews at the Central zone, where
holes were more likely to be 25 metres apart. Bre-X pointed out,
however, that it had an enormous target to test; the mineralized
zone extended for 7 km, whereas the strike length of the Central
zone was a piddling 900 metres.

Analysts were elated by the news, and intrigued to learn that
drilling was about to begin on Southeast zone No. 2 (previously
known as the North zone), which was "known to be mineralized
over a 6-km strike length." The gold potential of Busang showed no
sign of abating.

By now, Bre-X was faithfully pointing out in press releases that
it held 90% of the rapidly expanding Southeast zone. It also noted

that Indonesian exploration was being conducted through wholly owned subsidiaries incorporated in the Netherlands.

Felderhof topped the story off with some arm-waving from Jakarta: "A resource of 30 million ounces can be readily attainable in view of the recent results and visuals of the outstanding four holes."

There were more good drill results at month's end. But more interesting news came on February 20, when Kilborn Engineering reported another reserve calculation, this time for two sections across the Southeast zone.

The news should have depressed Bre-X's share price, as it showed that these two sections contained measured and indicated reserves of only 3.6 million oz. contained in 41 million tonnes grading 2.72 grams gold. But it did not, because the focus had shifted from quality to quantity. Once inferred resources from the two sections were included, the gold content was bumped up to 9.5 million oz. (110 million tonnes of 2.65 grams). And, once the contained ounces from the Central zone were included in the total resource picture, the number increased to close to 16 million oz.

In other words, the share price remained unaffected because the calculations represented only a small portion of the Southeast zone. Analysts calculated that 13 million oz. were contained in an area with a strike length of 330 metres, a width of 600 metres and a depth of 300 metres. In fact, Bre-X shares went up instead of down because the market was less interested in what was already in hand than in what was yet to come from a zone believed to extend for 7 km. And analysts had came to believe that the drills would keep on hitting.

This was the cornerstone — the secret, as it were — of Bre-X's remarkable success in 1996. From this point onward, the gold in the bush would always be more seductive and alluring than the gold in the hand. Busang was a tease and a temptress of the best kind — one that always delivered.

Professionals in the mining industry know that inferred resources are not "reserves," as the holes are not spaced closely enough to ensure that the mineralization is continuous. But many investors, many brokers and more than a few scribblers in the financial press do not. The Busang property became a factory whose assembly line produced "ounces" and "resources," not tonnes and grade broken up into categories of confidence.

Converts and skeptics

Nothing succeeds like success, which, in the case of Bre-X, converted many skeptics and silenced most others. But a silenced man

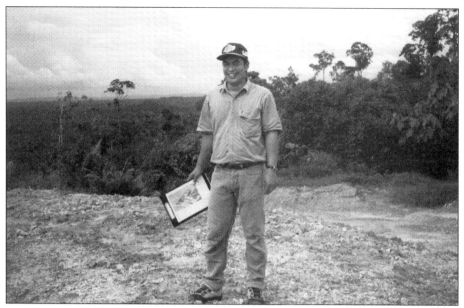

Cesar Puspos demonstrates Bre-X's all-smiles approach at Busang.

is not necessarily a converted one, as Bre-X would soon realize. By far the toughest nuts to crack were the geologists for Australian-based Murray Rogers Associates (MRA), who had previously drilled the Central zone. The skepticism of MRA's John Levings, in particular, was almost legendary in Indonesian mining circles and would soon find its way to North America.

Levings, an Australian, had been dumping all over Busang since Bre-X began its drilling. The audience that had played along in the past was now attributing his negative sentiment to the green-eyed monster.

"They [MRA] had egg all over their face because they did all the work for Montague Gold and didn't find the big zone," said Teck's Wayne Spilsbury. "They were in the same situation as me — keeping my head down for missing the world's largest gold deposit."

Another skeptic was Lawrie Reinertson, now deceased, who had watched the project closely while head of Placer Pacific, a subsidiary of Placer Dome. "I have a hard time believing the numbers," he said during cocktails at a mining symposium in early 1996, though he did not elaborate.

Closer to home, analyst Paul Esquivel at McDermid St. Lawrence Securities repeatedly warned that Mother Nature does not deliver gold on demand. "It [Bre-X's stock] is obviously overpriced, and people are getting overexuberant," he told *The Globe and Mail*.

Another vocal skeptic was Dale Hendrick, a retired Noranda executive who still worked as a consultant and was on the boards of a few junior companies. Hendrick was an avid trader who looked for undervalued companies using a back-of-the-envelope formula based on the number of shares the company had out on the market and his valuation of resources in the ground. His initial criticism of Bre-X was that its share price was always ahead of itself.

In 1995, when the value of Bre-X shares began to rise in active trading, Hendrick began plotting results from the drill holes in order to make his own resource calculations. The exercise proved more difficult than usual. Each time Hendrick completed his calculation, he found that Bre-X shares were always overvalued relative to the resources in hand. He resisted buying until the end of 1995, when the shares had fallen below his threshold. Over the next few months, he watched his investment closely and was "enormously pleased" with his returns. For a time, Hendrick was a believer — but only for a time.

Hendrick says his first clue that something was amiss at Busang came in early 1996, when he encountered Michael Gray, vice-president of Canadian exploration for the American copper producer Phelps Dodge Corp. The two men stopped to chat and, as invariably happened in those days, the conversation turned to Bre-X's latest drill results.

"They don't split their core, you know," Gray revealed.

Hendrick was astounded. Normally, after drill core is examined by geologists, it is split for analysis. Half is sent for assay, while the other half is retained for reference and possible re-checking of assay results. Not to split core goes against industry practice and, in Hendrick's view, was downright suspicious. He could think of no logical reason for anyone to assay whole core.

On February 18, while in Jakarta on business, Hendrick heard more unsettling news. Still jet-lagged, he met a group of Canadians for brunch in a smoky restaurant at the Grand Hyatt, where they were joined by Levings of MRA and a few Canadian geologists working in Kalimantan. Levings told Hendrick that he was one of three men who had drilled the Central zone at Busang in 1989 for PT Westralian's major shareholder, Montague Gold. Hendrick was naturally curious about the results.

"We got nothing, other than a sniff here and there," Levings replied.

"Well, what about Bre-X?"

"That's a joke," Levings said. "They have diddly-squit."

"Well, then they must be assaying diddly-squit with their own recipe," Hendrick joked, though still reeling from shock.

"Exactly," Levings replied.

Hendrick told a few people that Busang's Central zone had "diddly-squit." But no one was interested in the Central zone anyway; the action was at the larger, sweeter Southeast zone.

Besides, the rich Hemlo gold deposits of Ontario were once thought to have "diddly-squit" too, before Murray Pezim and his geologist David Bell showed the mining establishment otherwise. Donald McKinnon, the prospector who identified the project, was turned down by almost every major mining company in Canada before he found a believer in Pezim, who was just foolish enough to drill 76 holes and hit the motherlode.

Happy as clams

Toronto mining analysts, though, were happy as clams with Bre-X's performance. The stock had climbed by leaps and bounds to $60, $70, $80, then over $100, all before the end of February.

"We believe Busang will become one of the largest gold deposits in the world," wrote First Marathon's Kerry Smith.

Bay Street's top gold analyst, Egizio Bianchini of Nesbitt Burns, raised his estimate of total resources at Busang to 42.6 million oz.

"As a result, we are increasing our 12-month target price to $180 per share and our 18-month target price to $220 per share," Bianchini wrote. "In our view, the Busang discovery represents one of the most prolific and soon-to-be profitable gold discoveries over the past 20 years. Busang now becomes the corner post of what is already proving to be a world-class gold camp on par with the Witwatersrand [in South Africa] and the Carlin Belt [in Nevada]."

Bianchini ended his report with the comment that Bre-X should be viewed as a long-term investment, "much like Barrick Gold was from the mid-1980s to the early 1990s."

Bianchini's comments were taken as gospel, as he had been an early backer of Barrick, the pick that made his career. His strength was said to be an uncanny ability to see the big picture, and to see which direction the industry was going before it got there. His weakness was not paying sufficient attention to details. And the devil is always in the details.

Bianchini was too show-biz for some of the old-timers in the mining business, who believed that mining analysts should be dour, no-nonsense types with lots of grey hair and field experience. Bianchini had little of either and tended to think financially rather than technically. The old-timers preferred the opposite.

But other analysts were equally enthralled and loaded up with Bre-X shares. In late February, gold analyst Michael Fowler of

Levesque Beaubien Geoffrion, the brokerage arm of the National Bank of Canada, noted that Bre-X shares were already trading a fully diluted market capitalization of $3.5 billion. "We feel that the shares may well almost triple within five years," he wrote. His six-month target was $210 per share.

In early March, Bre-X announced it had raised gross proceeds of $30 million from the brokerage firms of Nesbitt Burns, Scotia McLeod, Levesque Beaubien Geoffrion and First Marathon. "The issue was significantly over-subscribed as investors continue to recognize Bre-X's potential growth as evidenced by its mineral exploration success in Indonesia to date."

Blind faith? Gold analyst Egizio Bianchini of Nesbitt Burns.

Back in Calgary, newsletter writer Ted Carter was amazed at all the fuss on Bay Street. He pulled out his notepad when Bre-X shares were trading at $150 and ran the numbers. "I said to myself, this is a $90 stock at best, or maybe, if you really stretch it, $112."

Carter also started hearing that Busang had the potential to deliver 50 million oz., and then 100 million oz. And the talk was not just coming from David Walsh and John Felderhof. "Those numbers were coming from the analysts," he said.

Meanwhile, at *The Northern Miner*'s newsroom in Toronto, subscribers were starting to complain that not enough attention was being paid to Bre-X Minerals and its Busang project. "You guys are asleep at the switch," one said. "This is the biggest story ever and you've already missed it. When's the last time you talked to David Walsh?"

The subscriber was right. The coverage had been minimal throughout 1995 and few details of the property's geology were known or had been reported. No one had called David in ages, and the stock had already reached $170. No one had talked to John Felderhof either; though he had recently been quoted in *The Globe and Mail* as saying, "I know I can do 30 million ounces with my eyes closed."

It was hoped that more technical details would be available at the company's annual meeting, scheduled for March 14 in Toronto, where shareholders would be asked to approve splitting Bre-X shares on a ten-for-one basis. They also would be asked to approve spinning off the Indonesian properties Sangihe and Sable (which had not gone anywhere and were dragging Bre-X down) to a new subsidiary that would be listed on the Alberta Stock Exchange.

Bre-X goes Broadway

They packed them standing-room-only into the ballroom of Toronto's Royal York Hotel on March 14. Retail investors jostled with fund managers and mining analysts for seats close to the stage and their heroes. The euphoria was scary.

Seated at tables along one wall was a veritable who's who of the business media. Peter Kennedy, a mining reporter for *The Financial Post* had his publisher, Douglas Knight, in tow. Jennifer Wells, author and columnist, was in attendance, which meant Bre-X was enough of a sensation to make the pages of *Maclean's*, Canada's weekly news magazine. Allan Robinson, the no-nonsense mining reporter for *The Globe and Mail*, was already taking notes. And a whole raft of other media representatives, who don't normally follow junior mining, had taken up the remaining seats. It was a full-blown outbreak of gold fever.

Although the event was supposed to be Bre-X's annual meeting, someone checked the company bylaws and said "oops!". The junior held its "real" special and annual meeting on May 10 at Calgary's Palliser Hotel, where shareholders approved a ten-to-one stock split, a shareholders' rights protection plan (a "poison pill," meant to thwart unwanted takeovers) and the roll-out of the Sable and Sangihe properties to a wholly owned subsidiary.

Bre-X officials nonetheless went ahead with the Toronto meeting, which was long on razzle-dazzle but short on substance. Walsh and Felderhof were the stars of the show, but the media were starting to take an interest in Michael de Guzman, a colorful character in his own right. Paul Kavanagh beamed like a proud father, and Stephen McAnulty, who headed up Bre-X's burgeoning investor relations department, wore his customary air of self-importance.

Bre-X started off by "postponing for 30 to 60 days" the votes on the proposed share split and property transfers, ostensibly because shareholders needed "more time" to understand the plan.

"This is ridiculous," fumed Dale Hendrick as he paced the floor. "They forgot to read their own bylaws. How Mickey Mouse can you get?"

The crowd of investors, which included many paper millionaires, had no complaints. Bre-X had paid their mortgages and guaranteed their children's education, with enough left over to retire comfortably to the Bahamas or Grand Cayman. And they owed it all to David Walsh, the little guy from Calgary who could. As a salesman, Walsh had worked hard to accumulate happy customers; here he had a room full of them, and more good news to deliver.

"We are confident we have a resource of 30 million oz. of gold, and we would not disagree with an estimate made by an Indonesian mining director who publicly described the resources as being 40 million oz.," Walsh boasted, adding that this number would increase as drilling progressed.

"Once that program is complete, we will consider inviting a senior partner to participate in and operate the project, but we intend to retain a 75% interest. And we would expect a bonus on any additional gold we find [after a deal is signed]."

Walsh acknowledged that majors usually expect a majority interest in the mines they operate. "But I think any senior company would be quite happy to have 25% of Busang and keep the 12.5 million oz." (Only minutes before, the resource was 30 million oz.; then Walsh "wouldn't disagree" with 40 million; once his speech got rolling, he thought a senior company would be happy with a quarter-share of 50 million.)

He also expressed confidence in his exploration team led by John Felderhof. "I think we understand the geological model of Busang better than our competitors do. We are far ahead of anyone else in the geological community."

Felderhof pushed the envelope a little further. "I think it's 30 million oz. . . . plus, plus, plus," he said.

Walsh said he was not sure what "each plus meant," though he probably has a better idea today. In town for the event, Michael de Guzman publicly acknowledged that Busang had potential for up to 100 million oz.

Later in the presentation, Felderhof made an offhand remark that crushed core was being analyzed by the cyanide leach method because of "problems with reproducibility using fire assay".

Peter Kennedy of *The Financial Post* was suddenly unnerved — he had honed his reporting skills at *The Northern Miner* and had seen scams involving unscrupulous operators who had added gold to cyanide solutions to get phoney assay results, and others involving promoters who had claimed, falsely, that conventional fire assaying, the standard technique for gold analysis, did not work on *their* gold.

In a story that appeared the next day, Kennedy pointed this out. It wasn't exactly news; Bre-X press releases since the end of 1994 had said that the gold concentrations in the core were determined from cyanide leach tests. But it was a cold shower for the market, which sold Bre-X down to $132.

Stephen McAnulty rushed into damage control and prepared a news release with remarks from Felderhof, who had returned to Jakarta. "A little knowledge can be more dangerous that none at all on any subject. I strongly suggested that those individuals commenting on the reliability of the cyanide leach assay method go back to school. I do not have time to educate them on the various grade determination methods for gold commonly used on a global basis in the mining industry."

Properly controlled cyanide leach tests are scientifically sound, unlike some of the "non-traditional" assay methods favored by hucksters. The process involves dissolving the metals out of the ore with the aid of a weak solution of sodium cyanide — a process which can be used on much larger "sub-samples" to defeat nugget effect (the tendency for gold to be unevenly distributed in a sample) and give a more representative analysis. Indo Assay, Bre-X's usual lab, was doing its test on 750 grams of rock. But Felderhof was protesting too much. The use of cyanide leach was enough of a departure from normal industry practice to warrant explanation, but rhetorical bullying, not explanation, was Felderhof's long suit.

The analysts weren't worried. They had already established the credentials of Indo Assay and ruled out the possibility that the lab would doctor its cyanide solutions. And they knew that cyanide leach was a legitimate choice for certain types of gold deposits, as the *Miner* pointed out at the time.

The more serious issue was that Bre-X was not splitting its core. The company sent most of its core for crushing and assaying and retained only 5% of each 2-metre core interval. The *Miner* wrote a report soon afterwards suggesting that, because of this practice, any major company interested in acquiring all or part of Busang would have to drill its own holes as part of the due diligence process. Later events would show that the paper should have placed more stress on this point.

Meanwhile, Kavanagh was having media problems of his own. Allan Robinson of the *The Globe and Mail* had found out that Kavanagh had told students from the University of Toronto that he believed Busang had potential for "one hundred million ounces." Robinson wanted clarification, but Kavanagh denied making the comment.

The controversy resulting from Kavanagh's remarks soon died down, as did concerns about Bre-X's choice of assay methods. The company described how more than 1,200 samples had been submitted to a third independent laboratory, which, using the fire assay method, "returned grades 5-7% higher than those reported employing the cyanide leach method."

The result wasn't surprising; fire assay determines the total amount of gold present, whereas the cyanide leach process measures only the amount that is extractable.

Concerns were further assuaged when Bre-X reported that metallurgical testwork, conducted by "internationally recognized" Kilborn Engineering, as part of its prefeasibility study on Busang, showed that Bre-X's gold assay results were understated by as much as 12.9%.

Beefing up the board

Until early 1996, Bre-X had done surprisingly little to strengthen its management team, even though the estimated ounces at Busang and the company's market capitalization had grown beyond anyone's wildest dreams.

Aware of this, Paul Kavanagh began suggesting some names which he felt would add experience and expertise to the junior. One was Rolando Francisco, a highly regarded financial executive who had held senior positions with several Toronto-based mining companies.

Francisco's appointment to Bre-X's board and his new position as executive vice-president was given an immediate thumbs-up on Bay Street when the news was announced on February 19.

Barry Tannock, then long-gone from Bre-X, thought it was the first sensible thing his former boss had done in years. "It was late in the game — why it wasn't done earlier I don't know."

Tannock said Bre-X's "fortress mentality" was a reflection both of John Felderhof's efforts to exert control and of Walsh's insecurity. "I think he [Walsh] was threatened by the idea of bringing in someone high-powered to handle the financial end of things,"

By this point, however, the brokerage firms were exerting their influence. In particular, they backed Kavanagh's efforts to beef up the team in Calgary. In Jakarta, Felderhof brought in Greg MacDonald, a former mining analyst, to help sort out administrative matters in Indonesia.

Meanwhile, Stan Hawkins had resigned from the board of Bresea. "We [Tandem] had a conflict of interest [with Bresea]," Hawkins said. "We were in the same joint ventures, and so I decided to resign."

He hinted, however, that there were other reasons behind his resignation. Despite repeated requests to both Walsh and Felderhof, he was never allowed to visit the Busang property. "I told them many times that I would love to see this orebody, because if you believed the results, as I did, it had to be one tremendous orebody. But they did not seem very anxious for me to see it."

As time went on, Hawkins' alienation increased. "David ran [Bresea] as his private company," he said. "Don't get me wrong — he wasn't dishonest or anything like that, but you never knew what the hell was going on, and you would hear about the deals only afterward."

By this time, Walsh and Felderhof had solidified into a team, with almost everyone else pushed aside. "David relied totally on Felderhof and thought he was the best of the best," Hawkins added. "I was a friend, but never a confidant."

But all was not rosy between the two head honchos at Bre-X.

Hawkins had already seen signs of a power struggle between Walsh and Felderhof. "There was some acrimony at times, and Jeannette couldn't stand the guy. She talked to Ingrid once in a while, but she sure as hell didn't like John.

"And I remember Mike [Duggan] saying once that Felderhof was leaving, or some God damned thing, while they were still drilling the Central zone. Then David would make a few remarks, from time to time, that there had been some sharp verbal exchanges, mostly about who was running the thing. I remember David saying, 'Christ, you wonder who is president of this God damned outfit' . . . and words to that effect, in relation to Felderhof."

The old school tie

In the spring of 1996, mining engineer Hermann Derbuch approached *The Northern Miner* with some interesting news.

Derbuch, a former Noranda executive, had just taken the helm of Minorca Resources, a small, Montreal-listed junior company that had formed a "strategic alliance" with one of Bre-X Minerals' Indonesian partners.

At first, Bay Street paid little attention to Minorca's partnership with the Syakerani family, whose company, PT Askatindo Karya Mineral (PT AKM), held a 10% interest in the contract of work (CoW) application covering the Southeast zone deposit. Their initial "co-operation and joint-venture agreement" involved not Busang but various other properties in Indonesia.

At a lunch meeting in the Toronto's King Edward Hotel, Derbuch explained that the Syakerani family would take the alliance one step further and sell part of its stake in Busang to Minorca. Why Minorca? Derbuch replied that the alliance was a case of the "old school tie" connecting Canada with Indonesia.

The family had approached Dr. Thomas Mulja, an Indonesian geologist trained at McGill University in Montreal, to see if he could help them forge an alliance with a suitable Canadian partner. Mulja was then working for Barrick Gold, and the word on the street was that he first took the deal to his employer. When it was turned down, Mulja looked elsewhere.

Prior to joining Barrick, Mulja had worked for the Syakerani family, advising them on property acquisitions and matters related to the location of *Kuasa Pertambanggan* permits (KPs), which are available only to Indonesian nationals and domestic companies. The family had put down the KPs covering Busang's Southeast zone. "[Whether] Mulja was involved in advising them to put them there or not, I don't know," Derbuch said. "I don't believe so; they got them some other way."

Mulja contacted James Bourne, one of his professors at McGill, and asked him for suggestions. Bourne recommended Alfred Lenarchiuk, a business associate who was Minorca's chairman.

These events took place in late 1995, just as Bre-X fever was beginning to hit Bay Street. Bourne and Lenarchiuk travelled to Indonesia to discuss the idea of a partnership. They met Haji Syakerani, the family patriarch, and one of his three sons, Ahmad Yani, who was then being groomed to become the family's business manager.

The discussions were productive and, before long, it was suggested that Mulja leave Barrick to become Minorca's exploration manager. The offer was accepted, and Mulja took up his new post in early March.

The first few transactions between Minorca and Syakerani involved various Indonesian properties, including one near Busang. The main objective of the alliance, however, was to pursue a final deal on Busang.

"The Syakeranis believed they would have to participate in financing Busang," Derbuch told the *Miner* at the time. "They were not poor, but the millions of dollars required was beyond them. So a deal was struck whereby Minorca would finance their capital requirements for Busang."

The Syakerani family agreed to sell Minorca 60% of its 10% stake in Busang for shares and cash. Put another way, Minorca would be entitled to a 70% interest in 6% of the production from Busang's Southeast zone.

The deal appeared to have caught Bre-X unawares and it did not take long for David Walsh to issue a news release stating that PT AKM did not have the right to enter into such an agreement without its consent. Minorca countered with its own press release stating that such consent was not required.

Bre-X's poor relations with one of its Indonesian partners was regarded by some as unsettling. The Syakeranis had complained they were kept in the dark by Bre-X and did not know much about what was going on at the property.

Contractually, the Syakeranis had the right to visit the property. "They never did, to my knowledge," Derbuch said. "They would have had to insist and that made them uncomfortable. Because of this poor relationship, Minorca was able to secure the deal."

Bre-X was criticized for not handling the matter with greater sensitivity, particularly as it had not yet obtained government approval for the Busang CoWs. The general view was: Why irritate your local partner, when the signature of that partner was necessary to obtain the contract of work?

Bre-X and PT AKM met in Jakarta on March 23 to discuss the issue and, when the meeting was over, all was rosy. Bre-X agreed not to interfere with Minorca's plans to become a minority owner in Busang.

Felderhof was still incensed about the whole affair, and was known to tell jokes based on the similarity between the names Minorca and South African mining giant Minorco.

Minorca paid US$2 million in cash and issued 3 million of its shares to PT AKM. It also agreed to pay a further US$2 million once a definitive joint venture was executed, plus US$3.5 million in cash within 30 days of the signing.

Mulja was made head of Minorca's exploration team and given a finder's fee of 300,000 shares for his role as matchmaker. Ahmad Yani, president of PT AKM, joined Minorca's board to represent the Syakerani family's interests.

Minorca was required to make another payment upon completion of a feasibility study that determined that Busang contained at least 12 million oz. of gold. The market responded to the transaction by bidding Minorca shares up over $6.

Felderhof commented in early April that "it would be in Minorca's best interest" to study the provisions of the CoW and regulations relating to foreign investments that protect the interests of Indonesian and foreign companies in a joint venture, as well as the interests of the government. He reminded everyone that while "Bre-X will not unduly withhold written approval of the agreement," it had not yet been approved by Bre-X or by Indonesia's Foreign Investment Board. "I understand that the agreement has been approved by the Montreal Exchange; however in Indonesia this agreement may have more holes in it than a lobster trap."

Felderhof's comments were meant to cast doubts about what Minorca really "owned" in Indonesia. But he might well have been talking about Bre-X, which would soon be hit by its own tidal wave of uncertainty.

No visitors please

Dale Hendrick had tried, on more than one occasion, to join a delegation of mining analysts about to visit the Busang property. The idea was always nixed by Bre-X management, who informed him that it was company policy not to allow consultants on the property.

However, Hendrick believes he was not welcome because he had publicly criticized some of Bre-X's practices, such as not splitting core in the normal manner. "I don't think they wanted someone like me poking around." But others say the increasingly paranoid Felderhof was beginning to suspect that Hendrick was really a spy for a major company, possibly Barrick Gold.

Mike Novotny, Felderhof's bush mate from the Jason/Pelsart days, also wanted to visit Busang, the property that had turned his own land-vending business into a roaring success.

Felderhof refused. "He told me he didn't want me to 'see the secrets,'" Novotny said. "He said if I saw what they had, we would know where to go and where to drill."

Novotny asked Felderhof why his team of geologists was not splitting core. "He brought up the whole issue of what had happened at Kelian and said they had coarse, particulate gold. He described it as 'lumpy gold' and 'nuggetty gold' and said that they were assaying most of the core."

Novotny also asked Felderhof how he was able to obtain long mineralized intervals from areas where Montague Gold had hit only spotty mineralization. "He told me they [Montague] had not been looking in the right place."

Felderhof was so adamant about the "no visitors" policy that he once overruled a decision made by Walsh. Barry Tannock heard about the incident after he left Bre-X. "I ran into Kevin Waddell, a geologist who had done some work for David over the years, and he was all excited because he was going to Indonesia. I ran into him a few weeks later and it was off — Felderhof wouldn't have him."

Waddell said Walsh had offered him work at Busang in February 1996 but that things turned sour when, a month later, he met Felderhof and Mike de Guzman at the Prospectors and Developers convention in Toronto.

Waddell, who was scheduled to leave for Indonesia on April 1, asked the two men what he should expect and what he should bring with him. "I wanted to know about the climate, bugs and snakes, and that sort of thing," he said. "I heard later that they were upset that I had asked questions on those matters, instead of asking about the rocks and geology."

Following the convention, Waddell returned to Calgary, only to receive a fax informing him that the position for which he was being considered was "no longer available," owing to a corporate reorganization.

"You would think that if the president of a company offers you a job, it's a done deal," he said. "But Felderhof and de Guzman didn't want me, which made me wonder who was running that company."

TSE Listing

Bre-X got its listing on the Toronto Stock Exchange on April 23, 1996, which made it eligible for inclusion in the TSE 300 and TSE 100 indices on, or after, November 1 of that year.

The listing document would even be skimpy by Vancouver Stock Exchange standards. It showed that Bre-X management held few Bre-X shares personally, though some may have held shares through trusts or holding companies. Of the company's 10 largest registered shareholders, only John Felderhof and Paul Kavanagh were represented. Felderhof held 1.8%; Kavanagh, 0.9%. Joel Raby of Westmount, Quebec, took ninth spot with 0.2%, which was the same amount held by Greg and Cathy Chorny of Aurora, Ontario. The four largest registered shareholders of Bre-X (which collectively held more than 95%) were unknown. Bresea still held an approximate 23% interest.

The document listed the options granted earlier that year to insiders, which included the key players at Busang — Michael de Guzman, Cesar Puspos, Jonathan Nassey, Jerome Alo and Roberto Ramirez — and Thomas Devlin, manager of special projects.

Devlin was a Calgary promoter who, because of his involvement with a bucket-shop brokerage firm of dubious quality, had been in trouble with securities regulators in the past. He had boiler-room experience, and the "special projects" he ran out of Bre-X's Calgary office required that he guide and advise the team of mostly young people who made up the investor relations department.

Bre-X's listing document did not contain much geological and engineering information, though Kilborn's resource calculations from the prefeasibility study were included.

Dale Hendrick was surprised to learn that the Toronto Stock Exchange did not send a consultant to visit the property.

The listing statement also noted that the Indonesian government had initialled the company's CoW applications for Busang II and III, as reported in late March.

When the development was announced, Bre-X pointed out that

while sixth-generation CoWs allow foreign companies the opportunity to retain up to a 100% interest in each project, "our Indonesian partner was invited into each contract area selected by Bre-X's technical team."

The partner referred to was the Syakerani family, not Jusuf Merukh, its other original partner in Indonesia. This would appear to have been something of an oversight, as Bre-X's Jakarta office was still telling the Indonesian government that all work at Busang was being carried out by PT WAM.

And PT WAM was still a joint venture owned by Westralian Resource Projects, the Syakerani family and Jusuf Merukh, just as it had been before Bre-X arrived on the scene. The Calgary junior still did not have any shares in PT WAM, as poor Roly Francisco would soon find out. Not only that, Bre-X was drilling the Busang property under exploration permits that would soon expire.

A few people were aware of all this, but the expectation always was that the Indonesian government would sign the CoWs and all would be fine.

Summer of Love

Spring had not yet come to Calgary or Toronto when Bre-X reported that the Busang property had blossomed once again.

On April 17, the company reported that reserves and resources had climbed to 24.87 million oz. in 267 million tonnes grading 2.8 grams of gold per tonne. While this was still far below Felderhof's "30 million ounces, plus, plus, plus," it was only for certain portions of the Southeast and Central zones. It did not include results from partially drilled sections or results from other drilled areas. The big picture was still hanging together.

By June 20, Kilborn had updated the numbers to 39.15 million ounces contained in 514 million tonnes grading 2.36 grams.

Business newspapers reported the "ounces," but rarely mentioned the tonnage and grade, nor the various resource categories, which tell a story all their own. Even at this point, measured and indicated reserves from the Southeast zone amounted to a mere 8.5 million oz.

In May, another group of analysts visited Busang. They returned predicting that Bre-X would soon be able to define more than 50 million oz. in resources and between 30 million and 40 million oz. in minable reserves. "We believe there will be enough resources to support an output of two million ounces per year at a cash production cost of US$100 per ounce, making Busang one of the largest and lowest-cost producers in the world," wrote Michael Fowler, an analyst with Levesque Beaubien Geoffrion. The stock was then trading at $27, which reflects the 10-for-1 stock split.

Fowler also projected that a 25% interest in Busang would be worth "about US$1 billion at current market prices." He said any potential buyer would have to pay an up-front fee of about $500 million in cash and shares and then invest $200 million into the project and arrange production financing.

Those were tough terms for any major to swallow. It began to look as though Bre-X finally was in the driver's seat. There would be no more basement offices for David Walsh and no more malaria pills for John Felderhof.

The hot spots of Busang

It took months of wheedling, but finally David Walsh agreed that *The Northern Miner* could visit Busang during the next tour by analysts. The invitation came suddenly, only days before the group was to leave, so the newspaper passed on this first opportunity in favor of another trip, scheduled for late July.

A flight from Toronto to Jakarta is a long, hellish trip in the cheap seats, and getting to the oil city of Balikpapan is no picnic either when jet-lag plays havoc with normal brain functions. Fortunately, there would be an overnight respite at the Dusit Inn, a modern hotel that would pass muster with any Lions Club. There, the group was to meet John Felderhof, who was waiting with his 10-year-old son, John Jr.

The next morning, everyone climbed aboard one of two helicopters bound for Samarinda, a refueling stop en route to Busang. As the choppers headed inland, the terrain changed from rice paddies and small settlements to miles and miles of sparsely inhabited swampland interrupted by winding rivers carrying heavy loads of sediment, the result of soil erosion caused by poor logging practices.

Felderhof took considerable pleasure in pointing out that most of his competitors south of Busang — Barrick Gold was specifically named — had acquired huge tracts of swampland. "Good luck finding anything down there," he chortled, with the peculiar "khee-khee-khee" that served as his laugh.

The group was met at the property by Michael de Guzman, Cesar Puspos and the hitherto unknown Jerry Alo, whose business card read "Site Manager — Metallurgist." The tropical sun and steaming humidity, the mud-brown rivers meandering through lush jungle, the Dayak villages and the symphony of sounds from strange birds and animals made it all seem exotic, but the mining analysts, and one mining reporter, had come to see one of the world's largest gold deposits, not scenes from National Geographic.

Geologically speaking, Busang's relation to "the big picture," is comprehensible. It is situated at the Kalimantan Suture, a major tectonic boundary in central Kalimantan which separates continental basement rocks to the northwest from shelf sediments to the southeast and forms the margin of a "magmatic arc" — a ribbon of volcanoes and intrusions that owe their existence to this weld in the earth's crust. The suture hosts the Kelian gold deposit, some 100 km southwest of Busang, as well as Mt. Muro and other known gold occurrences. The explanation made sense at the time, and still does.

Felderhof then laid out his maar-diatreme theory — a valid enough geological hypothesis, albeit one

Mike de Guzman prepares to tell yet another tall tale at the Busang property.

pumped up on steroids. Felderhof, whose principal academic interest was structural geology — the study of folds and faults — had observed, in a paper he wrote for Jason Mining in 1987, that the gold deposits at Mt. Muro, Muyup and Kelian all developed in maars. These are small, nearly circular ponds bounded by faults that were formed by the explosive eruption of molten rock and steam. The gold, Felderhof theorized, was deposited in fractures in the country rock surrounding the volcanic pipe.

Next, Bob Ramirez, who had been a field mapper at Benguet Corp., showed mining analysts drill core and explained site procedures. The core contained plenty of hydro-fractures, narrow veinlets in the rock that were said to carry the gold mineralization. The issue of not splitting the core intervals was discussed, but Felderhof pointed that he was simply following the practice carried out at the nearby Kelian gold mine, which, as everyone knew, had been involved in a lengthy lawsuit because its true grade had been understated when fire assays were used.

"They [operators of the Kelian mine] went to larger samples and cyanide leach to get a more representative grade, which is what we do," Felderhof said.

Next, the group was shepherded to a drill rig manned by Dayak villagers, but a second rig was not operating, and a third was being moved. Analysts also were shown stripped-off exposures of the Southeast zone that looked like prime places for gold deposits, as well as the original exposures of the zone found in the creekbed.

Tour guides de Guzman and Felderhof had no doubt that the rocks looked "right" for gold, and neither did anyone else. But, beyond that, visitors to Busang spent most of their time listening. First, there was a recount of the years of homework leading to the discovery, delivered by Felderhof. Then de Guzman discussed the latest assay results and resource calculations, as well as preliminary mining plans.

One analyst asked about geochemistry, but de Guzman said that a "depletion zone" sat on top of the deposit, that there was no gold in the overlying soils. He and Felderhof told their scornful tale of how one of Teck's geologists inspected the site and told them he thought they would have found some gold values in the overburden if they had what they told him they had. This "egghead," as they described him, was trying to force Busang into his own pre-conceived idea of what a gold deposit should look like. Now they were having the last laugh.

"We demanded an apology from Teck, and we got it too," Felderhof said.

For a Third World mine site, Busang looked impressive. Everything was well-maintained, clean and orderly. The grub was good, and the kitchen would pass muster at an mining camp in North America. A basketball court had been built to allow for some well-deserved recreation after a hard day's work.

Later in the day, de Guzman told analysts about Busang's "hot spots," a term used to describe areas where the main fault running southeastward through the property intersected a series of cross-cutting and radial faults. These intersections had the juiciest plumbing and, therefore, the highest grades.

De Guzman pointed out that while some of these "hot spots" had already been found by drilling, several more had been identified from surface mapping and air photos. These were not yet drilled, which meant that the exploration potential of the property was still wide open.

The visit also included a flyover of Bre-X's field camps, where early-stage exploration was being carried out in the search for new drill targets.

Felderhof hinted that this work was meeting with success. De Guzman agreed and told analysts that one of the areas had been named "the Egizio zone," after Nesbitt Burns analyst Egizio Bianchini, because he was the first to ask about work in this area.

The analysts were flown over ground held by other juniors north of Busang. "They're in the wrong rocks for gold," Felderhof shouted to analysts over the thump of chopper blades. "The ground up here is more prospective for copper or skarn deposits. We've got the best ground for gold."

All in all, the property visit was more about intangibles than tangibles, and more about what might still be out there than what was already in hand. Printed matter and any sort of technical data were skimpy, and they had not kept pace with the deposit's growing size and stature.

Part of the reason for this, Felderhof explained, was that it had taken the company years to unravel the geology at Busang. "We are now years ahead of anyone else in understanding where to look for these types of deposits," he told the analysts. "We are miles ahead of Barrick, and we don't want to give away all our secrets."

Jungle tales

Later that evening, mining analysts were escorted to the nearby Dayak village of Mekar Baru. Jerry Alo, who resembled a young version of the late Philippine dictator Ferdinand Marcos, tagged along as the group of mining analysts walked through the few streets of the small village.

Surprisingly, Mekar Baru was, in many way, similar to native Indian villages on the Pacific Coast of Canada. The Dayaks have totem poles and long-houses, just as the Salish and other West Coast tribes do, but with one noticeable difference. While the North American Indians used animals for inspiration in their carvings, the Dayaks carved intricate scenes of couples engaged in various kinds of love-making.

As might be expected, the Muslims were not amused by the carvings, or with the longhouses in which tribes co-mingled and engaged in activities that offended Javanese sensibilities. Individual family homes were built to encourage a more decorous lifestyle.

The Dayaks were former headhunters, though they are Asiatic and more closely related to Thai or Vietnamese peoples than to the Melanesians who inhabit Irian Jaya and Papua New Guinea. While incidents of headhunting are fairly recent in those areas, the practice

Bre-X staff pose with the July 1996 group of bewitched and bedazzled mining analysts and reporters at Busang.

was wiped out in Borneo long ago, in the 1960s.

De Guzman explained that the Indonesian government took action to outlaw headhunting after several missionaries were captured and killed by Dayak villagers deep in the jungle. "The army came in and strafed the place. Word of what happened went from village to village, and that put an end to headhunting."

He said the Dayaks living in the mountains north of Busang are fiercely territorial and, unless this cultural difference is respected, junior companies could have problems exploring in those remote and rugged areas. "They may not kill you, but they will make it clear who owns what up there."

De Guzman then recounted his experience in the jungle highlands when he had been taken prisoner by some irate local landowners. He knew of the few words of the local language and managed to reassure his captors that he meant no harm. It must have worked, as he was invited to a feast meant to separate the men from the boys. The main course was the head from a newly killed dog, roasted for a few minutes over an open fire. The skull was then split open so that everyone could partake of the brains.

"This was a ritual modified from their headhunting days," de

Guzman explained. "I passed that test and was given a special blanket so I could travel anywhere in their lands without problems."

Next, de Guzman told a gripping tale of how he had hiked and crawled for days and days from a remote site to seek help for a virulent form of malaria he had contracted while travelling deep in the jungle. At night, he slept wrapped in plastic garbage bags to keep off insects and ground leeches.

"I was so sick that when I laid down one day, I could feel myself dying," he recounted to analysts. "I forced myself up by sheer will and managed to make it the rest of the way to the river, where a boat was waiting."

The visitors from North America were spellbound.

Chapter Six:
THE BATTLE FOR BUSANG

Nothing except a battle lost
can be half so melancholy as a battle won.
Arthur Wellesley, Duke of Wellington

Seller's remorse

The guest bunkhouse at the Busang property has a wide, open-air veranda, ideal for nursing a cold beer after the supper hour and watching the sun set behind the jungle canopy. During a pleasant evening in the summer of 1996, a group of mining analysts, seated in comfortable rattan chairs, was doing exactly that as John Felderhof discussed his favorite subject; the geological marvel that was Busang.

Eventually, the conversation turned to the possibility that lawsuits might surface and delay production plans. This was a real concern, as almost every major discovery attracts a legal battle or two. In Bre-X's case, it was feared that one of the previous owners or partners might be tempted to claim rights to the property under some pretext or other. Felderhof did not rise to the bait, except to label all such people "opportunists." Legal complexities were not his strong suit.

Few people knew Bre-X had not obtained the shares of PT WAM it was supposed to have acquired three years ago for US$80,100. As a result, Bre-X never "owned" 80% of the Central zone as widely believed, though this did not stop the company from promoting results from the zone then, or at any other time.

The decision to sell 80% of PT WAM to Bre-X had been made by William McLucas through Waverley Mining Finance, which controlled Montague Gold and PT WAM's other foreign shareholder, Westralian Resource Projects.

By 1989, Montague Gold's subsidiary, Montague Pacific, had earned 50% of PT WAM under a farm-in agreement with Westralian. The two Indonesian partners retained their interests, but Westralian had been reduced to a 30% holding. Despite all this, Westralian was still registered in Indonesia as the foreign owner of PT WAM. Wayne Kernaghan, Montague's corporate secretary, said the shares reflecting the earn-in interest had never been passed along to Montague, at least not to his knowledge. "They were always held by Westralian Resource Projects."

Kernaghan was not able to shed much light on why Bre-X never got the shares of PT WAM for the monies paid in 1993. "They [Bre-X] never registered with the Mines Department. I don't know."

Peter Howe, who was on the board of Waverley at the time, doesn't know either. "Maybe Bre-X's legal people bungled."

Bre-X did more than bungle; it created an ungodly mess that fell in the lap of Roly Francisco soon after he joined the company.

Francisco knew Bre-X intended to sell a portion of Busang to a major, so he set about making sure the paperwork was in order. One can only imagine his surprise to learn that John Felderhof had never obtained the shares of PT WAM from McLucas, which then explained why Bre-X was not registered with the Indonesian mines ministry as PT WAM's new foreign owner.

Michael Novotny obviously was not joking when he described Felderhof as "a poor administrator." Small fires were burning all over the place. The door had been left wide open for McLucas to do more about seller's remorse than cry in his scotch.

The Scottish financier was upset that his agent, Felderhof, had sold Busang for a song to Bre-X and then made an important gold discovery that left him out in the cold.

According to Peter Howe, McLucas accused Felderhof of misrepresenting the potential of the Busang project. "I remember John was quite livid about that," Howe added. "He was a believer in the project since 1986."

McLucas grew more agitated as positive results began pouring from the Central zone and resource calculations were made. But he was in a bind. He knew, or at least ought to have known, that the skimpy results from past drilling did not show a resource of any size, shape or form for the Central zone. And, as a sophisticated player in the mining game, he would have known that de Guzman's wildly optimistic "resource calculations," based on six samples and some spotty past results, would not withstand the scrutiny of mining or legal professionals. Not only that; he had ignored de Guzman's recommendation to carry out a small Winkie drill program to "upgrade the viability" of the property's resource picture.

Felderhof countered accusations that he had misrepresented

John Felderhof plays show and tell with unsuspecting visitors at Busang.

the potential of Busang by turning the tables on McLucas. He produced the memo de Guzman had written after his site visit in late 1992. There it all was; tonnes, grade, the whole bit. It must have been a bizarre exchange.

Sources in the Jakarta mining community say the Waverley camp began looking for other ways to cook Felderhof's goose. David Hedderwick — who negotiated the original deal with David Walsh in 1993 — was rumored to be sniffing around Jakarta, trying to find some way to prove that Felderhof was acting for himself and Bre-X, rather than McLucas, when the deal was made with Walsh.

Whether he was successful in proving Felderhof had worn two hats at once is not known. But on July 27 Montague disclosed the "receipt of additional consideration" for completing a previous transfer to Bre-X of an interest in certain exploration joint ventures in Indonesia. Bre-X reported, a day later, that the transaction with Montague "completes the transfer to Bre-X of the full legal and beneficial ownership of the Busang I project commonly known as the Central zone."

Montague received US$5.6 million as "additional consideration," a big improvement over the original price. It also secured a net smelter royalty of one quarter of 1% of Bre-X's share of production after 3 million oz. had been produced from the Central zone.

The agreement that Francisco negotiated with McLucas still did not give Bre-X 80% of PT WAM, at least not directly. The settlement called for Bre-X to buy Westralian Resources Projects, which McLucas took private sometime in 1994. By settling the affair in this manner, Bre-X believed it would not have to obtain approval from the Indonesian government. Simply put, rather than buy 80% of PT WAM for $80,100, Bre-X waited three years and bought the offshore parent company that held this stake in PT WAM for US$5.6 million. Someone should have told David Walsh: time really is money.

Kernaghan later admitted that Montague was "surprised" when Bre-X began churning out better results than it had obtained from the Central zone. A bit skeptical too, he added — "definitely [skeptical], if you take the view we had a property that we put a [low] value on, which is suddenly the largest gold deposit in the world."

The entire event did not raise much of a fuss in the mining community, as few paid attention to the Central zone once the Southeast zone came into full flower. But it was a source of amusement to those who knew McLucas, as he was not known to have been an early backer of Bre-X. The joke began circulating that he did not invest early on because he "knew the property and knew the people."

"We always thought it was pretty funny that Willy was the only one not making any money off this whole thing," said one Australian mining executive with ground in Indonesia. "Though I gather he rectified that."

Peter Howe returns

Having been bitten once again by the gold bug, Willie McLucas teamed up with his old friend Peter Howe to join the Indonesian land rush.

Howe got the ball rolling. "I had lunch with John [Felderhof] again in July of 1995, after not having seen him for years, and he told me, 'You've got to come back to Indonesia because there are people here who remember you and would like to do a deal with you.'"

That September, Howe met with Felderhof and Mike Bird in Jakarta. Bird suggested that Howe's junior company, Diadem Resources, take a look at the Tewah alluvial project owned by Suharto's half-brother.

Howe agreed to acquire the project and to put McLucas on his board. Waverley bought shares in Diadem. Mike Bird joined Diadem and arranged some joint ventures with Bresea and Bre-X, thereby adding John Felderhof and Michael de Guzman to the exploration team. It was just like old times.

Diadem was not the only junior to take on Indonesian properties in 1996. Jakarta was crawling with Canadian mining executives scrambling to jump on the Busang bandwagon. The latecomers were caught by new restrictions imposed by the government as part of an effort to dampen the activities of land speculators.

Under the new laws, foreign companies had to pay an up-front fee of US$5,000 (non-refundable) and post a "seriousness bond." The juniors were asked to deposit US$4.25 for every hectare of ground covered by their CoW applications. This amounted to big bucks for anyone with large holdings, though the monies were refundable after certain work obligations were met.

Ears pricked up when it was learned that Barrick Gold had agreed to help out Yamana Resources, which had become one of the largest landholders in Kalimantan. The major put up Yamana's "seriousness bond," which amounted to millions of dollars, for ground in the area north and east of Busang. It was a short-term loan, but the deal also gave Barrick rights to acquire a stake in properties the American junior might find. This was a signal that the big gold producer was taking a keen interest in the area being worked by little Bre-X Minerals.

Bre-X heads for Wall Street

The Toronto mining community was surprised, and a bit shocked, when Bre-X turned to Wall Street, rather than Bay Street, to select its corporate and financial advisors.

After all, it was the large institutions in Canada that had given the small junior its biggest boost up the credibility curve. Not only did Bre-X's choice strike some as the epitome of ingratitude, it was perceived as a slight to the Canadian mining establishment, as Toronto was believed to have more expertise and experience in the mining sector (particularly with emerging producers) than New York, which dealt mostly with a handful of top-tier producers. "Toronto's a mining town," grumbled one industry observer. "New York ain't."

In early September 1996, Bre-X announced that Republic National Bank of New York would act as its corporate advisor, while J.P. Morgan would be its financial advisor. Their combined expertise was expected to help Bre-X negotiate "the most advantageous terms possible" with a potential partner.

The choice of Republic National Bank was believed by many to have had something to do with the fact that Paul Kavanagh's son, Ted, worked there. Whether nepotism came into play or not was deemed irrelevant, as Ted Kavanagh was respected by his peers as a bright and honest professional. Before the announcement was made, the younger Kavanagh had often expressed the view that Bre-X needed to add more talent to its team. And he particularly wanted to see someone more polished than the abrasive Stephen McAnulty head Bre-X's investor relations department.

About the same time, Bryan Coates, an accountant who was vice-president and controller at Montreal-based Cambior, joined Bre-X's Calgary office as a vice-president and corporate controller. And Bre-X announced that it had been approved for trading on the National Association of Securities Dealers Automated Quotations network (the NASDAQ exchange). The move to an American exchange carried benefits, Bre-X added, "[It will] augment shareholder value, as well as broaden and enhance both visibility and liquidity in the international capital markets."

These new developments did not escape the attention of one of Bre-X's Indonesian partners, Jusuf Merukh.

Yesterday's 'number one man'

In his glory days of the 1980s, Jusuf Merukh was the "number one man" in Indonesian mining circles. He was one of the first mining entrepreneurs — a role that earned him the title, "the Robert Friedland of Indonesia."

During the fifth-generation contracts of work, which included what later become Newmont Mining's Batu Hijau gold-copper mine and its new Minahasa gold mine, Merukh was the Indonesian partner in about 80% of the applications. His star had since faded, for reasons that have nothing to do with his being a Christian from Bali in a largely Muslim nation.

Merukh made his first faux pas by joining forces with an opposition party. Next, he obtained a small, vein-type gold mine that a foreign company was selling in Sumatra, operated it for a few months and shut it down. Sources say about 300 people were left unpaid, and the site was not cleaned up. As a result, Merukh became *persona non grata* with the mines department for some years and was conspicuously absent from subsequent rounds of CoW applications.

The absence of Merukh's company, PT Krueng Gasui, from Bre-X's efforts to acquire tie-on ground covering extensions to Busang

I was a little less conspicuous, because Bre-X had kept quiet about its obligation to bring its Central zone partners into the new property. Yet Merukh was a joint-venture partner in PT WAM, the legal owner and operator of Busang I. This opened up a can of worms called "fiduciary duty," and these worms had crawled all over mining companies in the past.

Peter Howe says John Felderhof had Haji Syakerani apply for the underlying KPs (permits granted only to Indonesians) because he knew the family from the 1980s but did not know Merukh well. Others say Felderhof knew Merukh but could not get along with his wily Indonesian partner.

Mike Novotny doesn't know, but shudders at the mere mention of Merukh's name. "Do not talk to me about this man. I was his technical adviser in the 1970s and he is not the nicest person."

Why Felderhof couldn't swallow his dislike or distrust of Merukh is not known. It is never a good idea to upset local partners in a foreign country, particularly a country as nationalistic as Indonesia.

Merukh later told Indonesian newspapers that he was shocked to learn he had been shut out of the Busang II and III CoW applications. He believed the applications were based on information gathered by a company he partly owned.

As far as Merukh was concerned, PT WAM — not Bre-X — had "discovered" the Southeast zone. And, as far as the Indonesian government was concerned, PT WAM was the operator during the period when Bre-X decided to apply for new CoWs covering the Southeast zone and other new targets. Merukh would later point out that relevant government filings made by Felderhof and de Guzman for this period were in the name of PT WAM, not Bre-X.

Merukh was furious, and there were rumblings in Indonesia that he was not planning to take this turn of events lying down.

Insecurity of tenure

Bre-X's land problems were not confined to the area covering the Central zone. The company's CoW applications covering Busang II and III had been initialled jointly by the Indonesian Department of Mines and Energy, Bre-X and its Indonesian partner, the Syakerani family.

But formal approvals and the signature of the president were still pending. Shareholders noticed that expected signing dates would pass and pass again. It began to look as though the whole process had come to a grinding halt.

At first, it was believed the delays had something to do with the

The skyline of Jakarta, Indonesia's capital and largest city, where the Suharto family manoeuvred for a stake in the "riches" of Busang.

fact that Busang had blossomed into something quite extraordinary. Rumblings were heard that nationalist sentiment had flared up, making the government hesitant to sign away something that still legally belonged to the people of Indonesia.

Sympathy in the mining business was largely with Bre-X, the small junior company that had gone to the jungle and made the find. It increased as reports began circulating that various "parties," believed to be unwanted suitors, had been telling government officials that Bre-X had no production experience and was not the right party to develop such a national treasure.

Bre-X Jakarta encouraged this conspiracy theory.

Few people knew that Jusuf Merukh, yearning for a bigger share of the Busang pie, was causing problems. The Indonesian businessman began discussions with Warren Beckwith, who was then running Golden Valley Mines in Australia. Together, they began demanding copies of PT WAM's records, geological maps, assay results, drill logs, financial statements — anything relevant to PT WAM's exploration activities at the Muara Atan CoW area.

As a partner (and a director) in the joint venture, Merukh believed he was entitled to all this material. And he may have been right. Merukh also complained that he had not been invited to some of PT WAM's meetings.

When Bre-X obtained its listing on NASDAQ, Merukh found the ammunition he needed to support his growing suspicions that he was being hoodwinked by his foreign partner. One of the requirements of the new listing in the United States was that documents had to be filed with the Securities and Exchange Commission, the agency that regulates the U.S. securities markets. The Muara Atan CoW document filed in Washington was different from the original lodged in Indonesia. The "missing" part was a provision dealing with his rights (and those of any Indonesian partner) to areas adjoining the CoW.

To Merukh, this could mean only one thing — someone at Bre-X had deliberately falsified documents in order to give the impression that he had no rights to ground adjoining the original discovery. Merukh's examination of the files also led him to believe that Bre-X was "misrepresenting" its interest in PT WAM.

Merukh went back to Indonesia and told all this to officials in the Indonesian government. His submission to the mines ministry was that the areas covered by Bre-X's CoW applications should be held by PT WAM. Whether he would have been successful in that argument is debatable and a matter for the Indonesian courts.

After that, the government saw Bre-X's conduct through a different lens. Merukh argued that Bre-X had used confidential information — obtained by an Indonesian company it never "owned" — to acquire adjoining ground which Merukh believed rightfully belonged to PT WAM.

From Bre-X Calgary's perspective, it began to look as though someone was asleep at the switch at Bre-X Jakarta. Little wonder Roly Francisco complained he had had "nothing but problems" since joining Bre-X.

Francisco tried to solve the problem by acquiring Westralian Resource Projects, which was then the legally registered owner of 80% of PT WAM. But this was not done until the summer of 1996, long after the Southeast zone was discovered.

The lobster trap

Felderhof's "lobster-trap" metaphor from the Minorca deal would soon come back to haunt him in other ways. Bre-X Minerals was drilling the Southeast zone under its SIPP, or preliminary exploration permit, which, interpreted strictly, allowed only surface work. Most companies wait until the CoW is formally granted to begin drilling.

This rule does not apply just to Indonesia. Few mining companies begin major drilling programs anywhere unless they are reasonably certain they have secure title to the ground being explored. To do otherwise is to run the risk of attracting modern-day claim-jumpers. That can happen anywhere in the world, including Canada.

Showing little caution, Bre-X began exploring its Southeast zone discovery without the security of having a CoW covering its area of interest. Not only that, it was running around the world telling everyone that it wanted to sell 25% of the project to a major partner for between one and two billion dollars.

Had Walsh and Felderhof been more politically sensitive, they might have realized that once this boast made its way to the inner circles of the Indonesian government, someone was bound to say: "You are going to sell what for how many billions of dollars? You don't own anything here."

Bre-X tempted the fates in the summer of 1996 and, for reasons that have more to do with its own carelessness or indifference, almost lost it all. The mess Bre-X made of things might be understandable if none of its principals had experience working in Indonesia. David Walsh had none, of course, but John Felderhof had spent more than a decade in the country.

"He knows these things," said Takala Hutasoit, an Indonesian who was once a partner with Felderhof on a mining venture. "He knows how to deal with Indonesians, he knows what is a contract of work, he knows what KPs are. He knows the regulations and the mining community."

John Felderhof had another huge hole in his lobster trap. Bre-X's exploration permit to drill Busang II had expired on July 20, 1996. It gained an extension a few days later, but, on August 15, that SIPP extension was cancelled by Kuntoro Mangkusubroto, director-general of the mines ministry.

The cancellation by one of the ministry's most senior civil servants is believed to have been triggered by the uncertainty cast on Bre-X's conduct in Indonesia by Jusuf Merukh, though Canadian press reports later suggested Barrick might be behind the cancellation — a suspicion which Felderhof and Walsh did nothing to discourage. But at the time, Bre-X neither told the public about the cancellation of the SIPP nor admitted anything about a dispute with one of its Indonesian partners.

Bre-X's cancelled SIPP came to light on October 4, when *The Globe and Mail* published a news story it was fed in late August. Merukh's company was claiming part of the Southeast zone, the story said, and the mines ministry had cancelled the preliminary exploration permit. The government was also looking into Merukh's claim that the Muara Atan CoW had been breached when Bre-X and the Syakerani interests had tied up the Busang

Barrick Gold personnel at the Indo Assay lab in Balikpapan, Indonesia, where Bre-X sent its bags of tricks for analysis.

II and III properties.

Determined to keep up its share price, Bre-X rushed into damage control. Walsh described Merukh's claims as "without substance" and said discussions with Indonesian officials, as well as with Merukh, had taken place. He asserted that the takeover of Westralian Resource Projects had sealed Bre-X's control of PT WAM, even though Bre-X's acquisition was completed only a few months earlier, when Francisco cleaned up the mess by making a deal with McLucas. Discussions were in progress, Walsh reassured the market, and the CoWs ultimately would be issued.

Bre-X thought it was justified in that the Syakeranis' Southeast zone KPs, which had expired in February 1996, were succeeded by the SIPP licence. Then, after the SIPP ran out in July, the company asked for, and received, an extension. That extension was cancelled on August 15, but Bre-X continued drilling, taking the view that it could continue work by virtue of its contractual obligations to the Syakerani companies, which were in the process of registering new KPs. The problem was that the KPs were registered almost a month after the cancellation, leaving a period when Bre-X effectively owned nothing. By now, David Walsh was probably too confused to understand the mess himself.

On October 15, Bre-X issued an unusually long press release in which Walsh poured cold water on Merukh's deal with Golden Valley Mines and their "false and misleading" claims against his Bre-X. "There is no evidence of a written agreement to support the alleged claims, and the holders of the existing CoW on Busang I have no rights under that CoW to participate in the pending CoWs on Busang II and III."

But at the same time Bre-X said it had met Merukh's representatives in order to "seek a resolution by negotiation."

The really bad news, though, came from the Indonesian government. Bre-X was informed that its new CoWs would be delayed until "resolution by Bre-X of the outstanding issue with its Indonesian partner in Busang I."

The Canadian and U.S. business sectors, influenced by the Bre-X publicity machine, saw the Indonesian government's actions as heavy-handed and arbitrary. Felderhof characteristically blamed it all on Barrick Gold, which be believed was trying to acquire Busang through a backdoor that was being pried open by Merukh.

It is said that all problems in Indonesia can be solved with diplomacy, the right connections and the right terms. Walsh was rarely in the country and had not yet learned the importance of paying courtesy calls to government officials. Fixers are everywhere in Indonesia. Had Bre-X been so inclined, it could have solved its problems with the cancelled SIPP and stalled CoWs by hammering out some sort of deal with Merukh. Such a deal would not have made everyone happy, and Bre-X's share price would have been clipped. But an open door to the Busang mansion would have been closed, and Bre-X would have had signed CoWs for Busang II and III, albeit with two Indonesian partners instead of one.

But Bre-X had waited too long. Merukh was gaining allies and the upper hand. He made it known that he would never be satisfied with only 10% of Busang I. He wanted up to 40% of the entire herd of Busang CoWs. If that was not scary enough for Bre-X, word was already spreading around Jakarta that Merukh was having "discussions" to ensure his views were known to all major mining companies interested in Busang.

Rumors were also circulating that Francisco's efforts to straighten things out in Indonesia were irritating Felderhof and de Guzman. At times, they browbeat their new colleague for questioning why certain things had been done. As David Walsh well knew, Bre-X Jakarta preferred running its own show.

Busang on the block

The Busang project officially went on the block on September 26, when Bre-X issued a news release stating that it would "pursue all available opportunities" to maximize the value of its Indonesian project.

A broad range of transactions would be looked at, David Walsh said, including a merger, acquisition, joint venture, or the sale of a majority interest in the deposit. This was the moment analysts, brokers and investors had been waiting for. The wonderful smell of money was in the air and everyone hoped the takeover would be as exciting and financially rewarding as the Diamond Fields takeover by Inco.

Because the deal was expected to be valued in the billions of dollars, all but the world's top gold producers were ruled out. Barrick Gold was the obvious contender. The major had the financial muscle to do the deal, even though it had just paid about $1 billion to acquire Arequipa Resources, a Vancouver-based junior with an interesting gold deposit in Peru.

Barrick starting eyeing Busang again when the Southeast zone started producing millions of ounces on a monthly basis. It was too good to ignore. Peter Munk, the entrepreneur who helped shape Barrick into one of the world's leading gold producers, had already decided he wanted to make his company the number-one gold miner in the world. Here was a project that looked as if it could rival his cornerstone operation, the fabulous Goldstrike in Nevada, which was then turning out almost 2 million oz. annually.

In the early months of 1996, Barrick staff had started investigating Bre-X as a potential acquisition. By May, the major had learned of the unusual filings of contract documents at the U.S. Securities and Exchange Commission and of Jusuf Merukh's claim to an interest in the Southeast zone.

Barrick opened an office in Jakarta. It began looking behind the press releases, behind the hype and behind the promotion. So did a few other major mining companies.

The salters at Busang were no doubt worried. They knew any potential buyer would carry out real due diligence programs, not the cursory kind done by mining analysts. Analysts cannot drill their own holes, look at all the technical data and take away tonnes of samples for examination. But any potential buyer of Busang would insist on doing all this, mostly because there were no split cores to examine and assay. The ounce factory was under siege, and devious minds went to work.

From here forward, the story is no longer about Bre-X.

It is about three Bre-Xs: the Canadian entity professionally managed by Francisco, Coates and the independent board members; the Indonesian shadow company operated by Felderhof and his technical team; and the promotional and marketing machine operated by David Walsh from Calgary or his beachfront house in Nassau.

Each Bre-X had its own agenda and the three rarely acted in concert.

Barrick Gold may have been the first to uncover Bre-X's multiple personalities. It certainly found that everything was not as represented. It learned that David Walsh spent almost no time in Indonesia and was only interested in stock-market side of the business. The job of running Bre-X at a professional level began to fall on Francisco's shoulders. And that put him on a collision course with Bre-X Jakarta.

Strategic alliances

With the process of securing property tenure proving slower than anticipated, and with rumors making the rounds that major mining companies had become aware of its precarious ownership situation, Bre-X formed a strategic alliance with PT Panutan Duta, a private company controlled by Suharto's eldest son, Sigit Harjojudanto.

Mike Bird is believed to have helped with the introductions, but who approached whom first is not known. By this point, Bird was doing some consulting work for Bre-X, mostly related to government relations and other legal and administrative matters.

The memorandum of understanding signed in late October was subject to several conditions, but, in essence, Bre-X retained Panutan as a consultant to assist in administrative, technical and other support matters, "including the identification of issues concerning the acquisition, exploration, development and production from mineral resource properties and other interests." And Panutan also got a 10% carried interest — that is, it would get 10% of revenues without putting up any money — in both the Central and Southeast zones.

Bre-X and affiliate Bro-X Minerals (which had been spun off that month and now held the Sable and Sangihe projects) maintained "the sole right and authority to determine the method of bringing their respective properties into production, including the right to select any major mining partner." The whole deal was subject to conditions, the most important being "issuance of CoWs for Busang II and III."

Then, in early November, Barrick confirmed reports that it had previously formed an alliance with the Citra Group, a construction and management company controlled by Suharto's eldest daughter, Siti Hardyanti Rukmana.

The news triggered controversy in North America. The local business community was more resigned and pragmatic; they had seen this all before. In Indonesia, politics is truly about who gets what, when and why. How could it be otherwise when the most powerful economic dynasty in the nation is made up of members of the Suharto family?

The Busang affair began to mirror an incident that began in 1988 when the Indonesian government invited bids to add telephone lines to Jakarta's telecommunications grid. Three of Suharto's children signed on as agents for different international firms. No one was surprised when all three companies made the short list. But that was only half the story. One of the three Suharto offspring had already secured the right to be the local manufacturer in the joint venture. So rather than choose between the two remaining offspring and their respective "partners," the government doubled the contract and asked the finalists to re-submit bids. Again, the Suharto children prevailed, with each company winning half the contract.

The antics of the family members competing with one another was a source of comic embarrassment, just as it became in the Busang affair, when two Suharto siblings began bending the ear of their father to intercede in the matter for reasons that were not altruistic.

Until Busang became "the largest gold deposit in the world," the Suharto family and their cronies had little direct involvement in the mining industry. They preferred big business: real estate, toll-roads, construction, oil and gas, and timber. Mineral exploration ventures they regarded as too risky.

As a consequence, Indonesia's mining industry was largely left in the hands of bureaucrats. The system put into place was not perfect, but it was workable, and the mines ministry had some capable people.

One was Kuntoro Mangkusubroto, a senior mining official who had earned the respect of foreign and domestic mining companies over the years. He was known a "pribumi" — a local term referring to an indigenous Indonesian who has risen through the ranks of his profession by merit, without patronage. The industry did not apply that same description to Gen. Ida Bagus Sudjana, the minister of energy and mines. When military men land in any ministry, it is usually a sign that the government (in this case, the Suharto family) is taking more than a passing interest in the business sector which that ministry represents.

Top down or bottom up?

A mining company typically decides to acquire a mineral project by having the project work its way through a hierarchy. Normally, property submissions are handled by field geologists who suggest acquisitions to upper management. The idea is that only the best projects survive the gruelling climb to the top of the corporate food chain.

The Busang project had circumvented this process by late 1996. Teck, Barrick, Placer Dome, Newmont Mining and others had taken a look in the early days and, for one reason or another, backed off. Some of their technical people were not keen on the project. But more often than not, things fell apart because Bre-X wanted an equity deal — that is, cash in its till — rather than a joint-venture partner.

The Southeast zone was now a whole new animal. The majors expressed renewed interest because Busang now promised to deliver lots of low-cost "ounces," which they needed and wanted. Very senior executives started pushing their subordinates to get a deal for Busang.

Placer Dome, which had previously looked over the Central zone, decided to look again as resources continued to grow. In 1995, the major company sent over a senior geologist, who brought with him someone who had been to Busang before, Stephen Walters.

There, they met with John Felderhof and began discussing the possibility of entering into a joint venture. By this point, Walters had evaluated all the available data related to past work at Busang, including work conducted by Magnum Minerals covering the Southeast zone. He also had results of exploration carried out in the same area by another company after Magnum had closed up shop.

Walters found it "strange" that while this zone went on for kilometres and had a huge amount of mineralization at surface, there was no surface indication of that mineralization (either from soil sampling or trenching programs); nor was there any explanation why this was so.

Walters also did not understand why Bre-X analyzed its core by cyanide leaching without splitting it first. "The answer that Felderhof gave [for this practice] didn't make any sense." And he was "suspicious" that Felderhof had a metallurgist, Jerry Alo, on site.

Placer Dome President John Willson was aware of all this, but decided the company should keep watching the project. It soon became too exciting to ignore.

Willson contacted Bre-X again early in 1996 and was told the same old story by Walsh: "We're drilling, have plenty of money to drill and no difficulty raising more."

Willson recalled: "They intended to keep drilling until the fall when they would have an auction to find a senior partner. We maintained contact and tried to convince them that we should be the partner of choice."

That fall, Willson began meeting with David Walsh. "We started talking about what we might do together. We were keen on it, because even with cautionary signs and red flags in the thing, it appeared there was a large deposit that would be almost unprecedented in the world. We believed we had to be extremely interested in that."

Willson knew that Bre-X was talking with other parties, including Barrick and Teck.

John Morganti, vice-president in charge of gold exploration for Teck in Vancouver, was showing renewed interest, even though he felt the risks were higher as Busang was already fully valued in the marketplace. "We kept initiating discussions, and finally, in November, we decided to go to Jakarta."

Morganti was excited because Walsh had told him that it "might be possible" to visit the property, which he badly wanted to do.

By this point, Jakarta's top hotels were crawling with executives from the world's leading gold producers. "I suggested we all get name tags," Morganti joked. "There were enough people around to justify a geological meeting."

While in Jakarta, Morganti met Roly Francisco and John Felderhof. "He seemed like a good bush rat — being one myself." But there was no site visit. "We discussed what was going on and were told that because 'Barrick had pushed in', there was no chance of visiting the property."

John Willson, who had Placer Dome's due diligence team lined up for a property visit, was told the same thing. "We had everyone lined up to go, but David Walsh said, 'God, guys, you can't. We're having this thing forced on us and we don't want to risk losing everything here. This government is giving us a strong message.'"

Barrick's competitors backed away, for the time being. Some were unnerved by the rash of lawsuit threats and property ownership problems Bre-X now faced.

"We were a bit surprised how many people came forward to say 'We can fix things,'" Morganti said.

Willson was similarly approached by local fixers.

Meanwhile, in the Toronto offices of Barrick Gold, Busang fever had reached a high pitch.

The mining industry was all abuzz that Barrick Chairman Peter Munk "wanted Busang so bad he could taste it." And if the deposit had even half of what John Felderhof and David Walsh were reporting, everyone could understand why.

The poison of hate

Mention Barrick Gold or Peter Munk to John Felderhof and his eyes turn cold and steely. He will say something nasty. His hatred is now legendary. To a lesser degree, David Walsh shared the sentiment.

"It was visceral all right," said Stan Hawkins. "They hated Barrick with a passion."

Felderhof often told the story of how the major company had "screwed" Bre-X in Sumatra by obtaining ground it knew the junior intended to apply for.

Teck's Wayne Spilsbury remembers the incident differently. Bre-X was eyeing some KPs (held by an Indonesian partner) and wanted a major partner to help it fund some CoW applications, as it had to lodge a bond and didn't have the money. The deal was offered first to Barrick, which turned it down, and then to Teck.

"We had a look at the property, but didn't think it was that great," Spilsbury said. "About six months or a year later, when Barrick opened an office in Jakarta, they went out and applied for a CoW in the area John had wanted both Barrick and Teck to help him apply for. He mentioned several times that he was going to sue Barrick over that. I suspect, though, that it was just something that slipped between the cracks. The Barrick office in Jakarta may not have even known of the old proposal."

One night, Felderhof confessed to Wayne Spilsbury that he had another, more personal reason for despising Munk, who had come to Canada as an young immigrant from Hungary.

"He had had a few beers when he told me this . . . but he said that when Peter Munk first came to Canada, the Felderhof family took him in as an immigrant student boarder. John felt that Peter had treated the family poorly, even though they had done a lot of things for him — given him money and whatnot. He said they never heard from him after he went on to do great things. And then he [Munk] came back as this corporate raider; it was too much. He told me many times that he would never do a deal with Barrick, because of Peter Munk."

The story is "nonsense," according to a member of the Felderhof family. It may well be. But Spilsbury was not the one to make the nonsense up.

Barrick's coup

While John Felderhof was vowing never to do a deal with Barrick, Roly Francisco had already approached Peter Munk in the summer of 1996. Representatives of both companies met in Jakarta later that month. With Barrick's Jakarta manager Neil MacLachlan and financial officer Randall Oliphant on one side of the table, and Francisco and Felderhof on the other, talks continued sporadically

John Willson, president of Placer Dome, one of the disappointed suitors of Bre-X.

over a course of months. And as the parties talked, tempting ounces rolled off the assembly line at Busang.

Having made the decision to go after the prize, Barrick went at it with guns a-blazing. Top executives were spending considerable time in Jakarta, pressing the company's case with government officials. Munk himself went to Jakarta, and the rumor mill said he had tried to talk directly to Suharto. Barrick confirmed that Munk had gone there, but would not say whom he had visited.

Brian Mulroney, former prime minister of Canada, and George Bush, former president of the United States — both members of Barrick's advisory board — were pressed into the company's service. Much was made of a letter from Bush to Suharto, though it proved to be a fairly innocuous note singing the company's praises. Journalist Brian Hutchinson, in a widely quoted article in *Canadian Business*, said an Indonesian source had told him a letter from Mulroney was given to Mines Minister Sudjana at a dinner in Toronto, identifying the son of a prominent bureaucrat as Barrick's agent in Indonesia; but Mulroney's letter in fact was sent later and said only that Barrick was interested in pursuing projects in Indonesia.

Barrick's lobbying efforts came to fruition when Peter Munk received a letter requesting his attendance at a meeting in Jakarta. Munk rearranged his schedule and flew to Indonesia.

The now-famous meeting took place November 14. Bre-X was represented by Walsh, Felderhof and Francisco, who brought representatives from Morgan and Republic with them; Peter Munk and an aide were the only Barrick people in attendance. Mines Minister Sudjana delivered instructions to the two companies that the government wanted them to come to an agreement to develop a mine at Busang.

Barrick sources insist that the mines ministry told the two parties to come to an arrangement that gave Barrick 75% and Bre-X

25% of the "foreign content" in the project. In other respects, it should resemble the deal that the two companies were basing negotiations on at the time. The mines ministry gave them until December 4 to come to an agreement.

The hard lines drawn around the terms amazed even Barrick. The gold producer was compelled to find a way to accommodate the government and, at the same time, work out a deal with Bre-X that would pass muster in North America. The parties had been discussing the possibility of a 60-40 deal, so earlier arrangements were restructured to give Bre-X an additional royalty based on the project's gross revenue. The two companies signed a confidentiality agreement on November 24.

The Barrick negotiators pressed ahead and, on November 26, the world was told Peter Munk had won the Battle for Busang.

In a tersely worded release, David Walsh announced that the Indonesian government "has given guidance to Bre-X to finalize a joint venture between Bre-X and Barrick Gold on the basis of 25% to Bre-X and 75% to Barrick."

The company was ordered to conclude negotiations with Barrick no later than December 4 and, "if the negotiations are not concluded by that date, the Indonesian government will take the necessary steps to prevent a delay in the development of the Busang gold deposit."

The Indonesian mines ministry also suggested a 10% interest in the project would be nice.

Bre-X was stunned and sent a letter to the ministry "to seek clarification as to whether certain other forms of transactions would be acceptable." It did not receive an answer.

The daily newspapers weighed in on Barrick's side, calling the deal a coup for the gold producer. News magazines began a sycophantic symphony of puff pieces. The usually hard-nosed U.S. weekly *Business Week* titled its story "Snatching the Mother of All Mines;" in *Maclean's*, Jennifer Wells called Munk a "King of Gold" who had "played his imperial hand beautifully."

The dailies and glossies, which love anything that smacks of shooting the wounded, were full of praise for what looked like Barrick's hardball tactics, yet people in the mining industry wondered who would ever be fool enough to make a deal with Barrick again. It is hard to find anyone in the mining industry who admires Barrick's conduct during that period, but even harder to find anyone willing to say so publicly. Privately, many believed that it was Munk — and not the highly regarded technical team at Barrick — who had put the company's reputation at risk. In their view, Munk was not a "mining man". He did not understand that in the mining industry the rules of the game had to be followed or a company would find itself out in the cold.

Among the few willing to give Barrick public lumps was Tandem's Stan Hawkins. "Coming in the back door like that was tacky. No class."

Norman Keevil, Teck's president, was outspoken too. "The whole thing was done behind the scenes," he told *The Northern Miner*. "We [for example] did not go in and ask the government of Newfoundland to issue an edict that Diamond Fields would give us 75% of Voisey's Bay."

Placer Dome's Willson also found the whole affair distasteful. "We said we don't think this is right. We think Bre-X should be allowed to exercise its natural right to conduct an auction and find a partner of choice rather than have [a partner] imposed on it."

The *Miner* also entered the fray and tried to remind the industry of its own tradition of fair play. Senior companies are not supposed to ride roughshod over prospectors and junior companies who make the discoveries in the first place. And David Walsh and Bre-X Jakarta were squealing like pigs being hauled off to slaughter.

Bre-X shareholders were scandalized by the government's writ, as it indicated that the big boys in Indonesia were pushing in on their winnings. Fearing that the final deal would be unfair to minority owners, a group of Canadian and U.S. shareholders, who held about 5% of the outstanding shares of Bre-X, retained law firms in both countries. One of the leading dissidents, lawyer Gregory Chorny of Toronto, told the *Miner* that the group knew it could not change the government's mind; rather, its aim was to ensure fair compensation to Bre-X in the form of cash or Barrick shares.

Paul Kavanagh delighted in the poetic justice of Barrick's all-out fight to secure control of Busang. "Ask them if they believe we have the goods now," he suggested on several occasions. At Bre-X's Christmas party in Calgary, Kavanagh made no secret of his displeasure with Barrick's conduct, which he blamed on his former boss. "Peter Munk is not fit to shine David Walsh's boots," people heard him say.

The two companies returned to the smoke-filled room but failed to reach an agreement by the government-imposed deadline. One reason is that the government appeared to be taking a more flexible stance, which brought new bidders into the open. Another is that Bre-X had started evasive actions that stymied Barrick.

More trouble from men in suits

The forced deal with Barrick was not the only bad news Bre-X's shareholders received in November. In the middle of the month, the company announced that Jusuf Merukh was planning to sue Bre-X and "19 other parties" if David Walsh or a suitable representative didn't show up for a meeting within a week.

The purpose of the meeting, Merukh's Canadian lawyers pointed out, was to "resolve the dispute" relating to CoWs for Busang II and III.

Merukh later told an Indonesian newspaper that the suit had to name so many parties because Bre-X's corporate organization was complicated and went in circles. "For example, Bre-X in Canada is given to Bre-X Amsterdam, and there are other Bre-Xs all over the world."

The letter outlined Merukh's claim and the remedies he would be seeking if it went forward. Merukh wanted the Alberta courts to force Bre-X to acknowledge Krueng's right to 10% of all the Busang CoWs and to declare that his option to acquire an additional 20% was "in full force and effect." The claim also asked for compensatory damages of about US$1.9 billion and "substantial punitive damages."

Bre-X said its lawyers would arrange a meeting. But it reminded shareholders that it had already met with Merukh's representatives, who had yet to turn over "pertinent information and documents," including the alleged option agreement that made up a key part of the claim.

Bre-X shareholders were worried, as threats of lawsuits always seem to inspire copycats. Little did they know Willy McLucas was already talking with lawyers.

As shareholders had feared, Merukh's legal salvo inspired others. On November 22, McLucas made it known that his seller's remorse had returned with a vengeance. Bre-X's Jakarta office issued a press release stating that it had received a letter from Canadian counsel "claiming to act for Waverley Mining Finance, Montague Gold, Westralian Resource Projects and William McLucas."

The letter stated that all the parties were investigating a number of claims against Bre-X and certain officers — claims which "mirror, in large part, the claims asserted" by Merukh's PT Krueng Gasui.

It was bizarre: the parties were all direct or indirect "vendors" of the 80% interest in PT WAM which Bre-X "acquired" in early 1993. "Vendor" and "acquired" may not be the right words — after all, Bre-X never received the shares. The "vendors" were now asking to be included in the meeting that was supposed to take place between Bre-X and Merukh.

Bre-X, of course, was outraged. First, it pointed out that it was the indirect whole owner of Westralian Resource Projects, and had not "authorized any person to make claims against it." In other words, Bre-X was not about to sue itself.

Next, the company pointed out that it had already reached an agreement with Montague "to complete the transfer to Bre-X of full legal and beneficial ownership of Busang I (the Central zone)." As part of that transaction, Bre-X pointed out, "Waverley, Montague and McLucas entered into a deed of release under which they jointly and severally released Bre-X, Bre-X Minerals Amsterdam BV, Westralian and their officers, directors, employees and agents from all losses or claims in connection with events that took place in 1993 and subsequently in connection with the proposal for Bre-X to acquire, and its acquisition of, an interest in, Busang I."

Bre-X pointed out that the deed of release had "effect throughout the world," dismissed the claim as "blatant opportunism," and stated that it was "entirely without foundation and, in the face of the deed of release, [was] unsustainable."

The Indonesian government was aware of Merukh's claims against Bre-X, but the latest legal salvo from Waverley, Montague, et al., was probably the last straw. Timely development of the Busang gold deposit was facing opposition on too many fronts. The last thing the government wanted was a bunch of foreigners battling in Calgary courtrooms to carve up the Busang pie into ever smaller pieces, delaying mine construction indefinitely. It decided to take action and head all this legal nonsense off at the pass. It would force the operators to bring the deposit into production, and thereby show the world exactly who was calling the shots.

All this legal uncertainty opened yet another door to the Busang mansion. It is hardly surprising that various parties slipped through to propose "alternative development options" with the government. After all, Bre-X had no CoWs, which meant Busang was a resource still "owned" by the Indonesian people.

The bidding war

The story of the negotiations between Bre-X and Barrick was already receiving plenty of attention in the Canadian press, which sought out any Indonesian foreign officers it could find. An official at the embassy in Ottawa said he had "no direct knowledge" of a deadline date; another, at the Indonesian consulate in Toronto, remarked that the government was ready to consider other development plans and implied that these plans might include parties other than Barrick.

That was enough for Placer Dome. The Vancouver-based company had been talking to Bre-X for the preceding two months, despite the misgivings of some of their technical staff. Placer's John Willson was wary of the project's "cautionary signs and red flags," but, like other major gold producers, he felt pressured by the investment houses and the large funds to make moves to secure Busang. The company made it public that it was ready to bid on Busang if the government would allow an auction process.

Aloof and serious, Willson was known as straight shooter in the mining industry, but he may have been too ready to trust in Bre-X's honorable character.

Down in Denver, executives at Newmont Gold were more discreet, but at the same time made no attempt to hide their interest in Busang. Newmont and Teck had already gone to Placer to suggest a three-party bid for the gold project, but after some preliminary discussions Placer said it would go its own way.

Bre-X's first countermeasure against the Barrick deal was the release of a new resource calculation. Kilborn Pakar Rekayasa put the size of the indicated resource at 316 million tonnes grading 2.27 grams gold per tonne, with an additional inferred resource of 464 million tonnes grading 2.3 grams. That was a total resource of 780 million tonnes at 2.28 grams per tonne, or 57 million ounces of contained gold.

Bre-X also announced that it had received Kilborn's intermediate feasibility report, which confirmed what the junior's Bay Street followers had already told the world: that Busang would become an immense, low-cost gold producer. Kilborn had drawn pit designs around the Central and Southeast zones; the big one, in the Southeast zone, showed 614 million tonnes of mineralized material in a pit with a stripping ratio of 1-to-1. The stripping ratio — the measure of the tonnes of waste the operator would have to remove in order to mine a tonne of ore — was low, implying Busang would have low mining costs. The report also said the gold was easily extractable with conventional metallurgical methods. Kilborn added up the charges and arrived at a cash operating cost of US$96 per oz. of gold produced — lower than any major gold mine in the world.

Negotiations between Barrick and Bre-X were going slowly. Bre-X's Stephen McAnulty persisted with the line that the government might allow an open bidding process. By mid-December, the two companies were ready to submit a deal that left Bre-X with 22.5%; Barrick, fronting US$1.5 billion to bring the property to production, would hold 67.5%; and the government would receive a 10% carried interest. The Merukh and Syakerani interests would be compensated by a cash settlement from Bre-X, with Barrick funding up to US$400 million. Also, Bre-X would get 20% of revenue on production from the project.

While the two companies waited over the New Year for the government to approve the deal, evasive action started again. Bre-X released results from another 12 drill holes, including one that showed 396 metres of core grading an average 12.56 grams gold per tonne. The press release described "high-grade pay streaks" between 50 and 200 metres long, 4 to 80 metres wide, occasionally bulging to 200 metres. Bre-X promised its shareholders it would look for some more of them.

It was stunning: a bonanza grade over a huge interval. "Pay streak," a placer mining term, is usually applied to high-grade gravel bars, not to zones in hard rock. The story had started to seem too good to be true, and should have met with some healthy skepticism.

Instead, the latest results had the effect — perhaps intentional — of lighting a fire under a rival suitor. In a letter to Walsh dated January 13, 1997, John Willson suggested a "merger of equals at a significant premium to the current market price," between Bre-X and Placer Dome. Those watching the events unfold pulled out their calculators and determined that a Bre-X share would have roughly equal market value to a Placer share, and that Bre-X shareholders would end up with about half of Placer Dome. David Walsh would become Placer Dome's largest single shareholder.

Placer was having none of the backroom shenanigans rumored to be going on in Indonesia. In a conference call to analysts and the press, the company let it be known that it would not enter into any agreements for services with influential powerbrokers or the Suharto family. Placer's style was to dangle a carrot quite openly: 40% for Indonesian interests, including the government. The company placed two conditions on its offer: it had to have access to the site to investigate the deposit, and the contract of work had to be issued.

"The offer was [made] on the basis — and only on the basis — that what [Bre-X] said was true," Willson said. "Anything we proposed was subject to due diligence — to getting on site and doing our own drilling, sampling and assaying."

The next day, the Merukh camp filed its threatened lawsuit against Bre-X. The Indonesian entrepreneur was determined that, if the Placer agreement went through, he would be in line for a settlement. Merukh had already been to see Placer Dome's people to make his position known.

"We knew his position," Willson said. "He told us if that we made a deal with Bre-X, we were going to have to deal with him, etc., etc. And we had talked with Roly [Francisco] and David [Walsh about the situation] at the Shangri-La Hotel."

Then the Indonesian government gave Barrick and Bre-X another month to make a deal.

With Placer Dome now a bright blip on the radar screen, more shenanigans started. A faxed message, detailing environmental problems Placer had at the Marcopper mine in the Philippines, made the rounds in Jakarta, with a fax identifier on top that listed a number used by Barrick Gold. Barrick, in turn, denied that it had sent anything of the kind to the press.

"It was an extraordinary thing," said Willson. "I do know it was Barrick's number, but where it came from I don't know. It was disparaging."

Barrick brought a group of Indonesian business reporters to Nevada to behold its huge and impressive Nevada gold-mining complex. It was Placer Dome's misfortune that, at the same time, it held a press conference to press its case as a contender to develop Busang. "We all had the people who had not gone to Carlin," said Willson, "and they were not happy about being left out."

One Indonesian reporter as much as told Willson that all the players had to deal with the [Suharto] family. "Don't you know that?"

"No," Willson replied. "We don't believe that's a necessity. We were making a deal with the people who owned it already."

Teck watched all this with amazement and decided to steer clear of a spitting match. At the same time, the company made its intentions known. "We tried to present ourselves in the best light. We said we were a technically diversified company that knew how to build and operate large mills," said John Morganti. "We didn't try to tear down other companies. We wanted to be a partner of choice."

Morganti's heart was no longer in the deal. "For me, the real deal was to be made in 1995. If things were as reported, that would have been the deal of the century. We continued to pursue it, but we could see the value being destroyed."

By now, it was obvious that Barrick had lost the inside track. There were rumblings that some Indonesians found Peter Munk arrogant. Placer Dome's deal was looking more attractive every day.

While one might think Walsh should have been grateful to Placer Dome for reopening the bidding war and helping stave off the supposed enemy, Barrick, he was nothing of the sort. Willson was "naive," Walsh said a month or two later. Asked what he thought of Placer's "merger of equals" offer, which won accolades from some business writers as being "attractive and politically sensitive," Walsh was brutal. "Who are they to give away forty per cent of something they don't even own to the Indonesians?"

It was a puzzling stance, and may have been a reflection of the feelings of Bre-X Jakarta. Perhaps some people there disapproved of Placer's proposal because it introduced the problem of what to name the merged company. Perhaps the salting crew at Busang, after careful consideration, concluded that "Bre-X Placer Gold" did not have desirable connotations.

Munk meets his match

In January of each year, the mining industry gathers to honor new inductees into the Canadian Mining Hall of Fame. Paul Kavanagh was on cloud nine during the black-tie event. Bre-X had just issued a news release about the latest developments in Indonesia. "Look who it does not mention," Kavanagh said. Sure enough, there was no reference to Barrick Gold.

Peter Munk had been upstaged by a powerful entrepreneur closer to Suharto's heart and home.

Mohammad "Bob" Hasan, an industrialist and a personal friend of General Suharto, was often described as a "lumber baron." He actually had dealings in a variety of industries and headed several large and influential investment funds which were closely tied to the government, the military and the Suharto family. He was a member of the country's ethnic Chinese minority, who had often been the target of attacks from nativist factions. Hasan had converted to Islam, and no matter that he may have done so out of genuine conviction, it did much to make him more acceptable in Indonesian society.

Ostensibly, Hasan stepped into the mess because he was concerned the actions of the Suharto children might damage Indonesia's reputation. The family could not afford to have open rivalry between a son and a daughter over the Busang deposit. Gen. Suharto was seen as being too indulgent of his many children and their controversial business ventures. One son had only recently tried to ban imports of all automobiles into Indonesia in order to have a monopoly for his automobile manufacturing business. His attempt failed, but the controversy had taken its toll on the national consensus.

Placer Dome was aware of all this and began discussions with Bob Hasan in December. Those continued into late January, when, according to Willson, the tide began to turn against Barrick. "We had a team of geologists ready to go to the site but were told [by Bre-X] that the government was still pushing Barrick. We did get some samples, but we didn't get anything we were comfortable with."

Placer Dome continued its efforts to make a deal, as did Barrick.

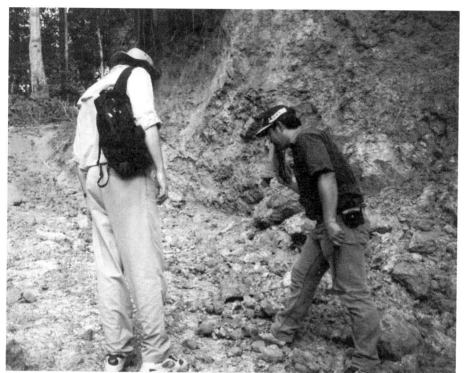

Cesar Puspos (right) examines an outcrop with a visiting investment analyst. Bre-X used its tours to sell Felderhof's geological concepts.

"We then went down a road with Hasan, who was presumably the delegate of the President, and continued negotiating," Willson recalled. "But there were other companies involved. For a while it appeared we and Barrick were the front-runners, but at the last moment he [Hasan] turned to Freeport."

Hasan is rumored to have offered Suharto the solution to the Bre-X problem over a golf game in early 1997. He would find a developer, broker the competing interests, and so keep the family out of a public controversy.

As Bob Hasan's role as a powerbroker grew, Barrick's influence declined. The major gold producer underestimated the strong nationalist sentiment that still dominated the thinking of many Indonesian bureaucrats, whereas Hasan did not. His deal would cut the government in for part of the revenues, and put a large part of the project in domestic hands.

Early in 1997, Hasan obtained a 10% stake in PT Freeport Indonesia, a subsidiary of New Orleans-based Freeport-McMoran Copper & Gold. But he had his eye on bigger and better things. He then made a deal to buy a 50% stake in Bre-X's minority Indonesian partner in the Southeast zone.

Hasan had talked with Placer Dome and Teck; he was greatly impressed with Norman Keevil, who pushed the idea that Teck, whose experience with big base metal projects gave it a better handle on how to run Busang's proposed giant pit, was the best choice. Had events taken a small turn here or there, Teck might have emerged as the victor in the Battle for Busang. David Walsh confessed in March that Teck would have been his choice as well. He liked Norm Keevil and his low-key approach to doing business. "He was fair and always helpful."

But Hasan would later say that the notion simply came to him that he knew someone in the mining industry that ran a big project in Indonesia. He prevailed on Freeport's chairman, James R. "Jim Bob" Moffett, to try the project on for size.

The Freeport deal

The deal was announced on February 17, only hours after the clock ran out on Barrick. Freeport would put up US$400 million of the project's estimated US$1.6-billion capital cost and arrange financing for the rest of the budget; Bre-X would keep 45%; and the Indonesian government would hold 10%. The Indonesian companies, in which Hasan and the Syakerani family had equal interests, would keep their 10%, and the remaining 20% would be held by PT Nusantara Ampera Bhakti (Nusamba), a financial group managed by Hasan.

The First Family got its cut: 80% of the Nusamba group was owned by three charitable foundations headed by Suharto, and 10% belonged to Sigit Harjojudanto (Suharto's eldest son, with whom Bre-X had already made a deal). The rest belonged to Hasan.

Approval came swiftly. The mines ministry, suddenly free of concerns about property tenure, announced that the CoWs would be granted shortly. But this didn't mean the problems were over; the Central zone was still outside the agreement and Merukh's Canadian lawsuit wasn't settled. Moreover, Freeport had clauses in the memorandum of agreement that forced Bre-X to reach a settlement with any party disputing ownership, or lose the deal entirely.

At the end of the day, with Freeport and Bob Hasan the apparent victors, most Bre-X shareholders were relieved the battle was over. "It could have been worse," many told themselves. Most analysts also believed that half a pie was better than no pie at all, particularly in light of all the backroom political intrigue that had taken place over a period of months in Indonesia. John Ing, a veteran observer of the gold industry and an executive at brokerage house Maison Placements expressed the prevailing sentiment when he remarked that Bre-X had no leverage; it should have secured its CoWs before launching into a major exploration program at Busang.

J.P. Morgan, Bre-X's financial advisor, was charged with determining if the Freeport deal was fair to Bre-X. Its evaluation work included comparisons with other offers, namely Barrick's deal, which was far more structurally complex. The conclusions of the New York-based firm were made public in a conference call on February 19. Analysts would be permitted to ask questions; news hounds had to be content to eavesdrop.

"We looked at it every which way and came to the conclusion that the current deal is indeed comparable to the share value of the Barrick deal," said Leslie Morrison, who worked on the agreement with Bre-X. "That [the Barrick deal] was a useful yardstick to determine if, at the end of the day, the [Freeport] deal was fair to the shareholders of Bre-X."

But not everyone was happy about Bre-X's reduced stake and the actions of the Indonesian government. Egizio Bianchini, Nesbitt Burns's star analyst, demanded an explanation on these matters from Morrison.

"In your fairness opinion writeup . . . how are you going to deal with the fact that the parliament of a sovereign nation had agreed to a contract of work on a 90/10 basis?" Bianchini asked. "I'm not trying to be a wise-ass here — I understand exactly what's going on — but I'm concerned about potential shareholder problems."

Morrison responded that, in light of national sentiment about ownership of natural resources, to expect Bre-X to have retained the stake that had been approved by the legislature was "unrealistic." Nor was it realistic for Bre-X to expect the Indonesians to pay for the stake they were provided, he added.

Bianchini was not satisfied. "The sixth-generation contract of work, at least on paper — and we now know what kind of paper its printed on — does not require an Indonesian partner. And I state again, the parliament of a sovereign nation had agreed to a 90% interest for Bre-X. We all know what's going on here."

Felderhof had a more direct explanation of the Indonesian government's actions to offer Bianchini. "I think what happened here is that we found too much gold, so therefore it becomes an issue of national interest. If we had found a lot less, this would have never happened."

Bianchini agreed, but did not let the matter rest. "I think we are just going to have to look at Indonesia in a much different light than [how] they have presented themselves at conferences and around the world at their roadshows."

Felderhof pointed out that there were benefits to government involvement at Busang.

"The government participation will ensure that this mine will get into production on time," he explained. "There is always a lot of permitting to be done, and having a large government participation here . . . the permitting will go very smooth."

Morrison said the issue — the rights and wrongs of tenure — was one that shareholders should not spend too much time thinking about. "We're all in the real world and we have to take decisions which are prudent in relation to those realities."

Suggesting that Bre-X's legal rights to ownership at Busang were tenuous at best, Morrison said it had been difficult, because of legal and political uncertainties, to use the normal yardsticks of an evaluation or fairness opinion. As he told one analyst: "The real question is, What effectively did Bre-X really own here?"

Indonesian smoke screen

The Battle for Busang made the perfect smokescreen for the salting crew toiling away at Bre-X's ounce factory.

The corporate intrigue and backroom dealings going on in Jakarta and in cities around the world had deflected attention away from the technical aspects of the project. By this time, virtually everyone thought Busang was the real thing. The few remaining skeptics were coming around to the view that there had to be something real behind this huge outpouring of energy, time and attention that had just been played out in the name of business on the world stage.

Bre-X had to have the goods, because what else was all the fuss about? Why else were companies fighting so hard to be the one? Why else were so many people lined up in the lawcourts to get a piece of the action?

Beating the odds is supposed to be what the mineral exploration business is all about. And *The Northern Miner*, like just about everyone else, believed that Bre-X Minerals had done just that. However clumsy its business dealings, the small Calgary junior had, it seemed, accomplished something rare — the discovery of a significant gold deposit.

The Busang project was the mining story of 1996. In recognition, the paper's editorial staff decided to name David Walsh and John Felderhof jointly its "Mining Men of the Year."

We should have waited; the story was not yet over. The rest of it was to prove sordid. We would soon learn the beginning had been too.

Chapter Seven:
OUT ON A LIMB

Boldness is a mask for fear, however great.
Lucan

True Confessions

The share price of Bre-X Minerals began its downward spiral during the Battle for Busang. It was showing further signs of weakness after the company announced its shotgun engagement with Freeport-McMoRan.

The old adage "buy on mystery, sell on history" was starting to kick in as investors realized the upside was limited and Busang would soon be yesterday's story.

Although John Felderhof and David Walsh had already taken some hefty profits of their own, they worked feverishly in early 1997 to keep the Busang story alive and reverse the slide in Bre-X's share price. Their efforts to defy gravity required nerves of steel and energy of manic proportions.

At the same time as it announced the development deal with Freeport, Bre-X released a new resource estimate for the Busang deposit. Total resources in all categories were 889 million tonnes grading 2.48 grams of gold per tonne. That was 71 million oz., up from the 57-million-oz. figure released just over two months earlier. But during a conference call with mining analysts, Walsh and Felderhof made it clear that Busang still had much upside to offer.

Felderhof was clearly the star performer on that occasion, though his brazen comments and arm-waving histrionics were overshadowed by a bombshell dropped by Walsh in his opening remarks.

Public speaking was never Walsh's strong suit. It was painful to listen to his clumsy attempt to let people know that, despite what they had "mistakenly thought" or been told by whomever, Bre-X

John Felderhof acquaints analysts with Busang's big picture, displaying the 10-centimetre remnants of core the salting crew saved.

did not own 90% of the Busang property. "That was never a practical reality, nor was it ever a basis for the evaluation of Bre-X's stock," Walsh preached. "It was always envisioned that we would share in the ownership with local interests and a development partner."

Reading from a script, Walsh acknowledged that mineral resources "belong to the people of Indonesia," with certain rights accruing to those who discover, develop and operate mineral properties. "Bre-X management recognizes that a larger share had to be made available to local entities than the 10% owned by our Indonesian partner. Given national statements about ownership of natural resources, it became unrealistic for Bre-X to expect to be paid for a portion of Busang that Indonesia believes belongs to it by right."

But the deal made sense, Walsh said, because it was in the interest of Bre-X shareholders to have long-term stability, and to have partners with the skills and financial resources to make Busang a success.

"This arrangement still leaves Bre-X with the largest direct share of Busang of any deal proposed by a major mining company acceptable to the government," he added. "This [ownership interest is] of the largest and most economic gold deposit in the world, with development and operations to be managed by Freeport, the perfect partner for Bre-X".

When New York talks . . .

After expressing the hope that this "better understanding" of the arrangement would be reflected in the stock market, Walsh stepped aside to allow comments from representatives of J.P. Morgan & Co., Bre-X's financial adviser.

Managing director Leslie Morrison told analysts that the capital expenditures to build a mine at Busang would be in the range of US$1.6 billion. Next up was Doug McIntosh, who provided technical detail about revisions to the previous mining plans. While the original study contemplated a production rate of 80,000 tonnes per day to produce around 2.5 million oz. per year at US$96 per oz. or lower, McIntosh said that concept was "no longer optimal" in light of the latest resource increase at Busang.

"Now we are looking at initial production of about 100,000 tonnes per day, with an expansion to 150,000 tonnes," he explained. "This would result in annual gold production in excess of 4 million ounces. And we expect cash costs to be significantly less than US$96 per ounce."

By this point, it was apparent that scientists and everyone else better throw away their textbooks and simply accept Busang's marvels. Never before had a gold deposit made the transition from being able to produce 2.5 million oz. per year to almost double that number in a mere three months.

And who better to muddy the waters of scientific thinking than John "Walk on Water" Felderhof? Having dropped all pretense of having Busang fit any sort of scientific straitjacket, Felderhof began his comments with his effective, but by now suspicious, catch-all disclaimer: "We are dealing with a very unusual deposit here, one of a kind in the world."

Without his usual preamble about Busang's geology and large structural setting, Felderhof pulled out all the stops and made the sky the limit. But the thought of Freeport and Bob Hasan poking into every hole and cranny of Busang must have been preying on his mind, for he was beginning to display subtle touches of jungle fever which may prove important (to lawyers, at least) at a later date.

"Once we finish the drilling program we are currently doing, a new resource estimate will be provided by mid-April. My estimate is 95 million ounces. Mike de Guzman, my project manager, estimates 100 million ounces. And if you would ask me what is the total potential, I would feel very comfortable with 200 million ounces. This is just within the Busang II area; it excludes the Busang III."

The Busang mine would be massive. "If you want my opinion, and that of Mike de Guzman, eventually we are looking at an open pit which would be the size of six kilometers by three kilometers. That's the geology of the area. And we've just started to drill. I'm just being conservative."

Putting his training as a structural geologist to uses that would no doubt shock his former professors, Felderhof had even more upside to offer. "In Busang III, we have five targets, one of which is very exciting. As far as I'm concerned, we have lots of blue sky."

Felderhof conceded that while Busang still has all this exciting potential, "at some point we had to make a decision to mine, otherwise my drill rigs would disappear beyond the horizon."

Having been primed and prepped, mining analysts were allowed to ask questions. The first off the mark asked if Bre-X would be left "free and unencumbered" to sell all or part of its interest in Busang after the contracts of work were in hand and the Freeport deal completed. The answer was "yes", though Walsh said government approval would be required.

Asked if he believed Busang could be expanded beyond 150,000 tonnes per day with six months of continuing exploration, Felderhof went out on a limb again. "I would expect daily throughput to be in the region between 200,000 and 240,000 tonnes per day."

As Egizio Bianchini of Nesbitt Burns pointed out, this would result in annual production of "much more than four million ounces."

"That's correct," Felderhof said. "My feeling — my gut feeling — from looking at the visuals and what we're getting now is that the grade will improve over the one we have stated. The visual results from holes currently being drilled . . . are all excellent. That's why I'm saying, 200 million ounces I'm quite comfortable with, and 100 million ounces is no problem."

Felderhof also predicted that the starter pit alone could contain 120 million oz.of gold. At this point, Doug McIntosh of J.P. Morgan stepped in to clarify Felderhof's comments and push the envelope even further.

"Freeport is very new in the game and they have not developed a concept, so the present concept is what we've been talking to Kilborn about," he explained. "The plan is for initial production of 100,000 tonnes a day. That's going to yield somewhere in the range of 3 million ounces a year. That involves two grinding lines. A third grinding line would be added as soon as practical to give you 150,000 tonnes a day, which should give you about 4 million ounces a year. As John alluded, if we're talking about resources that can be turned to reserves in excess of 100 million, I'd certainly think a fourth line would be contemplated; it's still not a very complex mill, although it's a big one," McIntosh added.

"That would get you up to 200,000 tonnes a day and, you're talking at this point — and we haven't given much thought about it — about 6 million ounces a year of production."

This was not wild-eyed John Felderhof, but New York, talking. And when New York talks, everyone listens.

The discussion then turned to Bre-X's plans going forward. Walsh told analysts that while "the 'for sale' sign is not in the front yard," Bre-X would not rule out discussions with a potential suitor "if the price is right."

Felderhof, whose optimism was by now pathological, expressed the view that Freeport's due diligence review would take less than the month allotted for it, perhaps as little as 10 days. He indicated that he would be meeting with their "top people" on the site, from March 1 to 3. And he said Freeport was "extremely pleased" with the excellence of the data presented to it so far by Bre-X.

"They were a bit worried that the data was all over the place," Felderhof said, adding that the major company had originally wanted 180 days to complete its review. But he was uncharacteristically nebulous when asked if, after the signing, Freeport would take over as operator of the project. "I hope so."

In light of subsequent events, Bre-X's conference call is a constant source of embarrassment for every mining analyst who participated in it. Business reporters, all made experts with the benefit of hindsight, later had a field day mocking the gullibility of the analysts who challenged none of these incredibly outrageous statements.

But Rome was not built in a day. Nor was the Busang delusion, and everyone, including the business press, had a hand in building that.

The aftermath

It did not take long before word of John Felderhof's arm-waving and David Walsh's ownership confession came to the attention of the Toronto Stock Exchange and securities regulators.

Some cold water was poured on the exuberance of Bre-X's senior officers, who wisely decided it might be appropriate to clarify "certain comments." As usual, the task fell to David Walsh, who said Felderhof's comment about "feeling comfortable with a potential of 200 million oz." was based on drilling results to date and "future drilling targets." It was *not* a new resource calculation.

A long-term drilling program would be necessary to confirm the 200 million oz. Walsh cautioned. In the next breath, though, he reminded everyone that "John Felderhof and the Bre-X technical team have been, to date, accurate in their projections."

A few days later, Bre-X "clarified" reports that it would not be allowed to sell its 45% stake in Busang, held through Dutch subsidiaries, to another party without the permission of the Indonesian government.

"Bre-X is free to sell its Dutch subsidiaries without a right of first refusal," Walsh said. "Bob Hasan acknowledged this right. However, there is no plan for such a sale."

But Walsh gave shareholders an idea of what the worth of such a sale, if it were ever held, might be. Busang has a "gross economic value" of US$24.8 billion, he explained, which meant Bre-X's share would be US$11.2 billion.

Walsh then tried to reassure shareholders that the worst of the "Busang adventure" was over. The company had been "victimized by its own success" in Indonesia, he explained, which caused all the problems with cancelled SIPPs (preliminary exploration licences) and lawsuits and behind-the-scenes shenanigans.

"We were handicapped by strict disclosure rules. Each time we released a higher resource calculation, we attracted the attention of modern-day claim-jumpers who wanted to share in our find."

Walsh also hinted that Bre-X might have obtained a better deal had it not been for the "various third parties" who conducted negotiations with the Indonesian authorities — negotiations "from which Bre-X was excluded." These activities, Walsh hinted, introduced "a percentage ownership mindset" which reduced its eventual negotiating leverage.

The mining community was taken aback by the whirlwind pace of the events that had taken place during the Battle of Busang. The deposit and its geological setting were now the subject of intense geological curiosity. Usually the industry shared information freely. John Felderhof changed all that and was keeping his geological marvel under wraps, which made it all the more mysterious.

During a lunch at the Toronto's King Edward Hotel in late February, Paul Kavanagh was asked exactly how he thought Busang fit in the geological scheme of things. The "glory holes" reported by Bre-X appeared to be similar in grade and width to some spectacular holes pulled in Nevada's Carlin trend, where Barrick Gold had its cornerstone gold mine. Yet, Busang was different. The bonanza holes at Carlin were deep; the mineralization was metallurgically complex and had to be roasted before it could be processed. Busang was hitting its glory holes near surface and most of the gold came off a gravity circuit.

Did Busang have some similarities to Carlin-type deposits? Kavanagh pondered a moment or two before replying. "Larry Kornze [a senior Barrick geologist] and I did see some evidence of that," he said, referring to his site visit in 1993.

The most amazing feature of Busang was its remarkable predictability. Egizio Bianchini acknowledged in the summer of 1996 that the use of the words "predictable" and "geology" in the same sentence is dangerous. Yet, he went on to explain that Busang was remarkably consistent because it had "more in common with a large base-metal porphyry" than with typical gold deposits.

Others in the Toronto geological community expressed similar sentiments. Boiled down, the prevailing view was that Busang was like the huge copper deposits being mined in the southwestern United States and Chile, except with coarse, free gold produced rather than fine-grained copper. Maybe Felderhof was right. Busang had to be "one of a kind in the world."

Felderhof had told analysts that a copper-gold deposit might exist below Busang and add to its overall potential. But later, he said the deep drilling done to test this tantalizing theory did not pan out. The salting crew must have breathed a sigh of relief. Trying to keep the gold factory going was hard enough without having to prepare all those copper shavings.

And so Busang remained a geological puzzle. The industry knew that Bre-X had always been focused more on drilling the deposit than on understanding its genesis and geological setting. Felderhof's maar-diatreme theory did not explain everything, and Busang was starting to play havoc with too many rules. With any luck, Freeport would get to the bottom of all the geological contradictions.

Meanwhile, in Indonesia, self-described genius Michael de Guzman did his part to keep the Busang story alive. That meant directing attention away from what was already in hand to what might still be "out there."

As every geologist knows, it is always more exciting finding ounces than proving them up. In interviews with local press, de Guzman preferred to talk about Busang's unexplored potential, rather than discuss mining plans or production rates. "The big one may still be out there," he would often say. "We may only have the tiger by the tail."

Down in the dumps

Poor Jusuf Merukh. All that huffing and puffing for nothing. The development deal for the Busang project brokered by Bob

Hasan failed to mention Merukh's company, PT Krueng Gasui. Shares of Golden Valley Mines, Merukh's "technical assistance partner," tumbled to 6¢ on the Australian Stock Exchange. Merukh still had his undisputed 10% stake in the Muara Atan contract of work covering the Central zone, but nothing was mentioned in the Freeport deal about his other claims to the remaining Busang CoWs.

Merukh told Indonesian newspapers that he wanted 40% of the whole pie; his original 10, Syakerani's 10 (in return for a US$32,000 unpaid debt Merukh claimed he was owed by Syakerani) and an "option" he claimed existed for another 20%.

Merukh had no recourse but to turn to the courts to recoup his "losses." He pressed ahead with his lawsuit against Bre-X, which still had a 45% interest in Busang, and the 19 other parties.

The suit was filed in Alberta's Court of Queen Bench on January 15. David Walsh immediately described it as "frivolous" and "completely without merit." Merukh would later find it was frivolous all right, but for reasons he never imagined.

William McLucas stepped down from the board of Diadem Resources. Howe says it was for "health reasons"; others say Howe had to "choose" between his old friend McLucas, who still wasn't over the trauma of selling Busang for a song, and his old friend John Felderhof, who had found "the biggest gold deposit in the world."

Falling stars

If David Walsh and John Felderhof were nervous about Freeport's due diligence review of Busang, they tucked away their worries and enjoyed the adulation that came their way during the March mining bash at Toronto's Royal York Hotel.

Both men were celebrities. They could not walk more than a few steps anywhere in the hotel without someone coming up to shake their hands and offer congratulations. Surprisingly, they were rarely together. Each had his own entourage.

On Sunday evening, Walsh and Felderhof escorted their wives to a dinner hosted by *The Northern Miner* at the Mercer Street Grill, a popular watering hole and gourmet restaurant for jet-setters and arty types.

It was no small measure of Bre-X's fame that almost everyone in the place recognized Walsh. The restaurateur fussed and the service was excellent. Diners would sneak glances, including two blonde aspiring actresses at the next table.

Ingrid looked like a new woman, and probably was. Gone was

the matronly blonde of several years ago; in her place stood a glamorous woman with long, glossy-brown hair. Tall and trim, she was dripping in gold jewelry, her left hand decorated with a huge, dazzling diamond ring. Jeannette, a likable down-to-earth type, favored a less ostentatious look.

After a sumptuous meal punctuated by several breaks to allow Walsh and Felderhof to puff their cigarettes, *Northern Miner* Publisher John Cooke presented the two honorees with their "Man of the Year" trophies — brass miner's lamps imported from Wales and suitably engraved for the occasion.

Walsh seemed genuinely appreciative, and Felderhof's acceptance speech, too, had the ring of sincerity. "I will always treasure this," he said, adding that he agreed with a recent editorial in the newspaper that bemoaned the proliferation of lawsuits in the minerals industry.

The remark triggered a response from Ingrid, who made quite clear her displeasure with those "nasty people" who had made John's life so difficult in recent months. "My wife gets very upset when I'm attacked," Felderhof explained.

Ingrid, who confessed she had never been to Busang, appeared to be relieved that her husband's involvement with the project would soon be over. She was anxious for her life to return to normal. John's long absences had been a strain, and the steady stream of visitors who passed through their home on the Grand Cayman had monopolized his time.

"I'm taking control of my life, and you should too," she advised Jeannette, who merely shrugged and said, "David does whatever he wants to do."

Felderhof was now spending more time in the Cayman Islands. He had previously bought a home in West Virginia but later decided to move offshore, ostensibly for tax reasons. Perhaps that decision had been Ingrid's, who probably had learned that John was not the best administrator of the family finances. After all, he had made and then lost a small fortune before. Ingrid was known to take a keen interest in business; a year or so earlier, in Jakarta, she had been spotted toting around Alex Doulis's book *Take the Money and Run*. The joke quickly circulated that she was doing some "estate planning" for John.

The Walsh family were in the process of remodelling their waterfront home in Nassau, The Bahamas, where they had kept the common touch, maintaining contact with many of their old friends. Since hitting the big time they had refrained from putting on airs.

Even Felderhof had kept in touch with his Bluenose roots. He told the story of how he had brought one of his geology professors from Dalhousie University to visit the Busang property. "He was pretty old and it was a long trip," Felderhof admitted with a touch of guilt. "But he wanted to look at everything because he was so excited. It was a big thrill for him."

The evening was meant to be a sociable one, and neither man expressed any interest in discussing the technical aspects of Busang. A general question about Bob Hasan was met with stony silence, and Felderhof offered no hints as to where he intended to start looking for his next maar-diatreme.

Walsh did volunteer that he had "personal reasons" for selling a large block of shares the previous summer, though he declined to mention what those reasons were. Many of the shares had been sold after Bre-X's exploration permit had been cancelled by the Indonesian government and during a period when other questions about property ownership were being raised. Walsh didn't like the way the issue had been "played up" by the financial press.

As the women continued chatting about "taking control of their lives," David briefly outlined his next venture, Arm-X Resources, which was to begin exploring for gold and base metals in Armenia. The company would involve members of Jeannette's family, who were from there.

Walsh also stated that the accomplishment of which he was most proud was building his investor relations team. It was a peculiarly superficial comment, given that his company had supposedly found one of the largest gold deposits in the world.

Walsh was in good spirits. He told a few anecdotes related to his encounters with Peter Munk during the infamous Battle for Busang. "The man would call me 'darling'," Walsh said, with his boyish smile. "What is that? Is he related to Zsa Zsa Gabor, or is it some sort of Hungarian thing?"

That set Felderhof off on a litany of Barrick's alleged shenanigans, starting with the Sumatra property affair — "we got an apology from Munk for that" — and ending with numerous allegations about the gold giant's heavy-handed conduct in Indonesia. His contempt for the company was palpable, perhaps paranoid — if there wasn't a Barrick guy hiding under the bed, there was one lurking in the bush. One almost expected Felderhof to accuse Peter Munk of destroying the ozone layer.

"Barrick people are all like that," he said, lumping in even the company's new president, John Carrington.

That was too much for the *Miner*'s Cooke, who politely told Felderhof that he had known the Carrington family for decades and that John was regarded as a man of integrity in the mining industry.

"He'll be corrupted before you know it," Felderhof insisted.

The Last Supper: David Walsh's son Brett (left) and Indonesian geologist Jonathan Nassey (right) head up the Bre-X table at the PDAC convention.

"Wait and see."

Cooke disagreed and the matter was dropped, but not before Felderhof indicated that he had kept detailed notes of the meetings that took place during the Battle for Busang. Geologists are trained to be meticulous note-takers, so it is not surprising that Felderhof would have documented events on a daily basis. He added, however, that he has stored these notes in a vault so that, after all the dust has settled, he will be able write his version of the Busang story. "The real story," he teased.

'Find your own'

The highlight of the annual Prospectors and Developers convention is the awards banquet, a black-tie event where industry professionals gather to honor their own.

It would be a night of glory for Bre-X, as John Felderhof was there to pick up the "Prospector of the Year" award for having discovered Busang, and also for his role in finding Ok Tedi.

The night was doubly glorious for Felderhof. His archenemy, Peter Munk, had been named "Developer of the Year" for having built Barrick Gold into one of the world's largest producers, but was unable to attend the ceremony. Accepting on Munk's behalf was John Carrington.

The convention was buzzing with speculation that Felderhof, and perhaps other Bre-X insiders, had threatened to boycott the event if "that arrogant man" had attended. The Bre-X team played along, suggesting that, yes, the indignity of Felderhof's having to occupy the same table, let alone the same room, as Munk would have been too much to bear.

Felderhof had his "Team Indonesia" people, past and present, on hand for the occasion. Mike Bird was there, along with Peter Howe. Mike Novotny skipped the event, and was later dressed down for his ungracious absence by both Bird and Ingrid Felderhof.

Felderhof's senior team at Busang was present; Michael de Guzman, Cesar Puspos and Jerry Alo. Mandy and Candy and their friends were absent and supposedly keeping the home fires burning. Walsh brought in his entire investor relations team from Calgary, a group of fresh-faced, youths under the tutelage of the brash Stephen McAnulty and Special Projects Manager Tommy Devlin.

The awards banquet was held on March 10 in the Hotel's Concert Hall. The menu included roast pepper-crusted, demi-rack of lamb, with tiramisu imperial for dessert. Felderhof was seated with other award-winners at the head table on stage, with Ingrid placed at a table immediately below, near several tables occupied by Bre-X's Calgary team.

In his acceptance speech, Felderhof paid tribute to David Walsh, Mike de Guzman and his wife.

He praised Walsh for always providing the money needed to continue exploration at Busang. Felderhof harkened back to his college days and likened his partner to a father who always "sent money" when it was needed. And he told the audience that Ingrid had been "deeply hurt" by recent events in Indonesia and by the "attacks" made on him as he defended his discovery.

Felderhof also praised his colleagues at the Busang site, particularly star geologist Michael de Guzman. In an eerie foreboding of events to come, he paid tribute to "comrades lost in helicopter accidents," mudslides and other natural disasters. But he saved his best for last.

At times, award recipients have used the occasion to get something off their chests. Royal Oak Mines President Margaret "Peggy" Witte, for example, lashed out at the British Columbia government upon accepting her Developer of the Year award in 1994. Her criticism was directed at the government's decision to expropriate her company's Windy Craggy copper-cobalt deposit and make it part of a public park.

Nothing, however, can compare with the chutzpah unleashed by Bre-X's vice-chairman on the evening of March 10, 1997.

"We have a development that goes against my grain. When you find something, someone wants a piece of it." he intoned. "I think we should expand the PDAC to include the tree-shakers . . . those who shake other people's trees to see what might fall out. The only jungle they know is the concrete jungle, and the closest they get to rocks is a scotch on the rocks. To them, I say 'Go find your own gold.'"

The crowd was stunned. Everyone knew he was talking about Barrick and Peter Munk.

John Felderhof goes out on a limb at the PDAC convention in Toronto.

Some cheered, some clapped, while others sat silent.

John Felderhof went out on a limb that night, propelled by the dark instincts that had brought him to this fleeting moment of glory. It would be only a few short weeks before someone with a real grip on geology chopped him down.

It could not have been easy for John Carrington to ignore those barbs and step up to accept the Developer of the Year award for Peter Munk. As he approached the podium, a group of people from the Bre-X tables left the room in protest, mostly young hotheads from the company's investor relations team. Roly Francisco stayed put, as did Peter Howe and several others.

Carrington did not rise to Felderhof's bait. He delivered his comments with dignity, congratulated Felderhof on behalf of Peter Munk, and returned to his seat.

After the presentation, a few people came up to Felderhof and praised his "courage." Many felt that while the PDAC awards ceremony was not exactly the best time and place to launch into a diatribe, Felderhof had a point. There were too many "tree-shakers" in the mining game. It was not difficult to see that the whole Busang affair had been deeply divisive for the industry.

The flamboyant Ingrid supported her husband wholeheartedly. A Bre-X shareholder seated at the next table asked how she coped with her husband's long absences at Busang. Ingrid replied that because her husband had the talent and drive to do "great things," it was important to give him the freedom he needed to achieve these accomplishments.

There were more than a few rough moments that night. Stephen McAnulty lost his cool when a shareholder swung by the table and said: "Good sale at twenty-eight dollars, Steve." The $22-million public-relations man flushed at the obvious reference to his insider trading record and stood up, ready to defend his honor. Brett Walsh interceded. "Settle down," he told the ruffled McAnulty.

The issue of insider trading was a sensitive one for Bre-X insiders, as most had been sellers in the latter half of 1996 when ownership problems and "predators" began to surface. Paul Kavanagh was one of the few whose name did not routinely appear in the Ontario Securities Commission's *OSC Bulletin*. He was, in his own words, "a believer", and continued to exercise his stock options without selling the stock. He did, however, use his paper wealth to patronize the arts, making a gift of 11,500 shares just before Christmas in 1996. Some were used to help the family of a young pianist, then training in the United States. The rest went to the Toronto Symphony Orchestra, which reciprocated by inviting Kavanagh to a black-tie dinner. There, he was seated next to a senior executive of *The Globe and Mail*, whom the paper had recruited from the food industry. "I never spoke a word to that soup man," Kavanagh said.

Roly Francisco and Bryan Coates, who came on board after Bre-X started making waves on the market, both received options, but only the former was reported to have cashed in on them.

The OSC released records showing that David Walsh had sold $7.5 million in shares between April 23 and August 27, 1996, and that Jeannette Walsh had sold $20.8 million worth between April 23 and October 22. Any shares the couple accumulated during the same periods were from options exercised at zero cost. Stephen McAnulty took in $3.1 million, and his wife, Nancy, another $3.1 million, between April 23 and September 30.

But John Felderhof was the champion inside trader, having sold off a full $35.3 million in shares between April 10 and September 11. Records show he also exercised options for more shares, which cost him $22.3 million. On one day (May 15, 1996), he sold almost $6.4 million worth of Bre-X shares into the market. The average size of his individual sales into the market was just under $340,000. Felderhof was to insider trading what Michael de Guzman was to sex.

The sales figures do not tell the whole story, since some of the options to acquire the shares were exercised before April. But estimates at the time put Felderhof's profits at more than $30 million, with the Walshes, taken together, in the black by a similar amount.

Many shareholders of Bre-X had held on to their stock throughout the Battle of Busang. Some were disappointed the Freeport offer did not have a buyout provision that would have put cash in their pockets; some grumbling was heard that, perhaps, Barrick's deal might have been better in that regard. Then again, most shareholders assumed that the Barrick arrangement would be fair in a North American context; otherwise, lawyers would have a field day. No one knew the exact terms.

Suspicion was growing, however, that Bob Hasan had not structured the deal in anyone's interest but his own.

The bloom was starting to come off the rose. The reality was that Hasan effectively controlled the 40% of Busang held by "Indonesian interests," which cost him little or nothing. He had picked the operating partner of his choice, Freeport, which was to receive a 15% interest in return for developing the mine. Ostensibly, a joint-venture committee would be set up and Bre-X would have representation, but this was Indonesia. David Walsh would *not* be calling the shots. A Freeport buyout of Bre-X's 45% interest seemed the logical outcome.

Bre-X said nothing publicly about Freeport buying the rest of Busang, though the junior's investor relations department had been dropping hints to analysts and investors. Some claimed to have heard about the buyout from Brett Walsh. Dollar figures for the supposed buyout were even floated as trial balloons. In any event, by the time the PDAC convention rolled around, the Royal York Hotel was buzzing with rumors that a Freeport offer was imminent. Once again, people simply dismissed or forgot about Jusuf Merukh and his lawsuit against Bre-X and "nineteen other parties."

During the four-day event, David Walsh showed up at a cocktail reception hosted by Kilborn, which Bre-X had hired to carry out geological and engineering reports at Busang. A few people said later that they had noticed "tension in the air" and that no one from Kilborn was speaking with Walsh.

Mike de Guzman and Cesar Puspos were seen wandering around the convention floor. De Guzman appeared to be in good spirits, though perhaps somewhat subdued given the celebratory nature of the event. He said he had dropped by several company booths to learn how Canadians explored for massive sulphide deposits (base metal deposits, usually found in volcanic rocks), as he expected he would soon be working on this type of project. Cesar was his usual self: quiet, nervous but invariably friendly. He always looked like a guilty teenager caught with his best friend's girl.

De Guzman also visited Freeport's display booth, which was popular with Bre-X investors as the company was giving away promotional keychains featuring rock chips from the company's Grasberg gold-copper mine in Irian Jaya.

One investor was standing in the booth, talking with Freeport officials, when de Guzman dropped by, his apprentices trailing behind. The investor naturally wanted to know how things were coming along at the Busang site.

"We're getting along great since the fire," de Guzman said.

The investor, who prided himself on keeping abreast of Bre-X developments, was shocked. "What fire?"

The gist of the conversation was that de Guzman had been upset because Freeport had accused Bre-X of deliberately setting the fire in January that had destroyed some of the company's geological records. But following a "review from both sides," the misunderstanding had been resolved, de Guzman explained. Both parties agreed, for the sake of friendship, that the fire had been an accident caused by a short in the electrical wiring.

A time bomb ticks

While John Felderhof was being honored for discovering Busang and Michael de Guzman was amusing himself with the latest in a string of lady friends, Freeport's Jim Bob Moffett was making a few discoveries of his own, none of which was pleasant.

Results were already in hand from several drill holes, but no senior Bre-X people were on site to answer questions about the disturbing results. The salting team had gone to Toronto to watch their boss accept an award for his role in discovering the world's biggest ounce factory.

Moffett had tried to reach either Walsh or Felderhof at the Royal York Hotel to report that "a problem" had arisen. When he finally established contact, he got the same runaround that Stan Hawkins had to endure.

Moffett explained that he had received information that needed to be discussed. There were "real problems with the initial results" which required an explanation. Moffett wanted a senior person to come to the property immediately.

"I don't know anything about all that; I'm not a technical guy,"

Walsh told Moffett. "You'll have to talk with Felderhof."

Felderhof brusquely told Moffett he was "confused" and had probably "mixed up the samples," a story he would stick by for weeks to come. Moffett ignored this slight to his mental faculties, the insult to his technical team, and the barely credible explanation. "I hate to mess up your party, but you've got to send someone out here."

After some discussion, Bre-X management decided that de Guzman would return to the property to meet with Freeport officials and straighten out the whole mess. Moffett and his team waited for de Guzman to show up with answers.

Later that evening, Walsh appeared at the convention's Kirkland Lake Night, alone and visibly drunk. He was asked why he was not on the dance floor with Jeannette, celebrating his good fortune. He replied that she had a "terrible headache" and had gone to bed.

Later, Walsh was heard mumbling into his beer, "I hope that God damned Felderhof is right."

Chapter Eight:
RED FLAGS OVER BUSANG

The eye of each man sees but what it has the power of seeing.
Andrew Lang

Debunked in a basement

The gold company David Walsh built from the basement of his Calgary home unravelled in the basement of Jan Merks' home, just outside Vancouver. Merks took on fellow Dutchman John Felderhof and debunked his gold deposit without ever having seen a rock or a grain of gold from the Busang property in East Kalimantan. And it all happened before Freeport's due diligence team landed at the jungle property and discovered what Merks already knew, but had to keep secret.

For most others, the credibility of Bre-X Minerals began its downward spiral on March 18, as reports swept around the world that Michael de Guzman was missing and presumed dead after falling 240 metres from a helicopter while en route to Busang to meet with Freeport officials.

"This is a tragic development, and our hearts and prayers are with Mike's family," Bre-X Jakarta stated.

When word of de Guzman's disappearance reached Freeport President Jim Bob Moffett in the middle of the night, he reacted quite differently. His gut instinct told him something insidious was afoot.

"I've been around this business too long," he later told reporters in a conference call. "You don't fall out of helicopters. Once [de Guzman] disappeared, I had an airplane in Balikpapan and I had my guys out of there two hours later. Because you never know what's going to happen next. When people get desperate you have to assume desperate things might happen."

At first, mining analysts thought it was some sort of freak accident caused by a storm or sudden turbulence and were sympathetic. But big dollars were at stake, and some began to worry. It was hard to imagine how a geologist with plenty of helicopter experience could simply fall from the sky.

Worry turned to panic the next day when Bre-X reported that de Guzman had left a suicide note saying he was "giving up on life" because he had contracted acute hepatitis B. The prognosis was poor, Bre-X officials said, owing to his many bouts of malaria.

For those who had seen de Guzman days earlier at the mining convention in Toronto, the story was tough to swallow. While he may have been ill, hepatitis B is rarely fatal; it is easily treatable, and the symptoms often disappear on their own. And he had access to the best medical attention money could buy. De Guzman's work at Busang was nearly complete, the pressures of the job almost over, and he was wealthy enough to spend the rest of his life relaxing on a beach with a pretty nurse.

"I was shocked, like everyone else," said Stan Hawkins, who had spent an evening with de Guzman just days earlier. "I thought he looked as healthy as a horse. He was lucid and didn't seem depressed at all."

The more logical explanation was that the due diligence review was not going well for Bre-X. It is never a good sign when geologists go "missing" at such critical times. The incident cast the first real doubts about the size, grade and economic viability of the Busang project.

Those doubts found fertile ground in the *Miner*'s newsroom. Editor Vivian Danielson had a hunch and called Jan Merks in Vancouver. Merks, whose firm, Matrix Consultants, often does trouble-shooting for mining companies that run into sampling problems, is not a geologist or a mining engineer. He is a statistician. That, and not his thick Dutch accent, makes him difficult to understand at times.

Merks is a classical mathematician who talks about variances, standard deviations and laws of probability with a fervor that causes most people's eyes to glaze over. He is a purist and despises the burgeoning practice of manufacturing data from data to arrive at mathematically unsound conclusions that can be steered this way and that. To Merks, this is not science; it's "the people-pleasing business."

Merks also is a scam-buster, though an inadvertent one. He had already toppled Ronald Markham, also known as "Runaway Ron," an aging playboy promoter described by securities regulators on several continents as "the ultimate con man." That is another story

— one that made it all the way to the upper classes of London society — to be told later in this book.

As it turned out, Merks could say nothing about Busang or Bre-X, for "legal reasons." Those few words convinced Danielson, who had worked with Merks to expose Runaway Ron's phantom gold deposit in Oregon in 1993, that Barrick must have found something wrong in its samples from Busang. She was well-aware of the kind of work he did.

It was clear that the gold producer must have been given either a data set, or some samples to test while engaged in discussions with Bre-X.

Merks could say nothing; he was party to the same confidentiality agreement that bound his client. So Danielson laid out her suspicions. The story was not hanging together. There were too many niggling inconsistencies, too many bizarre things said by de Guzman and John Felderhof. Normally, geologists love their discoveries. Something was wrong here. Busang, instead of being proudly turned over to Freeport, was being publicly dumped.

Merks listened, took pity and said, "Find your own proof."

The *Miner* had one lead. We knew that in earlier controversies Merks had used a statistical technique called the "analysis of variance". Its principal premise goes like this: in any set of data, the differences between individual measurements — the "variance" — comes from a number of sources. If the measurements are examined in a properly designed test, that variance can be split up into components which come from each of these sources.

In practical terms, what it meant for someone examining a set of assays from drill core was that there would be differences in grade from one sample to the next, and that the *overall* difference would start with the differences Mother Nature put there — Merks called this the "intrinsic variability." The variation from other sources would be added to it — he called this the "measurement variability." But in any natural process, the intrinsic variability must be greater than the measurement variability for there to be any proof that a concentration of metal exists.

We realized that if Merks had been brought in to do statistical analyses on the data from Busang, that the data must have shown unusual and unnatural variability. That meant Busang might be unnatural too.

It was a devastating, sickening moment of certainty. There was inner turmoil and self-doubt, but no tears, only grim determination to get to the bottom of things. While it took a few days for the shock to wear off, there was, from that day, never a moment of doubt that Busang was anything but a total crock. "Jungle-dirt," we called it, with a few expletives for emphasis.

Reality hit that day, and it hit hard. Gold deposits do not grow as big and as fast as Busang without a lot of fertilizer. Gold deposits do not have marvellous metallurgy, dreamy geology, pay streaks and glory holes. Gold deposits cannot be custom-made. Real gold deposits are tough to find, and even harder to define. Real gold deposits are broken up by faulting, turned upside down by folding and stretched to nothing in places. The big ones have murderous metallurgy or skimpy grades or, because they are in the middle of nowhere, cost a king's ransom to develop. The little ones hide, torture and tease. Real gold deposits are never, ever this easy.

Suspicions were heightened days later by press reports from Indonesia that suggested Freeport's due diligence was not producing results similar to those previously reported by Bre-X. Obviously concerned about its confidentiality agreement with the Calgary junior and its Indonesian partners, Freeport responded by stating that it "had not commented on the progress, to the press, in this regard," and that due diligence was continuing. It was not a denial.

Soon afterward, Daniel McConvey of Lehman Brothers, a New York City-based investment firm, downgraded his rating on Bre-X stock to "neutral" from "outperform." It was somewhat surprising that many others did nothing at all.

But the doubts were as contagious as the euphoria had been months earlier. The analysts began burning up the phone lines to one another, swapping theories. They were unnerved, rattled, biting their nails. Investors were spooked. The smart money bailed out fast. The smell of scam, thus far contained, was now in the air.

Deaths and fires

Salting scams — the really infamous ones — have involved either death or fire. Bre-X's Busang, which the *Miner* now suspected was the Mother of all Gold Scams, already had both.

Michael de Guzman was supposedly dead, and two mysterious fires had occurred at Busang, one in 1996 and another in early 1997. The first was small and resulted in minor damage to a pump room, according to David Walsh. The second destroyed geological records, though Bre-X's damage control team, led by Stephen McAnulty, tried to reassure shareholders that duplicates were retained elsewhere.

Dessir Resources also tried to reassure investors when suspicions were first raised in 1991 about its gold deposit in northern California. John Kilburn, a reporter with the *Miner* at the time, was sent to investigate when drilling returned suspiciously high-grade gold over wide intervals. He came back unimpressed, despite spectacular results such as 76 ft. grading more than 2 oz. of gold per ton.

A short while later, the bad news was out. Joseph Montgomery, the man who had found placer gold at Tapin Copper's project in Oregon, found the same thing in Dessir's samples. Gold does travel from its source, but how placer gold from the Yukon found its way to an underground deposit in California cannot be explained by the migration theory.

As it turned out, Dessir had allowed the vendor of the property to operate the work program and take samples for assaying. Normally, this is not done. When it is done, it is stupid — the vendor is hardly a disinterested party, particularly if shares are part of his compensation. This particular vendor got 200,000 shares, plus a cool US$1.4 million cash.

The vendor took the samples to one lab, where they were crushed. He "changed his mind," packed up the samples in the back of a pickup truck and dropped them off at the second lab, which did the assaying. At the second lab, gold was detected; at the first, it was not. Both were reputable, so the problem was not inside the lab. When the U.S. Federal Bureau of Investigation was called in, someone panicked. The lab that found the gold was burned to the ground, destroying much of the evidence. The vendor disappeared and the investigation went nowhere. Dessir went defunct.

The *Miner* later received a call from an unknown party who claimed that the "vendor" who had carted around the samples from one lab to another didn't own the property after all. The real owner was behind bars and had just "lent" the property to a former cellmate. The case would not be solved, we were told, because the suspected perpetrator was now in a witness protection program involving some Colombian drug-smuggling operation. We threw up our hands. This story went way beyond geology.

No one died in the Dessir scam. But a young man named Michael Opp was shot once in the head and killed on the night of November 14, 1982, possibly because he knew too much about the New Cinch stock and salting swindle in New Mexico. That bizarre story involved a cast of colorful characters, a cover-up and an unsolved murder.

The scam went along nicely for a year or so but began to unravel when a senior mining company bought shares of New Cinch Uranium Ltd. at a cost of more than US$25 million — big money at the time. It took its own samples and found no significant gold.

New Cinch officials argued that there was an assaying "problem." They said it would have been "extraordinarily difficult" for anyone to tamper with the samples for two years and produce consistent results. Some bewildered shareholders bought the story and hung on to a shred of hope that the "assaying discrepancies" would soon be resolved.

A consulting firm began studying the problem while shareholders waited and speculated on the outcome. The whole thing blew up when finally it was announced that the original samples had been contaminated, possibly by salting, though falsification of assay data also was suspected.

New Cinch officials professed to be shocked and appalled by all that had been going on under their noses. The senior company that bought the near-worthless shares sued. New Cinch officers claimed they were "victims," and the matter was settled out of court for pennies on the dollar.

It would soon sound eerily familiar.

Naysayers and short sellers

On March 24, David Walsh told the world that he, too, felt like a victim.

The share prices of Bre-X and Bresea were sliding down the slippery slope of uncertainty every day, putting in jeopardy all his work of the past four years. More forces of darkness had to be at work than a few negative press reports from Indonesia, which were getting far more attention than they deserved.

Walsh reminded the world that Bre-X's board had "absolute confidence in the integrity and accuracy of [the] assay results and resource calculations" that had been reported since exploration began in 1993. "Unfortunately, when the first ounce of gold is poured at Busang, I am sure the naysayers will complain about the color."

Walsh threatened legal action against "certain parties and publications" that were continuing a "proliferation of falsehoods and misinformation." It was pure bluster, for Walsh already knew there was "a problem" at Busang. Jim Bob Moffett had made that quite clear.

Convinced that short sellers were behind the fall in his company's share price, Walsh sought advice from Andrew Racz of Bishop, Rosen & Co., in New York City. Racz had been helpful before, during the Battle of Busang, when he wrote to American senators calling for them to intercede and ensure Bre-X got fair treatment in Indonesia.

Racz also had helped Walsh in his efforts to inform the market that Bresea shares were undervalued relative to Bre-X. He issued a report, dated March 18, predicting that major mining companies might be interested in buying 100% of Bresea "to gain control of its 49 million shares of Bre-X." Racz named Barrick, Placer Dome,

Newmont Mining and Freeport as possible contenders. He suggested that, in the event of even a partial takeover, the 23% interest of Bre-X held by Bresea appeared to be the cheapest Bre-X stock around; Bresea was selling at a "holding company discount." David Walsh had been trying to make this point for months.

There were a few other eyeopeners in Racz's report. One was that Bre-X had a whopping 240 million shares outstanding. The other was Racz's comment that David Walsh controlled about 35% of Bre-X, through "outright ownership" of about 35 million Bre-X shares and his 16 million Bresea shares.

Racz met Walsh in New York, and later in Calgary, to discuss the downward pressure on Bre-X and Bresea shares.

Racz said Walsh was "mesmerized" with the idea that a short-selling conspiracy was behind the erosion of the share prices. He had been stalking this bogeyman for months. "My answer was to tell [Bre-X] to clarify their legal position in Indonesia and get down to work. That is the only way to stop short selling."

Walsh was clearly unnerved, Racz said, and still obsessed with the notion that short sellers were behind his problems. "He was afraid of something very badly." During a visit to Bre-X's Calgary office and a tour of the investor relations department, Racz became convinced that Walsh's sole interest was the market. "The whole thing was about stock promotion; there were few professional people." He said he decided then that it might be wise to back away from the whole story.

Meanwhile, on Bay Street, analysts had their own problems. Michael Fowler of Levesque Beaubien Geoffrion tried to reassure investors that it was "premature" to jump to conclusions about Freeport's review, based on a few negative Indonesian newspaper articles that "occurred on the heels of one of the biggest tragedies in recent exploration history." He was referring to Michael de Guzman's apparent demise. "We do not see any material effect on the stock price from this shocking event," he said.

First Marathon waded in a day later and called Bre-X a speculative buy. "We believe Kilborn has completed adequate due diligence on the drilling, sample preparation and assay techniques prior to completing their resource estimates," wrote analyst Kerry Smith.

But the most frightening comments of all came from Egizio Bianchini of Nesbitt Burns on March 25. "Our sources indicate that Freeport's initial sampling of the deposit has indeed come up well short of Bre-X's announced grades," he wrote, though cautioning that this had not been "substantiated" by Freeport.

Bianchini predicted the discrepancy might have something to do with the sample preparation procedures used by Freeport.

"Freeport has conducted its initial assaying without consulting Bre-X," he wrote, forgetting what due diligence was all about. The two companies were now talking, he added. "We are of the view that if indeed an assay discrepancy exists, it will be resolved within a short period of time. The gold is there!"

The gist of the message was that John Felderhof would solve the problem once he showed Freeport his protocol for sample preparation procedures that "must be followed in order to obtain accurate assay results."

Those comments sent a chill through the *Miner*'s newsroom. We'd heard those same words years earlier from none other than Runaway Ron Markham and his geologist when problems surfaced on their gold project, then known as "the largest in the world." The world's "ultimate con artist" also had a strict protocol for assaying, which never failed to find gold major companies could not detect.

We'd been there, heard all that, and knew better. Assaying, whatever some may say, is a science, not an art. *Plus ça change, plus c'est la même chose.*

The Busang fortress

Bud Laporte is the quintessential diamond driller. Crusty, cynical and not easily fooled, he knows good rocks when he sees them, as most drillers do. Just ask their brokers.

Laporte suspected Busang was not all it was cracked up to be a while back, for one main reason. During a trip through Southeast Asia to drum up business for his company, Major Drilling Group International, he heard local suppliers and contractors complaining that Bre-X was not buying the normal range of supplies and services usually purchased for an exploration project. And trying to see anyone at Bre-X Jakarta was nearly impossible. "I know," he said. "I tried. They were always too busy to see me."

Laporte started hearing strange things. PT Drillinti Tiko had 15 drills, ostensibly for Bre-X — its only client — but only two or three were going at one time. "It didn't make sense. I heard it was because they didn't want many people on site, particularly North Americans or Australians."

Laporte heard that Bre-X wanted only Dayaks manning the rigs. They might be perfectly competent at the job, he added, but they wouldn't know good rocks from bad. "I found that suspicious."

While in the Philippines, Laporte talked with a local geologist who had previously worked with Mike de Guzman. He asked how many Canadians were at Busang. "None," he was told. What about geophysical companies? Same answer.

"They could put out all the razzle-dazzle information without fear of having to substantiate it as there were no Canadian geologists on the property to dispute it," Laporte said. "The crew were all [de Guzman's] drinking buddies."

Laporte had a point. With de Guzman missing and presumed dead, it became painfully obvious that no senior geologists from North America or Australia were working at Busang. So who was minding the shop now that Felderhof was spending most of his time in Jakarta and the Cayman Islands?

Answer: a small band of unsupervised Filipino geologists with stock options. There was goofy young Cesar Puspos, who might have been a good field geologist in his day. But was he experienced and seasoned enough to run a project as large as Busang? Hardly. And there was Jerry Alo, a frightening enough figure long before his shady dealings at Benguet were even suspected.

While all this might sound bigoted, the money to fund work at Busang was not coming from the Philippines. Most of it was coming from North America. Shareholders might have appreciated having one or two reputable Canadian geologists checking up on things from time to time.

"It would have been a helluva lot easier to check their credentials," Laporte said. "Especially with all those investors flocking to Bre-X like brood mares to Secretariat."

Bre-X Jakarta's obsession with secrecy extended not only to the Busang site, where a strict no-visitors policy was always in effect.

The company's office was in the city's downtown core, and not in Cilandak Estates, where most mining companies and their suppliers were based. Geologists working for other juniors would drop by Bre-X's office on some pretext or other to try to glean more information about Busang's geology information which they hoped they could use to guide their own exploration efforts.

"It was sterile," said John Ball, a Canadian geologist who visited the Bre-X office a few times. "It was like a doctor's office. There were no maps or cross-sections on the wall and no rocks and specimens of any kind. There was nothing to say 'We're proud of what we've found.'" They told me all that kind of stuff was at the site."

Ball also thought it strange that John Felderhof would become livid if anyone hired away his Indonesian geologists. "It happens all the time in the industry, but John would say competitors were trying to 'steal' his people. He yelled at one of the Barrick guys for that."

Indonesian geologists did, indeed, work at Busang, but their role was confined to geotechnical logging: they examined the core for fracturing, calculated how much was recovered in each interval, and observed anything which might have an effect on slope stability or groundwater flow. They didn't look for the mineralization or describe the rocks; that part of the core logging was left to the Filipino geologists.

The Busang story took another strange turn when reports surfaced that de Guzman had two wives. Then another wife surfaced, and then another. Laporte was somewhat amused by it all. "No wonder he committed suicide."

But analysts were not laughing. The affable and intelligent Michael de Guzman they thought they knew had taken on a complexity of character they had never imagined.

There had been reports that de Guzman kept a mistress near the site, but this was something quite different. Mining men, like travelling salesmen, sometimes forget they are married when they are far from home. As the old saying goes, these things get a bit blurred when the moon is bright, the beer is flowing and the girls are pretty. Clarity comes later, when most trundle home with their varying burdens of guilt. But de Guzman's secret life shocked even the most hedonistic of mining men. Most could understand having a girlfriend here and there, sequentially of course, but four wives? That required a level of duplicity few men had the energy or will to muster.

"Mandy," who spent five days in Toronto with de Guzman just before his fall from grace, and the sky, was not surprised to hear he was married. This was true of many of the men who frequented her club. But she was surprised to hear that he was more married than most. So were each of the wives, who probably wished they had carried out more due diligence of their own.

Due diligence

Due diligence in mining is not a young man's game.

The mining industry has plenty of folksy adages, but, as Freeport's exploration staff descended on Busang, John Felderhof must have feared this one the most.

"Due diligence" is one of those terms that has made its way into everyday speech from the language of contracts. It is the legal draftsman's phrase for that timeless counsel of caution, "Look before you leap." Most mineral property agreements have a provision which allows the company coming on to the property (the purchaser or the new joint-venture partner) a period of time, before the deal finally closes, to confirm the representations the vendor or property-holder has made about exploration results and land tenure.

The new agreement between Bre-X, Freeport and Bob Hasan's

Nusamba Group was no exception. Freeport, which might never have ended up with Busang had there been an open and fair bidding war (because, at the time, its financial resources were directed towards proving up reserves at the huge Grasberg mine in Irian Jaya) had until April 30 to look its gift horse in the mouth.

A due diligence review on a mineral property is usually done by a team of people with experience in geology, mining and metallurgy. The team typically has a senior technical person from each profession, with intermediate and junior professional staff to help. The senior people most often have operating experience at producing mines; each one needs to know enough about the other two disciplines to be able to talk to, and work with, the others.

The property-holder's files are opened to the team: they look at geological maps and cross sections, to gain some understanding of the deposit's shape, size and host rocks; at sampling procedures and assay records, to determine that reserve estimates are reliable; and at metallurgical work, capital and operating cost estimates and material contracts, to ensure that estimates of development and production costs are reasonable. The reviewers are expected to be skeptical, suspicious, hard to please: that's what the review is for. And always at the centre are the reserve estimates. Seasoned mining men know that while mills and mining methods can be designed and developed, geology, grades and tonnages have to be lived with.

And, of course, the geologists pore over the drill logs and compare the split core with the records. But Bre-X's unconventional practices didn't allow for that.

All this has to be done before the team can review the owner's estimates of tonnage and grade. If the information used to calculate reserves is not properly acquired and evaluated, the end result is a house of cards. Under certain circumstances, a company entering a project will drill new holes, sample and re-assay.

The task is formidable, as the team usually has only a few weeks in which to acquire, assimilate, evaluate, judge and report on work which required many years and millions of dollars to accomplish.

Before Freeport set foot on Busang, John Felderhof told mining analysts that initial mine plans were based on the intermediate feasibility study and an annual production rate of 2 million oz.

"Freeport has upgraded this to four million ounces per annum. So what we are looking at, from what I understand, is that we may start at two million ounces in the year 2000 and then upgrade it to four million ounces within two years."

But the reality was somewhat different. It was true that Freeport was engaged in financing discussions with its banks to raise the money it would need to build a mine down the road. But on site, it had gone back to square one. Jim Bob Moffett was not taking anything at face value. "We had no idea what we were going to uncover," he later told reporters. "That's what due diligence was all about."

It also became obvious that Bre-X's drilling program had a somewhat different rationale than the programs typically carried out by senior companies to prove up reserves. The Calgary junior was a lot more interested in finding ounces than proving them up. Freeport's bankers are rumored to have been a bit taken aback by the widely spaced drill holes. Bankers are not speculators. Their job is to assess risk and make sure the risk is mitigated before they sink their dollars into a mining venture. They did not give a hoot in hell about Felderhof's eyeball assays and blue sky potential. To ensure Bre-X's results were as reported, they wanted independent tests and results from twinned holes.

The world would soon be surprised to learn that Freeport's program was the first time confirmatory work of this type had ever been done at Busang.

Doctor Doom

The professional team at Bre-X Minerals, led by Bryan Coates and Roly Francisco, did not run around the world looking for short-selling conspiracies. They took action to get to the bottom of a problem that threatened to ruin their careers.

Shaken by Freeport's results and de Guzman's apparent suicide, Coates called Graham Farquharson, who ran his own consulting firm, Strathcona Mineral Services. The two were acquainted from Coates's time at Cambior, where Farquharson was on the board of directors. Coates asked Farquharson to come over to the offices of Bennett Jones Verchere, Bre-X's Toronto lawyers, to meet with him and Roly Francisco. When he arrived, Coates broke the news.

"He said they had a problem over at their Busang property," Farquharson recalled. "They'd had a phone call from Freeport, and also, that same day, their chief geologist had had an accident. Their lawyers had recommended they'd better get an independent review, so they thought of our firm."

Coates and Francisco both asked whether Farquharson thought it was possible such a massive exploration program could be a complete fraud. Farquharson's initial impression was that the scale of the program was simply too massive to make it possible. He told Coates that he thought Strathcona could do the review, and consulted his partner, Henrik Thalenhorst, who agreed they would go ahead.

Farquharson enjoyed a reputation as a plain-talking consulting engineer, one who would deliver bad news without candy coating, one who could be counted on to appraise a project critically, even severely, but always fairly. He had just finished an investigation of the troubled Anvil Range open-pit zinc and lead mine at Faro in the Yukon. He had worked in hard-rock mines as a young engineering student, graduated with a degree in mining engineering from the University of Alberta, then worked at operating mines and with the prominent Toronto consulting firm Watts Griffis and McOuat before starting Strathcona in 1973.

Strathcona's first job was the construction and operation of the Nanisivik zinc mine in northern Baffin Island. It is among the most difficult environments in the world in which to construct a mine, and Strathcona's success gave the firm credibility from the start.

He had worked for lenders and investors through a period in the mid-1980s when a number of gold mines met with spectacular failure; his work dissecting those failed projects earned him the nickname "Doctor Doom," but no one dared deny that Strathcona was among the most competent engineering practices in the industry.

Thalenhorst, Farquharson's partner, had joined Strathcona in 1986 from the Canadian arm of the German metals conglomerate, Metallgesellschaft. He had earned a PhD from the University of Munich and moved to Canada in the 1970s, working both in exploration and production. His beat included the Nanisivik zinc mine on Baffin Island in the Northwest Territories, which Strathcona had developed and managed for a consortium which included Metall.

A few years after joining Strathcona, Thalenhorst brought a former associate at Metall, Reinhard von Guttenberg, aboard. Von Guttenberg, who had been running a one-man consulting firm, also sported a PhD in geology, though he wore it so lightly that some colleagues didn't even know it existed. These three, plus another Strathcona geologist, Douglas Dumka, would form the crew that shut down Busang.

The day following their first meeting with the Bre-X people, Farquharson and Thalenhorst were back at the Bennett Jones offices, where they met with Coates and Francisco, along with Bennett Jones lawyers Michael Melanson and John Sabine. Joining them this time was Paul Kavanagh, who had brought some drill hole plans and sections. Kavanagh, though he had recommended rival consultants Roscoe, Postle & Associates for the audit, still thought highly of Strathcona and was cordial and helpful.

Farquharson had to be at a Cambior board meeting in Montreal on March 21 but returned to Toronto the next day. He, Thalenhorst, and von Guttenberg then piled on a plane to Indonesia. They had a copy of Kilborn Pakar Rekayasa's intermediate feasibility study, which Kavanagh had provided, and they spent the long flight passing it around. "Henrik and Reinhard were very good about spotting the red flags . . . by the time we landed, we at least knew what we were up against." What Thalenhorst and von Guttenberg had found particularly alarming was that almost all the gold in the samples from Busang was coarse, between one- and four-tenths of a millimetre in size.

Arriving at Jakarta at noon local time on March 24, they got in touch with Bre-X's local office and began arrangements for permits to travel to Kalimantan. They also had their first phone conversation with John Felderhof, who had just arrived in Jakarta and who didn't make Farquharson feel welcome. "He wasn't too happy to hear we were there."

It was little wonder Felderhof was grumpy. That same day, Freeport (probably in the person of geologists David Potter and Steven Van Nort, who were in Jakarta at the time) showed Felderhof its preliminary drill results, plus mineralogical observations that its in-house lab, Crescent Technology in New Orleans, had made on some of the crushed material Bre-X had given it from storage.

Three of the Freeport drill holes had been "twins" — holes that had started about a metre and a half away from holes that had been drilled by Bre-X, and drilled in the same direction and with the same dip. Not only had samples from those holes failed to duplicate Bre-X's results; they were found to contain virtually no gold at all. Freeport drilled two "scissor" holes — where Bre-X drilled southwest, Freeport drilled northeast, so as to cross the mineralized structures Bre-X had found from the other direction. They still found nothing. Freeport's other hole was drilled parallel to the main structural trend. There was still nothing.

Freeport had tried both standard fire assay analysis and Indo Assay's cyanide-leach procedure. It had sent its samples to Indo Assay, to two other labs in Indonesia, and to its own lab in New Orleans. None of the labs got anything.

Freeport sent away crushed material that Bre-X had provided. That stuff had gold, but the grades often disagreed violently with what Bre-X's records showed for the same sample interval. Portions of the same sample went off to Crescent, where the mineralogists found only coarse gold grains, ranging from a tenth of a millimetre to 2 millimetres across. Crescent looked at the Freeport cores and found tiny amounts of fine gold, in grains 0.03 to 0.09 millimetres across.

The Freeport geologists hesitated to say it, but Crescent's work had clearly shown that the gold in the Bre-X samples wasn't at all like the gold in the core. Paul Kavanagh would later say that Felderhof "didn't bat an eyelash," but it couldn't have been a good day.

At this point the trio knew none of this. They made their way over to the Bre-X office and spoke to Greg MacDonald, who was anxious that they stay out of sight. He presented them with some memos and more reports, which they carried back to the Grand Melia hotel and reviewed through the afternoon and evening of March 25. Von Guttenberg, who had seen the results of the metallurgical studies in the Kilborn report, was struck by a report from Vancouver geologist Anne Thompson, whose firm, Petra Science, specialized in microscopic examination of rocks and ores. Thompson had examined 103 samples from Busang in 1996, and stated clearly that she had found no free gold grains, nor any occluded in sulphide minerals. "That told me there was something weird," von Guttenberg said later. "All that free gold going into a gravity concentrate, and yet no free gold in any of the sections."

The Strathcona team must have wondered how Thompson's report was received by Bre-X's technical team and, in particular, which part of the report's "no gold" conclusion it didn't understand. Peter Howe, who knows John Felderhof better than most, has some idea, though he does not know if his former employee even read the report. "When John believed in something, he believed in it wholeheartedly. If he saw something like that he might say, 'Bullshit, they don't know what they're talking about.'"

That afternoon, Strathcona met with J.P. Morgan's Doug McIntosh, who was the first to provide them with a fax showing the initial results of the Freeport drilling. It was worse than Farquharson had thought; in 1,000 metres of drilling, Freeport had not had a single hit. Farquharson sympathized with McIntosh, who had been blindsided by the recent turn of events and badly needed an opinion he could count on. "He didn't know what was going on," Farquharson recalled, "but he was an enthusiastic supporter of the audit."

Paul Kavanagh arrived that night and met with the Strathcona team early the next morning, still unable to believe the Freeport results. "There's gold there," he told Farquharson and von Guttenberg, "Barrick found it." What Barrick had found were five random hits in library core Felderhof had given them, and a number of mineralized sections in bags of core from the Bre-X office in Samarinda — bags that had already been doctored.

At 10 that morning, Dave Potter and Steve Van Nort delivered a verbal presentation of the results Freeport had been getting at Busang. Farquharson was astonished, but impressed by the work the Freeport geologists had done, and full of admiration for their low-key style. "The Freeport people just sort of shrugged their shoulders," he recalled. "Dave Potter did a superb job; he never once pointed the finger or insinuated anything. He just said, 'We haven't found any gold yet.' I could never have done that."

By then the Strathcona team had heard enough to have strong reservations about Busang. The uneasy feelings had crystallized in Farquharson's mind, and he felt sure there was only one way to handle it: Bre-X would have to announce that it had engaged an independent consultant to audit both programs. Both McIntosh and Kavanagh blanched at the implications, and Kavanagh argued that since the Strathcona people had not been to the property, any announcement would be premature. Farquharson felt otherwise. "We realized it would hurt a lot of people. But we didn't want widows buying the stock."

They headed back to the hotel and mapped out the procedure, schedule and costs of a six-hole drilling program that would give good coverage over the Southeast zone at Busang. They estimated that the program would cost about $900,000, including the fees paid to the drilling contractor and to the analytical labs that would do the assays. Strathcona's own fees were only a small part of the budget. Farquharson, Thalenhorst and von Guttenberg checked the arithmetic and telephoned the crestfallen McIntosh and Kavanagh with the news.

It was about 5:30 p.m. in Indonesia, and 5:30 a.m. on the same day in Toronto. Farquharson at last could bring himself to awaken Roly Francisco at his home in Oakville, west of Toronto. "Roly," he said, "there's a problem here. We don't think there's any gold."

"I can't believe this," replied Francisco.

"We haven't been to the property yet," said Farquharson. "But there are an awful lot of signs here that there's a big problem."

"This project," lamented Francisco, "has been nothing but trouble for me since I signed on."

Farquharson promised Francisco that the lawyers at Bennett Jones would have his letter outlining the proposed work at the start of business. He hung up the phone and wondered what he was going to write.

Farquharson called his wife, Anna-Liisa, at their house in west Toronto. When he had started his consulting business, she had joined the firm as his secretary, and, 23 years later, Farquharson was pressing her back into service. "Get your stenographer's pad," he said, "you're about to take down the most critical letter I've ever written." Anna-Liisa Farquharson drove to the office, typed the letter, and faxed it to the hotel. Graham checked and approved the letter, and Anna-Liisa hand-carried a copy to Bennett Jones, where Roly Francisco was waiting. Francisco called the Toronto Stock Exchange and notified them there was news to come from Bre-X, and by 10:30 a.m. Toronto time, Bre-X was ready to shock the world.

The left-right punch

Bewildered Bre-X shareholders were thrown a double whammy on March 26, when Bre-X Minerals and its potential partner at Busang, Freeport-McMoRan Copper & Gold, each released some alarming news.

First, Bre-X said it had been advised by Strathcona Mineral Services that "there appears to be a strong possibility that the potential gold resources on the Busang project . . . have been overstated because of invalid samples and assaying of those samples."

Bre-X's release said the company was retaining Strathcona to do an independent investigation, though nobody thought to tell Farquharson, who later said, "We took the press release as our authorization."

One half hour later, Freeport told the world why one of Bre-X's geologists might have jumped. The company had drilled seven holes within the Busang II project area to confirm holes previously drilled by Bre-X. "To date, analyses of these cores, which remain incomplete, indicate insignificant amounts of gold."

The American company also told its shareholders about the findings of Bre-X's own consultant, Strathcona Mineral Services, which already had advised its client of the strong possibility that samples from Busang were "invalid."

The exchanges had already halted trading in Bre-X at the company's request, and now Walsh was on the phone to Rowland Fleming, president of the Toronto Stock Exchange, pleading for the stock to remain halted until Strathcona had completed its audit. Fleming wouldn't go along with the request, insisting that the market had to open unless Bre-X had some more news to make public.

When trading reopened on the afternoon of March 27, not only Bre-X — which fell $13 in half an hour to settle at $2.50 — but all the junior exploration stocks were hit, especially the ones that had been flying high on recent exploration results.

The days of doubt

People wondered exactly what these "invalid samples" were, and argued semantics. But *The Northern Miner* knew exactly what Farquharson had meant; we had heard those words before. That

Please God, let the gold be there.

evening, Vivian Danielson appeared on the television program *Business World* and pulled no punches when asked about the invalid samples. "It means they [Bre-X] are back at square one. It means that what has been reported in the past can not be relied upon." And she reminded viewers that the words did not come from Freeport, which was already being viewed with suspicion as a company intent on stealing the rest of Busang from poor David Walsh. The words came from Bre-X's own consultant, Strathcona, which had an impeccable reputation in the mining industry.

The next morning, the hate mail started.

Red flags fly

The *Miner* laid out some of Busang's red flags in a front-page story dated March 31 that went to press five days earlier.

We still had no proof that Busang was a scam other than gut instinct and our faith in an unknown Dutchman with a computer in his basement, crunching numbers we would never get to see. Libel was a big concern, as David Walsh had already threatened to sue publications that printed "misinformation" and caused erosion of Bre-X's share price. And Bre-X had deep pockets.

If Busang was a scam, it was the perfect place to carry it out. The rocks were right. It was remote and difficult to visit. The geological theory was plausible, if a little grandiose. And Felderhof and de Guzman had experience in this part of the world and the scars to prove it.

The big picture Bre-X had painted began to change; a lot of little red flags began to unfurl, one by one. Before long, there were more flags flying over Busang than ever flew at a May Day parade in Red Square when Joseph Stalin was at the height of his power.

One of most obvious danger signs was always Busang's incredi-

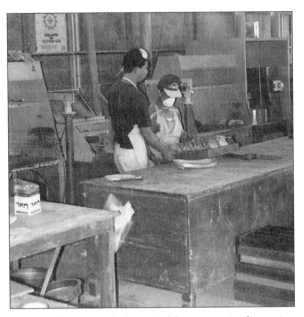

The Indo Assay lab in Balikpapan, Indonesia, where Strathcona picked up samples prepared at the Busang ounce factory.

ble size. In February 1996, Bre-X reported total resources of 152 million tonnes averaging 2.7 grams gold per tonne, or 13 million oz. A year later, total resources had proliferated like a malignant cellular disease to 890 million tonnes averaging 2.5 grams gold per tonne, or 71 million oz. But the market was paying bigger rewards for finding ounces than it was for proving them up, so only a small percentage was ever moved into the proven category by close-spaced drilling.

But was Mother Nature really that generous?

And what about Felderhof's boast that he could increase existing resources to "200 million ounces" in a year? "I could do that," he once told mining analysts, "if I had six drill rigs going." And there was his boast to a newspaper reporter: "I know I could do 30 million ounces with my eyes closed."

The Grasberg-Ertsberg mine in neighboring Irian Jaya had huge reserves of copper and gold, but those took decades to drill and develop. If Busang was the ounce factory it appeared to be, it had help on the assembly line. So began the process of picking apart Bre-X's story piece by piece.

Bre-X had raised some eyebrows in March 1996 when it announced that, because of problems with reproducibility using fire-assay techniques, it had adopted the cyanide-leach method to test core samples from Busang. At the time, the controversy blew over; but now it was back, with analysts and investors speculating that the reason Freeport's results did not agree with those of Bre-X stemmed from some sort of "assaying discrepancy." It didn't matter that Freeport, in announcing its results, had said clearly that both sets of results were from cyanide leach. A lot of people long in Bre-X stock needed to believe that this cloud would just go away.

To the staff at the *Miner*, this explanation simply didn't wash. A year before, Bre-X had sometimes noted with satisfaction that it sent its samples to the highly reputable Indo Assay Laboratories, saying it was "the lab Freeport uses." It seemed unlikely that the Indo Assay staff had forgotten how to do cyanide-leach analyses. There had to be another reason for the discrepancy, and we would have to find it ourselves.

An obvious place to begin was with Felderhof's decision not to split the core, a decision which had long puzzled those mining analysts who had troubled themselves to think about it. We could find no logical reason for destroying the entire sample. Early in 1994, Felderhof had told a senior mining geologist that the previous operator at Busang had "lost mineralization" because it had fallen off during splitting of core. He made similar comments a couple of years later when Daniel McConvey of Lehman Brothers asked why Bre-X did not, like everyone else, split its core.

McConvey was told that the gold was "about 90% free, loose and powder-like" and that the ore itself was fractured, which made for "delicate cores." Bre-X had told the analyst that "the more you split up and cut the core, the more gold that falls off like dust before it is sampled." For this reason, McConvey added, "John Felderhof decided to sample the whole core."

Staff writer James Whyte was puzzled by this explanation, snarling that it was "absolute bloody nonsense." We decided to get to the core of that matter and cut through the assaying controversy.

Felderhof argued that a 13-kilogram sample was necessary to provide sufficient material for a representative sample because of the coarse size of the gold grains, which were later found out to be mainly between 100 and 400 microns in diameter.

But even if the gold particles were as coarse as that and large samples were needed, a 2-metre section of HQ-size (63.5 mm) core weighs about 14 kilograms. A split core, leaving a 7-kilogram sample for crushing, would still be sufficient for cyanide leaching of nine samples, each one weighing about 750 grams. It is the amount that is analyzed, not the amount crushed, that controls the reproducibility of gold samples.

The other defense was that the gold at Busang was "loose and powder-like," which makes for delicate cores. The more you split and cut the core, Bre-X told analysts, the more gold falls off.

But it is debatable whether splitting would actually disturb gold anywhere but on the core surfaces, and the unweathered core at Busang appeared to be generally competent and produced good core recoveries. It was just not the kind of rock that gold falls out of.

The faith is shaken

Diamond drills are not called "truth machines" for nothing. And they finally delivered the truth about the Busang property on March 27, when Bre-X released the results of confirmatory drilling conducted by Freeport.

The results showed just what Freeport's geologists had told Bre-X and Strathcona. Every Freeport hole had been drilled in a place where Bre-X said it had gold; the holes had gone to the same depths and intersected the same structures that Bre-X's holes had. And every hole came up cold. The best grade Freeport could muster was a paltry 0.06 gram gold per tonne, from an interval where Bre-X's holes had averaged 3.2 grams.

Rob Robertson, who runs *The Northern Miner*'s Vancouver office, had no doubts once he saw the numbers. "When Freeport got nothing, that was enough for me right then." But not everybody was aware of how minuscule the chance was that two holes could be drilled side by side and get such different results. So began a month-long orgy of speculation, most of it uninformed and some of it deliberately designed to serve the ends of investors who held Bre-X shares, or had sold them short expecting the price to fall.

Freeport's credibility was already being undermined by reports on the Internet that accused the company of having a bad environmental or human rights record at its Grasberg-Ertsberg operation in Indonesia. Investors developed theories about how Freeport was trying to undermine Bre-X's share price to make the company an easier takeover target. Even in Jakarta, Graham Farquharson sensed Freeport's position, telling us later, "They were under a lot of pressure in Indonesia with claims that they were trying to steal the project from the little guy."

Bre-X, of course, had had its credibility undermined by the drill results, though many people just couldn't bring themselves to believe it. If Busang was phoney, then they had been played for fools and their stock was worthless. It wasn't pleasant to look down that road, but instead of turning back, they shut their eyes, trading knowledge for peace of mind.

The daily press scrambled to find the experts, some of whom were still in denial themselves. Each new opinion they sought out blew them in another direction. Some were being told that the gold was there, and dutifully published the reassuring news. Others smelled a story but couldn't find it. And each new piece of information was dissected and over-interpreted.

Journalists without stories are prime targets for propagandists.

Sources, mostly anonymous ones, began making oracular pronouncements about how it was physically impossible to salt thousands of samples, and whispering darkly about conspiracies to knock down Bre-X's share price to make a takeover bid less expensive, or to make money for short sellers. Columnist Barry Nelson at the *Calgary Herald* took a brave walk to the very end of the limb when he wrote: "There may not be 200 million ounces at Busang. There may not be 71 million. But it's safe to bet there's gold and lots of it."

The easiest mark for Bre-X's spin doctors turned out to be the *Calgary Sun*. It assigned Joseph Warmington to the story, and Walsh soon took to the young reporter, giving him regular personal interviews while failing to return others' phone calls. Warmington's stories, which were sometimes picked up by other *Sun* papers, were openly sympathetic to Bre-X's version of events.

Walsh fights back

Walsh was angry with the world in general, and with the Toronto Stock Exchange and the media in particular. On March 31, he issued a press release which dealt mainly with the TSE's decision to open Bre-X for trading without waiting for the results of the Strathcona audit. But, as an aperitif, Walsh fired off a warning which was clearly directed at *The Northern Miner*.

The tone of the announcement was threatening enough: "John Felderhof and the entire technical team at Busang, as well as the Canadian management of Bre-X, have initiated a thorough review of all recent statements and actions by persons, parties and publications responsible for the proliferation of misinformation that has served to tarnish personal reputations and the integrity of the Busang project, with the intent to take legal action where warranted."

Having got that off his chest, Walsh got down to business and released the contents of a letter he had written to TSE President Rowland Fleming. In it, he argued that holders of Bre-X shares would suffer "enormously and unnecessarily" from a resumption of trading, and then launched into a long explanation of Busang's problems.

Walsh called Busang "a complex orebody with an equally complicated assay process," and provided a text authored by "our chief metallurgicallist [sic] under the direction of John Felderhof, both of whom are currently at the Busang site."

The metallurgist was, of course, Jerry Alo, and Bre-X Jakarta apparently knew enough not to name him. The alarm bells would have gone off for Birl Worley and others who knew of Alo's shady activities at Benguet.

The explanation of the company's sampling methodology was telling. In it, Walsh mentioned that the geologists had discovered the problem of poor reproducibility between duplicate samples early in the project's life. First, they had sent the full, instead of split, core for crushing; then they had abandoned the 50-gram fire assay in favor of the cyanide leach analysis, which used 750 grams of material.

Felderhof's account went on to say that "the Kelian mine, which has similar geology to Busang, had the same assaying problem," one it had solved by having its samples analyzed with a cyanide leach. The implication that Kelian's operators also sent the whole core, and didn't split it, was very clear.

But the most stunning revelation — one that few people noticed at the time — was that in one test, a crushed sample had been poured through a sieve with 0.1-millimetre openings, and the two portions (one retained on the sieve, and one that passed through) had been assayed separately. The test showed that 80% of the gold was in particles larger than 0.1 millimetre.

If Jan Merks had read that, he may have fallen out of his chair. He may well have been doing statistical tests that showed similar findings. In any event, Strathcona later pointed to these same results as evidence that coarse gold, from another source, had been introduced into the Busang samples.

The letter was a brazen attempt to obfuscate Freeport's drilling results, but it did not succeed. For the scam-hunters at the *Miner*, it merely revealed more inconsistencies in Bre-X's story, particularly the presence of coarse gold. We also checked with the manager at the Kelian mine, a hearty Australian named Alan Roberts. When asked if there was any truth to the suggestion that Bre-X was using Kelian's sampling procedure, he answered immediately : "We don't destroy all our samples, for example."

Devilish details

More little crimson banners popped up. One staff writer headed down to the Toronto Stock Exchange, finding that Bre-X had not filed a new prospectus to list on the TSE. Instead, it was permitted to provide a much less extensive "listing statement" and use the original prospectus under which it had listed on the Alberta Stock Exchange.

Another disturbing fact was that Bre-X's disclosure was largely by press release, which does not require full, plain and true disclosure of the type required in a prospectus. The company made liberal use of its home page on the World Wide Web, where it posted favorable news stories and reports by mining analysts.

Another red flag was the lack of concern placed on making sure that paperwork related to property agreements and government filings was in order. Records now show that, until Roly Francisco came along and tried to clean up house, such matters were given scant attention.

John Ing, an analyst with Maison Placements, had been spooked by all this months before Bre-X's problems came to light. But Bre-X's storyline for public consumption always was that everything was in order and that the problems were the work of "claim-jumpers" and "predators." While there might be a grain of truth to that, the lack of concern about property ownership started on day one, when someone either forgot or didn't care about getting the shares of PT WAM from William McLucas and registering a change in ownership of the joint-venture company with the Indonesian government.

The obvious absence of local miners at Busang was another puzzle. John Felderhof was once asked once by a mining analyst whether Bre-X expected local opposition to its mine plans. It was a valid question, as operators in many developing nations have problems with illegal miners swarming their properties. Not only that, some of the indigenous tribes in Kalimantan, Irian Jaya and Papua New Guinea are fiercely territorial.

"I've operated in other areas of Indonesia controlled locally by Dayaks, and they do tend to keep everyone else out," Felderhof replied. "At Busang, we have no illegal mining operations and no influx. It's unique; other companies have major problems with illegal miners. The Dayaks are very much land-conscious [and] very travel-conscious."

Michael de Guzman told analysts that he had been attracted to the Busang area by reports that local Dayak villagers were panning for gold in the streams and rivers draining the property. Those reports predate de Guzman's involvement with the project, but the areas being worked were the drainages of the Central zone.

The gold in the Southeast zone must have been of a different type, as there were no local miners at all working the drainages of this supposedly huge mineralized system. A flight over the property revealed no signs of alluvial mining activity, despite the fact that a Dayak village was only a few kilometres away.

Canadian geologists working near Busang asked locals about this curious fact and were told that, yes, villagers had rushed to the property after the discovery was announced in hopes of adding a few rupiah to their meagre annual intake.

"They had no luck at all," said John Ball. "They best they got in one day was maybe 0.2 gram — hardly worth the effort." He later asked Felderhof why no local miners were working in the area. "His eyes turned steely," Ball said. "He told me they don't have any problems because they had a big security force over there."

John Stackhouse, a reporter from *The Globe and Mail*, found his way to the Dayak village after suspicions were raised about Busang. He found that the locals came to the same conclusion years earlier when they tried to extract some of those ounces in the local rivers and streams.

Yet Doug McIntosh of J.P. Morgan had already mentioned the coarse gold in Bre-X's conference call. "It's a very coarse grind for a gold operation," he said, adding that the design demanded only that 80% of the ore had to be milled to a size below 0.15 millimetre, "and that's one reason for needing the gravity circuit, because the residence time in the CIL [carbon-in-leach] mill would be very long if one did not recover the coarse gold in a gravity circuit."

Which prompted the remark by Egizio Bianchini: "It will be one helluva gravity plant."

"Yes it is," McIntosh agreed, "if you're talking about two to three million ounces coming off a gravity circuit. That's a heck of a gravity circuit."

Had Byron Knelson heard this conversation, he might have done a jig on a tabletop. Knelson's Canadian company sells gravity circuits to mines all over the world. He has sold several to the Kelian gold mine near Busang, where about 40% of the yellow metal is recovered by gravity concentrators.

Had Busang been the real McCoy, Knelson could have sold dozens of his namesake concentrators to Bre-X. Then *he* could have retired to the Bahamas or the Cayman Islands.

The labs get some new clients

Unnerved by de Guzman's apparent suicide and growing doubts, several mining analysts rushed off their souvenir core samples from the Busang property for assaying.

The *Miner* followed suit, sending off a sizable chunk of core — supposedly mineralized as it had plenty of hydrofracturing and sulphide staining — to Chemex Labs for assaying.

Chemex faxed back their result in early April — below 0.03 gram, not detectable, which was the same as the results obtained by several analysts. Some caution had to be read into all this; Bre-X's gold was reported to be coarse-grained, and assay results would be erratic. But, statistically, someone should have had a hit or two if the gold had been there.

Later *The Globe and Mail*'s Terence Corcoran would make sport of this, reasoning that if one needed to analyze thousands of samples to prove a gold deposit was somewhere, then one would need to analyze thousands to prove it wasn't, as well. Corcoran's mockery only showed how little he understood about sampling theory.

With the whole of Bay Street comparing notes about core samples and site visits, it wasn't hard to ask around and get pieces for the jigsaw puzzle; we kept assembling the ones that fit until a recognizable picture started to appear.

For instance, someone should have seen some gold at Busang. But no one who had been there remembered seeing any in the Southeast zone — not in core, not in outcrop, and not even in samples in the geological office. A Canadian geologist had a similar experience when he worked at Busang for three months in early 1995. His duties included splitting core, and he later told people he never saw a grain of gold the entire time, which might explain why he was given the bum's rush off the property by Michael de Guzman.

It is common not to "see" the gold in a gold deposit, since plenty of them have gold so finely disseminated that it is not visible to the naked eye. We had thought this was the case at Busang, since the average grade — around 2.5 grams — was relatively low. The early descriptions of gold mineralization in a paper written by Bre-X's technical team also implied that the grain size was fine.

But if that was the case, where was all the "nuggetty" gold — the coarse-grained stuff that Felderhof said would "fall from the core" if the core was split? And what about all the coarse gold coming out of the gravity circuits? All that gold was big enough to see, and nobody recalled seeing any.

And, with the average grades that Bre-X was now reporting, particularly from the glory holes, someone should have seen a spot of gold. "I'd agree with that," said geologist Birl Worley, "because gold is never so finely disseminated in an epithermal deposit that you can't see it."

The proliferation of red flags did not prove that skulduggery was being perpetrated at Busang. Technical evidence was required, and that came sooner than we expected. A kind soul from somewhere faxed over a few pages of a metallurgical report we had never before seen. Underlined were a few passages that made our eyes pop. To this day, we refer to it "the smoking gun from Down Under."

Chapter Nine:
THE DOWNWARD SPIRAL

You must not think to put us off with a flim-flam story.
Miguel de Cervantes, *Don Quixote*

The Normet report

Around the middle of 1995, Mike de Guzman invited a Perth-based engineering firm, Normet Pty. Ltd., to manage a metallurgical study of samples from the Central zone at Busang. Normet farmed out the technical work to another Perth consultant, Oretest, and the two companies produced a preliminary report in September of that year. Normet and Oretest then did some supplementary testing and contributed a section on the metallurgy to Kilborn Pakar Rekayasa for inclusion in the preliminary feasibility report.

Metallurgical testing is a controlled experiment, in which the material from the mineral prospect is run through a set of "test circuits" — tabletop versions of mineral processing plants. These test runs allow the metallurgist to compare the amount of metal recovered by each processing method; he does so by assaying the material that goes into each step in the process, and the product and waste that comes out. The metallurgist starts with a "head assay" — a determination of the amount of metal in the untreated sample. The recovered metal, plus the amount found in the "tails" or waste, should match this head assay. The process with the highest recovery, and the smallest amount left in the tails, wins.

The Normet and Oretest metallurgists found that the head grades of the Busang samples were "very variable, making accurate assessments of the head grade difficult." That result pointed to a sampling problem and implied that the samples contained coarse gold. Their second finding echoed the first one: after the samples were ground, much of the gold was recoverable in a gravity circuit, a very simple metallurgical device that mechanically separates heavy grains from light ones by agitating the ground ore and flushing it with water.

Gravity concentration works best on coarse material, since smaller particles, even the densest ones, can stay suspended in the process water and end up in the tails. Hard-rock mines use gravity concentrators only as a first step in the whole recovery process, to recover coarse gold quickly and cheaply. The tails from the gravity circuit then flow to some other recovery process, because most of the gold in a hard-rock deposit is too fine-grained to be recovered by gravity.

Normet and Oretest also found that the samples released 92% to 94% of their gold to direct cyanidation, a process used in many gold plants in which sodium cyanide solutions dissolve gold from its host rock. Cyanidation, a big brother of the cyanide-leach assay that Indo Assay Laboratories had been using to test the Bre-X cores, should work better, and faster, on more finely-ground samples. Smaller grains are quicker to dissolve than larger ones, and finer grinding breaks up grains of other minerals that can shield smaller gold grains from the cyanide solution.

But finer grinding didn't help, which told the metallurgists — for the third time — that the gold in the test samples was coarse. Normet noted those results, but all that mattered to Bre-X, and seemingly also to Kilborn, was the high recovery figure, which Bre-X released publicly on December 15, 1995.

Normet followed the instinct that built many a successful consulting firm: it advised further work, in the form of a larger testing program. De Guzman and the engineers at Kilborn agreed, and Bre-X engaged Normet to do a full set of metallurgical tests on two large bulk samples from the Central zone and two from the Southeast zone. Each bulk sample was to be prepared by blending hundreds of bags of crushed core that were stored at Bre-X's sample warehouse on the riverfront near Samarinda. These were all samples that had been analyzed for gold by Indo Assay in Balikpapan, and had been returned to Bre-X because it was Indo Assay's practice to send any crushed material that had not been consumed at the lab back to its clients.

Normet signed up Oretest once again, and beefed up its team with a mineralogist, Roger Townend, who ran a small specialist consultancy. Adding a mineralogist at this stage of the work was routine: any serious metallurgical research has to find out which minerals carry the metal, how large the mineral grains are, and whether any other minerals in the rock are likely to present metallurgical or environmental problems once the mine is in operation.

Tony Showell, the Normet metallurgist who carried the Bre-X job file, and Sean Waller of Kilborn headed to Samarinda in March 1996. There they joined the Bre-X staff in blending the individual samples — each one a bag of crushed rock weighing about a kilogram, and each from a different drill intersection at Busang — into four composite samples. Each composite weighed several hundred kilograms. By April, the drums carrying the samples were in Perth, and the new program, which would ultimately last until the following October, was under way.

The head assays of the new samples showed the same high variability that the earlier ones had shown. What was new this time was that the metallurgists at Oretest also did "screen" assays, passing the samples through a sieve and assaying the two fractions separately. Sure enough, 73% to 80% of the gold was in grains that were coarser than the sieve's 0.1-millimetre openings. Other screen assays, using a set of five sieves with different openings, showed that most of the gold grains were 0.15 to 0.6 millimetres in size. A shipment of 40 portions, each weighing 750 grams, was sent to Indo Assay for a cyanide leach analysis. Indo Assay found less gold than Oretest, but the larger samples showed less variability. This suggested that the larger sample was more representative, just as Felderhof had argued in his defence of the cyanide-leach assay.

Direct cyanidation worked well as a recovery method, too, pulling 96% of the gold from the samples. And finer grinding still didn't improve the recovery. But this time, Oretest had taken measurements of the gold content in the cyanide solution periodically through the 48-hour leaching test — measurements that showed that the leach was working unusually slowly, just as it might do on coarse grains.

And still the samples gave up their gold willingly to the gravity circuit. The concentrator recovered 89% to 94% of the gold in the samples, but the heavy concentrate, which would have included gold and an assortment of other dense minerals, made up only 6% to 11% of the sample. That meant that a high proportion of the heavy concentrate was gold — 35 to 70 grams per tonne. This, too, was an unusual result.

Meanwhile, mineralogical consultant Townend had made a set of polished mounts — crushed material set in plastic and polished for examination under an ore microscope — and confirmed that the gold grains were mostly 0.1 to 0.4 millimetres across. Every so often he found a small one, a few thousandths of a millimetre in size. But that was it: there were large grains, small grains, and almost none in between.

There were some sulphide minerals as well: pyrite, marcasite and pyrrhotite, all iron sulphides, plus galena (lead sulphide) and sphalerite (zinc sulphide).

But it was the shape, not the size, of the gold grains that stood out. Townend described them as "rounded, with beaded outlines." The metallurgists at Normet would later say they had not realized the significance of the shapes, but the rounding and beading are characteristic of placer grains, which are milled down and abraded when they erode from primary hard rock and are transported into stream beds.

Townend also put some of the sections under a scanning electron microscope, which, apart from showing a much-enlarged view of the material, can be used to determine the composition of individual mineral grains and even of tiny spots on the grain. Some of these abraded gold grains had cores of gold-silver alloy, which graded outward to a rim with more gold. This was another clue: hard-rock "gold," more often than not, is actually an alloy containing some silver. But when the grains are re-concentrated as placers, wind and water work on them; the silver reacts with air and water, leaching away and leaving a spongy, gold-rich edge.

The report's conclusions about the mineralogy also didn't match the descriptions Felderhof, de Guzman and Puspos had put in their research paper on Busang — the one Bre-X was handing out to the analysts. The Bre-X geologists were telling the world that the gold was partly enclosed by sulphide minerals, and partly in "free" grains that occupied the interstices between larger grains of other minerals. That implied that most of the gold should be very fine-grained; but the metallurgical tests proved that couldn't be true. Busang was breaking another one of Mother Nature's rules — if there's coarse gold in a hard-rock deposit, there's always plenty of fine gold along with it. We noted that the gold grains were much larger than the other mineral grains; Townend's photographs were truly worth a thousand words. This was solid evidence of salting, which no amount of blustering could refute.

Normet also suggested that to gain further confidence in the resource estimates, Bre-X should drill several parallel holes adjacent to existing holes and send the core to Perth for metallurgical testing. As we later learned, Bre-X Jakarta never complied, arguing that it could not take a drill off its aggressive stepout drilling program to drill these twinned holes.

The PR war

On April Fool's Day, 1996, Mark Heinzl, the Toronto reporter for the Dow Jones news service and the *Wall Street Journal*, called David Walsh and Stephen McAnulty in Calgary. Heinzl had talked with Walsh before; the promoter had called him in November 1994 as Bre-X began to cast around for partners, and they had spoken occasionally as the big gold producers fought over who would have Bre-X's hand. Heinzl's post at the *Journal* had given him some preferential access to Walsh and McAnulty, who may have been eager for coverage in the American news media.

The pair's response to Heinzl's questions about the sudden turn of events at Busang was that Freeport must have goofed, that it was physically impossible to salt 48,000 samples. Walsh trumpeted the line that became the trademark of Bre-X bravado in the early days of doubt: "We stand behind John Felderhof, who spent half of his career in that part of the world . . . we stand by our analysis and our reserve calculations." Heinzl brought up the unusual problems that the Kelian mine had experienced with millhead grade. McAnulty chimed in, saying they were "confident Bre-X is correct, and has been correct with its procedure and the results of its procedure."

Walsh told the young reporter, "I don't lose a moment's sleep" over the doubts about the find. Heinzl was no Joe Warmington; his shrewdness made up for a limited technical background, and he pressed Walsh hard for an explanation of the discrepancy between the Bre-X and Freeport results and was told only that "outside forces" were responsible for the problems and the attacks on Bre-X's credibility. He kept at Walsh for specifics, but Walsh wouldn't elaborate.

All this time, Walsh and McAnulty, who were on separate phone extensions, continually put Heinzl on hold, in order to confer with each other and someone else — Heinzl later learned it was Paul Kavanagh — to get their story straight. The conversation turned to the subject of Strathcona's recommendations, and the trio, obviously taking their cue from the argument Kavanagh had made to Farquharson in Jakarta, accused Strathcona of jumping the gun, of "assuming" there had been tampering when they had neither seen the site nor talked to John Felderhof. McAnulty, who could always slip comfortably into the role of geological expert whenever scientists were out of earshot, informed Heinzl that Busang was a "particular type of deposit of which there are only three in the world." Walsh got into the spirit of the game and named Kelian, Porgera (in Papua New Guinea) and Busang.

Walsh then asked Heinzl, "Who would benefit from tampering with the core?" Heinzl quite reasonably suggested that anyone owning Bre-X stock could have gained, at which Walsh's sensitivities got the better of him. "Are you saying that 13,000 shareholders are part of a conspiracy?"

McAnulty waded into the fray. "Our reputation is pristine. Every time we've been challenged we've come out on top . . . We don't think we have to explain an anomalous situation . . . We're confident that the outcome will be that Bre-X is correct and has been correct all along."

With the lab results still at the centre of the controversy, Heinzl asked about the check programs that Bre-X had mentioned in previous news releases. But the spin doctors in Calgary weren't up to speed on that subject. McAnulty named Indo Assay as the company's main lab, but Walsh broke in to contradict him. They put Heinzl on hold, then came back to tell him that Indo Assay was indeed Bre-X's usual lab. Checks had been done at labs in Jakarta and Perth. Heinzl, reasonably enough, asked for names. McAnulty said he would let him know if they had the names at the Calgary office; Walsh said, "We don't have them."

Heinzl, astonished by the reply, said, "You don't know what labs they were sent to?"

"No, I don't," said Walsh. "They were reputable labs, but they don't come to mind and I don't have their names here." (Heinzl again asked Walsh to name the labs in subsequent interviews, but to no avail.)

A beginner's guide to salting

Once we had read Normet's report, the very last of our doubts faded. The sizes and shapes of the gold grains were consistent with a placer source: gold from lodes is most often described as delicate or wiry in shape, not rounded; and typical placer deposits have gold in exactly the size range that Townend had reported. The high recovery from the gravity circuit also was astonishing; to our knowledge, there was not an underground gold deposit in the world where that much gold could be recovered by gravity. It mattered little how finely the ore was ground: cyanide could recover it, because the gold was already liberated.

At first, we had only the main chapter of Normet's report, with the general metallurgical observations and the results of Townend's mineralogical examinations. But it was enough that we were able to conclude that what came out of this metallurgical test had to have been what went in. It was obvious that the Busang samples had been salted with placer gold. We already knew that Freeport had noticed "visual differences" in gold found in Bre-X samples from the small amounts that showed up in Freeport holes. But we wanted to know how it had been done. Usually, salting is crude and easily detected because of its erratic, unbelievably high grades. When the Busang samples were salted, the job was done with a degree of precision never before seen. And it was this, more than anything else, that fooled the mining world.

Nobody in the *Miner's* newsroom would admit to having any direct experience in designing a salting scam, but one writer, a geochemist by training, had enough lab experience to have mastered the requisite skills. A few minutes over a calculator convinced us that the salting scheme could be executed pretty easily. The right amount of gold to yield a geologically believable assay result, averaging around 2.5 grams per tonne, had to be added to each 13-kilogram bag of core. For duplicate samples from the same interval to match, the bag's contents would have to be salted before the 750-gram sample of crushed material was divided off.

It would take 32.5 milligrams of gold in a 13-kilogram sample of rock to give Busang's typical grade of 2.5 grams of gold per tonne. It would be possible to weigh out the right amount of placer gold, but easier still to weigh out the right amount of a gravity concentrate from a placer operation, containing a known grade of gold along with other heavy minerals. After a little experience, the salter could dispense with weighing entirely, and just measure out the right volume into a marked vessel — something like a test tube or a measuring cylinder — to speed up production at the ounce factory.

It wouldn't have cost much. A single troy ounce of gold could salt about 950 samples. And it wouldn't have been difficult to find: gold is not hard to get your hands on in Indonesia, or in many other parts of the world for that matter. Local miners will deal cash for alluvial gold, no questions asked. And if a salter already has occasion to stop by a placer dredge, he could beg, borrow or steal some concentrate easily enough. And there were plenty of dredges around Kalimantan.

Geology students from the University of Toronto later took our numerical exercise one step further, and figured that it would cost less than $30,000 to salt all the samples reported by Bre-X, which is not a bad return on investment.

We knew the samples had been salted, and we were pretty sure we knew how. Where and when were less obvious. At this point, we had no idea that Bre-X had its own, on-site sample preparation laboratory, complete with everything needed to ship crushed samples, rather than core, to Indo Assay.

The building with the pretty flowers in front spelling out BRE-X MINERALS was not part of the analysts' tour of the Busang site we had joined in late July.

'The gold is there'

On March 27, Bre-X had promised the Toronto Stock Exchange it would soon release a report from Kilborn Pakar Rekayasa, detailing a check-assay program carried out by the consulting engineers on samples from Busang. It was a curious coincidence that a study such as this should be waiting in the wings, just as suspicions about Bre-X's resource figures had begun to surface. Bre-X got its report on April 1, buying a little time with the TSE by claiming the document was "extensive," and saying the technical team would need time to review it.

Whyte wrote an analysis based on Normet's findings in the April 7, 1997, issue of *The Northern Miner*. The issue hit the newsstands on Friday, April 4, emblazoned with the headline: "Bre-X's credibility undermined as suspicions mount." Early on the previous morning, only hours after the issue had gone to press, Whyte awoke to the sound of his clock radio. The local radio station announced that Kilborn's check-assay study had been published, proving that Busang had gold. His wife asked what he was laughing about. "They haven't got a clue," he told her. The morning's *Financial Post* was waiting for him when he got to the newsroom; the headline read: "Busang has gold."

Kilborn's "extensive" study, it turned out, had proved nothing. The consulting firm had simply taken some crushed rejects Indo Assay had returned to Busang, and had duplicates analyzed at two Vancouver laboratories: Chemex and Acme Analytical. The two Canadian labs confirmed Indo Assay's results. All Kilborn's study had proved was something many companies operating in Indonesia already knew — that Indo Assay was just as good at its job as reputable labs in developed countries, and that salted samples sent on long plane trips were still salted when they arrived.

When the Normet story broke on April 4, the dailies abruptly changed course. Both the *Post* and its crosstown rival, *The Globe and Mail*, phoned the *Miner*'s newsroom to get more background. Normally, journalists from competing publications do not share information. But we knew that what we had was important and that the dailies had a much larger circulations than our paper. We decided to spread the word.

Strathcona starts to drill

Graham Farquharson, Henrik Thalenhorst and Reinhard von Guttenberg flew to Balikpapan on March 27 and checked into the Dusit Inn. John Felderhof and a number of the geologists from Busang were passing through to attend Michael de Guzman's funeral, so the parties had lunch together. Felderhof was surly, and when Farquharson asked why he thought the Freeport geologists might have got the results they did, Felderhof was contemptuous. "If they drill in the wrong place," the great man snorted, "they won't find any gold." He didn't say how a twinned hole could possibly have been put in the "wrong place," but there seemed to be little point in arguing.

Strathcona's attempt at scholarly debate having gone nowhere, the trio repaired to Indo Assay Labs and found a clean and well-run facility. They came back to the lab the next day and packed up some crushed samples from Busang that were still in storage, sending these to a highly regarded assaying and metallurgical lab, Lakefield Research, in Lakefield, Ont. That done, the three took off for Busang by helicopter, to be greeted at the helipad by Alex Mihailovich, a young Canadian mining engineer employed on one of Bre-X's scout drills and the most senior man left on the property. He showed them around and they made their final plans for the drill program.

The next day Strathcona got to work moving the drills to the sites, under the watchful eye of Freeport geologist Colin Jones. Over the next two days, Jones was joined by Imang Suangdi and Paulce Daud Wenas, two Indonesian mining engineers in the employ of the Nusamba Group, Bre-X's other potential partner. Technicians from the country's mines ministry were also on hand.

Jerry Alo, the shifty metallurgist, and geologist Robert Ramirez also showed up, and the Strathcona staff found them busy and persuasive helpers. The trio also met Rudy Vega, Alo's assistant, and Farquharson asked what he did.

"Well," said Vega, "I work on the metallurgy." The Strathcona engineer did not pursue the subject further.

Farquharson, with characteristic diffidence, later reminisced that "there were a lot of people on site" as the consulting firm got down to work. John Felderhof arrived as the drillers were starting the first hole and took every opportunity he could to upbraid Farquharson's crew. "I found it difficult," Farquharson later told us. "He was our client, after all."

Ingrid Felderhof, who was accompanying her husband, showed that she, too, possessed a peculiar conception of the relationship between client and consultant when she haughtily informed Farquharson that, after the audit, he would be sued for everything he had.

The relations between Felderhof and Farquharson, as they developed during the audit, provide insight into the dynamics of the investigation; they also provide clues to Felderhof's later behavior. "The discussions improved as we went along," Farquharson recalled, and Felderhof came to agree that Strathcona had picked the right places to drill, despite his view that the Strathcona geologists should be out looking at outcrops

The maar diatreme 'big picture' that John Felderhof pitched to analysts.

and mastering "the big picture" instead of wasting its time pulling samples from the ground.

The same chopper that had brought Felderhof had left Doug Dumka behind. The fourth horseman of Bre-X's apocalypse, Dumka had been plucked from a project in Central America when Farquharson realized he would need a larger force on site. Dumka, who had been denied space on the flight because John and Ingrid were needed at Busang, cooled his heels on the coast until the next day, then joined Henrik Thalenhorst on the night shift, with Farquharson and von Guttenberg supervising the daytime drilling.

The drilling itself largely went without incident. The crew from Strathcona sealed each box of core with steel strapping, then painted it over so that if the box was opened, the paint marks could not be matched. The core went into a locked container on site, guarded by Indonesian military police.

Felderhof's next tactic was to bring geologists Gregory Corbett and Terence Leach to the property to help convince the meddling outsiders from Toronto that Bre-X had the goods. Corbett and Leach were Australians with wide experience in the Pacific Rim; they were interested in seeing the big picture at Busang, and had been asking Felderhof for a tour for some time.

It was left to the Strathcona geologists to show Corbett and Leach the little picture at Busang: the one with no gold in it. Selecting a piece of library core from an interval that had been assayed at 60 grams gold per tonne, Farquharson and von Guttenberg asked if the pair saw any visible gold. "You just saw their faces get longer and longer," recalled von Guttenberg, "as they realized there was no way this ran 60 grams."

Strathcona also discovered that the geologists on site had gone blind from staring too long at the big picture. The audit team kept the Bre-X drill records close at hand during the drilling, and consistently found that the junior geologists had identified silicification — the addition of quartz to the rock by mineralizing solutions — where none could be seen. Quartz is hard, and silicified rock is usually glassy and impossible to scratch.

Challenged on this, the juniors shook their heads and said that Cesar Puspos and Michael de Guzman had told them it was silicified. "We'd ask why they said it was silicified, and we'd take a nail, or something, and scratch it along the core," von Guttenberg told us, "It was very soft, totally carbonatized, with very little silica." Corbett and Leach saw this display on one occasion, and their faces fell again.

Thalenhorst tried to schedule a meeting with Cesar Puspos, intending to discuss some of Bre-X's recent drill holes, which had not shown any gold. True to form, the most senior man on site after John Felderhof did not want to talk, claiming instead that he had "something else to do."

Twisting in the wind

Ted Carter watched the events unfolding at Busang with considerable interest. The newsletter writer had been out of the stock for a long time, but the story was still captivating. After the Freeport results were released, Carter called David Walsh. "There was no doubt in my mind that he believed the stuff was there," he said. "I think it took him a while to realize that probably Felderhof and de Guzman had pulled the wool over his eyes."

By all accounts, Walsh was shocked by Freeport's results.

"He was pretty stunned, naturally, and couldn't believe that it wasn't there," Stan Hawkins said. "I think it was his genuine view that Freeport screwed up, though maybe in his heart of hearts he had serious doubts."

David Walsh was not used to having doubts or doubters. He had become accustomed to wealth, fame and glory. He enjoyed being recognized when he walked down Toronto's Bay Street, Vancouver's Howe Street and any street in Calgary. It was a thrill to have people shake his hand and congratulate him or thank him for making them rich.

Now, analysts were openly pooh-poohing the Busang story. "Quite frankly, if you own Bre-X, dump it," advised Doug Leishman of Yorkton Securities. Paul Carmel of Bunting Warburg in Montreal, once a believer, also saw through the Bre-X bluster. Others followed suit.

When the tide started to turn against him, Walsh's personality began to change. Gone was the affable promoter; in his place was a mean bulldog with teeth bared. He went on the offensive, lashing out at "mining reporters that know nothing about mining," and, in a shot clearly aimed at *The Northern Miner*, which had already published the Normet findings, he slammed those who used information delivered to them in "brown manila envelopes."

Only Joe Warmington was keeping the faith. The *Calgary Sun* scribe quoted a source in Indonesia who claimed Bob Hasan had taken out a huge loan to buy Bre-X shares. Some Bre-X insiders encouraged the suggestion that "smart money" was buying Bre-X.

Walsh ranted and raved about the actions of the Toronto Stock Exchange and told reporters that Bre-X was looking at pulling itself off the senior exchange. Next, he told reporters that it would be impossible to tamper with core samples; that it would take "an army of people, or a helluva big salt shaker."

Walsh also confessed that he "wasn't that concerned" when told the bad news by Moffett. Nor was John Felderhof, he added. Walsh told the *Calgary Herald* that he was "somewhat surprised" by Freeport's findings, "but only for a moment, because of the well-oiled misinformation campaign that's been going on for a year."

Walsh was suspicious of everyone, and spent considerable time with McAnulty and another old crony, Tommy Devlin. Devlin had worked as a broker-dealer with Hampton Securities in Toronto before going west, where he ended up in hot water with regulators. Devlin was an unemployed jack of all trades when Walsh's star began to rise. He called Walsh looking for work, and was promptly brought on board to help out. "I think he was only around a little more than a year before it all blew up," Hawkins said.

By this point, Walsh had divided the world into believers and non-believers. Devlin and McAnulty were believers, and so were the rest of the investor relations team. And Walsh thought the biggest believer of all was John Felderhof. He hung onto the master's every word and guided himself accordingly. As time went on, Walsh's belief that Freeport had made a mistake hardened into a fanaticism, bringing out his aggressive, confrontational temper. He bought wholesale the idea that Freeport had "screwed up." He told some people that Freeport had "assayed the wrong core" and that the whole affair could end up being "the biggest bungle in mining history."

Stan Hawkins, meanwhile, was being pulled in the opposite direction. A former mining reporter with considerable experience in the industry itself, he knew what a gold scam smelled like, and that particular odor had started to come from Bre-X. "The thing that always really mystified me — and I could never get a straight answer from anybody [at Bre-X] — was why there weren't any surface results," he said. "In order to drill something you have to have a target, either an anomaly or surface results; you just don't go out in the jungle and drill because you think something might be there."

Hawkins put the question to mining analysts who he knew had been on site. "I called Chad Williams of Research Capital and asked what the hell they [Bre-X] had on surface. Chad said, 'Felderhof told us there were no results on surface, and no geochem either.'

"I said, 'Oh really' and asked how they explained that. Chad said Felderhof had some theory about how they drilled — if they drilled a certain way, they got gold, and if they drilled another way, they didn't. It sounded real cockamamie to me and I was left scratching my head. But then I thought, Felderhof has a good reputation, and maybe he's right."

But more doubts came to surface which Hawkins was not able to dismiss. After talking with analysts who had been on site, Hawkins grew suspicious that Bre-X had stripped off the mineralized exposure of the Central zone and shown this to analysts, pretending it was representative of the Southeast zone.

Walsh worked over

On April 8, Stephen McAnulty granted Mark Heinzl another interview. Intent on controlling the damage caused by the leaked Normet report, he told Heinzl that Busang's gold had "three different shapes," and that the diverse types explained the Normet results — an odd contention, given that the Normet studies had found that most of the gold was of just one type, coarse rounded grains.

McAnulty said Busang had "largely free gold that has a nuggetty effect" and that some of the gold was "rounded." He didn't know what the third shape was.

McAnulty's unspecified gold types were not enough to satisfy Heinzl, who extracted a promise to have Paul Kavanagh call and explain.

Kavanagh called the same day and levelled with Heinzl. "I don't know about three types of gold," said Kavanagh. "There are only two explanations here. This is either a massive salting operation or Freeport is wrong."

Heinzl asked how Freeport could be so wrong, and Kavanagh couldn't answer; he just told Heinzl to wait for the results of Strathcona's drilling. Kavanagh still found it "inconceivable" that 48,000 samples had been systematically salted, and he clung to the belief like grim death, saying that a salting operation could never produce grades that consistent.

Heinzl, taking advantage of an opportunity few reporters had during the days of doubt, asked Kavanagh for a little insight on the Freeport meeting and the Strathcona investigation. The veteran geologist described the meeting as "three or four hours of unrelenting doom.

"I just listened," he said. "They just kept talking and talking. They hoped there would be gold there, but they didn't find it."

Not for the first time, Kavanagh tried to stake out the high ground of sober professional responsibility, painting Farquharson, Thalenhorst and von Guttenberg as trigger-happy mine-killers. "Strathcona were very moved by Freeport's presentation; so moved that when it was over I tried to caution them that they hadn't talked to John Felderhof and hadn't been on site. But they felt it was their professional responsibility to report [their findings to Bre-X and Bennett Jones] at the time."

Such was the hold Felderhof had over Kavanagh, over Walsh, over analysts like Bianchini and Fowler. Doubters had only to talk to John, learn from him, and they would have no trouble believing the gold was there. For Kavanagh, there was faith in Felderhof on the one hand, and desolate dim night on the other, and he was sure the dour Scot and his grim Teutonic henchmen were firmly in the dark. Kavanagh's condescension for the Strathcona geologists showed as he told Heinzl, "With a lot of hindsight, it would have been better and more responsible for Strathcona not to say anything until they had at least spoken to John Felderhof and been on site."

Heinzl sensed that Kavanagh was close to lifting the curtain on the communications between Freeport and Bre-X. He worked at his quarry by asking about the geology at Busang, letting Kavanagh talk at length about how the deposit was a big brother to Kelian, how the Busang intrusive dome had provided the structural preparation for a vast gold deposit. Then Heinzl steered the conversation around to Felderhof, asking how he had reacted to Freeport's results. Kavanagh, little knowing how his answer would undermine Felderhof's later defence, told Heinzl that Felderhof "was presented with the data the day before" Farquharson and

Kavanagh had seen it.

"He didn't bat an eyelash," Kavanagh said of his hero, adding that Felderhof's view was that "the audit drilling is going to support Bre-X."

The feeding frenzy

Normet, besieged by phone calls from the press, sent out a faxed statement that their work had "confirmed a high-grade gold deposit," and that client confidentiality prevented them from going into greater detail. Client confidentiality did not, however, stop the firm's managing director, Philip Hearse, from telling the *Calgary Sun* that he did not doubt that the samples Normet tested had come from Busang. "If I had stock in Bre-X," he told the *Sun*'s Michael Platt, "I'd certainly be hanging on to it."

A horde of Canadian journalists descended on Indonesia. *The Globe and Mail* freighted two of its reporters to Jakarta, one of whom remained in the city while the other made his way to Busang. Coverage by the paper's mining reporter, Allan Robinson, was overshadowed by confusing and speculative reports from Indonesia written by reporters who all too obviously lacked Robinson's discernment and experience.

The *Globe* promoted Rudy Vega, the suspected sample-salter from Busang, to "senior Bre-X official." Vega disseminated the odd tidbit of truth sealed in a crudely crafted pack of lies. In short order, he began telling reporters that both Barrick and Placer Dome had been given intact core that contained gold. He may have been acting as a mouthpiece for his immediate boss, Jerry Alo, who, given his widely known history at Benguet Corp. in the Philippines, could not speak for himself.

Bre-X officials had stopped talking to anyone from the *Miner*. No one replied to a suggestion that Bre-X should bring some pieces of library core to Canada to settle the gold debate once and for all. Stephen McAnulty was outraged when James Whyte told him directly that he suspected cores from Busang had been salted. "So you people are regulators now?"

The Internet wars

The most bizarre part of the Busang story is that a great many people stubbornly refused to believe Freeport's results and Strathcona's comment about invalid samples. Bre-X's investor relations team went into overdrive, and the stock began to rise from the dead. Before long, rumors swirled that Freeport had absentmindedly assayed for copper and not gold, or that Jim Bob Moffett had been forced to resign in disgrace because Busang had actually turned out to have tons of gold.

Attacks on Freeport picked up in intensity and number as the deadline date for Strathcona's report loomed, surprising even Jim Bob Moffett, who heard about the reports at Freeport's head office in New Orleans. "Everybody was still in this never-never land," he later told reporters. "[They] were asking, Who the hell is Freeport? But we've looked at gold grains before and know the difference between gold and no gold. We're pretty competent at that."

Even some industry people began to have doubts, thinking perhaps the gold, or at least a portion of it, was still there.

Much of the speculation was posted on the World Wide Web; over the previous year or two, more and more people with home computers had hooked up to the Internet. As the Web gained reach, a number of interactive Web sites sprang up that enabled "surfers" to post investment-related queries and messages and respond to those of others.

Jeffrey Berwick, Vancouver-based operator of the *Stockhouse* Web site, found that visits to his site increased drastically during the Busang fever, as investors with Internet connections looked in for the latest news. He called the Bre-X affair "the first high-level, highly publicized scam in which the Internet community was able to play a large part."

Surfers who subscribed to *Silicon Investor*, another large investment web site based in San Jose, Calif., created a Bre-X "thread," which grew to include more than 20,000 postings. "Lurkers" — the eavesdroppers who merely looked at other people's messages for free — were too numerous to count.

A large part of the Internet crowd peddled, with childlike faith, the message that Bre-X would be vindicated and that the gold was there. If they thought it would help, some would have posted that pigs could fly. The believers outnumbered and out-shouted the skeptics, and frequently maligned the *Miner*'s coverage of events. One accused us of taking a million-dollar payment drawn on an Indonesian bank and threatened suit against us (we never heard from his lawyer). Several accused us of being part of a press conspiracy, linked with Barrick, against Bre-X.

Under cover of anonymity, Web "posters" played at being geolo- gists, analytical chemists, lawyers and gumshoes. They developed weird theories about how assaying works, saw conspiracies behind every tree, and generally provided a sea of entertainment for every drop of useful information. It is unclear whether they ever actually moved the price of the stock, except on April 23 when a rumor that Jim Bob Moffett had resigned from Freeport drove the stock up $3.15 to $5.75 in a matter of minutes, then a denial of the rumor got on the Web and the stock retreated again. As one poster pointed out later, the investment-related Web sites were where the rumor was debunked, not where it was started.

One of the most prolific and polemical posters used the nicknames "Drumbeat" and "Mike Sloan." A writer at Vancouver-based *Canada Stockwatch*, a news disseminator and source of market news, tracked down the poster, who turned out to be David Walsh's brother Merrick, a resident of Vancouver. His postings, spiced with misinformation and personal attacks on other posters, consistently defended David Walsh and Bre-X management.

A few posters had tried to unfurl the red flags that are now flying full mast in the Busang story. But as every *toreador* knows, waving red flags in front of bulls only enflames their passions. Skeptics, such as "Bigdude," who shot down the rumor that Moffett had resigned, got gored for their efforts.

Please welcome your host . . . Jerry Alo

During the days of doubt, the *Miner* was scolded regularly via E-mail. The greatest volume came during the days following April 11, when, departing from usual practice, the paper posted a story on its own Web site several days prior to publication of its print edition. The story dealt with the Busang core preparation lab, which we believed was a salting shack.

Venture, the Canadian Broadcasting Corporation's televised business program, had obtained a videotape shot by Nesbitt Burns analyst Egizio Bianchini on his June 1996 trip to Busang. It included a tour of the sample preparation lab, and *Venture*'s Wendy Trueman was interested in what the *Miner* thought about the whatever revelations the tape might contain.

Bre-X's spin-doctoring facility had been trying desperately to make the question of sample handling disappear. But every time they insisted that Indo Assay had received intact core, more evidence would surface that Bre-X had its own sample lab.

The facility, which the *Miner* never knew existed until the video surfaced, showed that the building contained crushing and grinding equipment and riffles to split samples into equal portions — equipment that enabled Bre-X to ship crushed samples, rather than core, to Indo Assay. It didn't take a professional assayer to realize that anyone with the equipment that allowed for samples to be crushed already had the means to salt them as well.

In the video, Jerry Alo pointed out the lab's crushing and grinding equipment, its sample-splitting riffle, and a tray of newly crushed samples. The controversies over sample-handling meant that the video's revelations were news, and we decided to include video clips with the Web story.

The Bre-X believers were scandalized. Faxes and E-mails warned us of pending lawsuits. One subscriber denounced the paper as a "sensationalizing tabloid," and demanded that we retract our "lies."

"The negative articles you have painted Bre-X and David Walsh with are the grossest example of YELLOW JOURNALISM I have ever seen," wrote one angry subscriber. "Not only is your paper trash, it is below that of supermarket tabloids. I am aware of a lawsuit being initiated against you [Vivian Danielson] and *The Northern Miner*. I just wish that I was a Bre-X shareholder [so] that I could join in."

Another believer — the same who had the goods on our million-dollar payoff — vented his feelings in a Web posting on *Silicon Investor*: "If Bre-X does have the mother lode I will personally see that *The Northern Miner* pays deeply, and I mean a major lawsuit for this disgusting story. A group I know will do a deep investigation into every employee and every director of this paper to see all the dirty laundry the [sic] are hiding from the world."

Each of us checked our closets for skeletons and, finding the usual number, settled down to wait for the investigators. They must have had a flat tire. The wrath with which our disclosure was greeted did not surprise us, for, by this point, Busang had become a widespread delusion. A great many people had a stake — either materially or emotionally, or both — in the little company that could.

Bre-X's defence was that the core crushed at Busang was from sections which the geologists had examined and decided were unlikely to be mineralized. Nonetheless, in the Bianchini video, Jerry Alo is shown pointing out that part of the sample was reserved for metallurgical testing — something unmineralized material never needs. And we already knew the metallurgical tests showed gold, lots of it. Jerry obviously had the Midas touch.

Turmoil for Kavanagh

All through the days of doubt, there was an unresolved contradiction. One man said the page was white, while the other said it was black. Logic would dictate that it had to be one or the other. But it ended up grey, because many thought finding the truth meant splitting the difference. While the consensus of the Internet-users was that the gold was there, most people interested in the Busang saga opted to avoid taking sides and chose, instead, to compromise.

The prevailing view was that perhaps the 71 million oz. were not there; perhaps it was more in the order of 10 or 15 million oz., which at least left the door open for the shares to have some value at the end of the day.

As a scientist, Kavanagh knew that if two contradictory answers are given to a question, one must be wrong. But still, it was obvious he was hoping Freeport's answer was the wrong one. On Sunday, April 6, he sent a fax to the *Miner*, in response to the "voluminous reports and editorial on Bre-X in your April 7th, issue [printed May 2]," which he felt did not sufficiently stress the point that Strathcona was still carrying out its six-hole audit drilling program.

"One should wait for the assay results of that program before drawing any conclusions," Kavanagh cautioned.

His suggestion was not heeded. More and more evidence was coming to light that supported the salting theory, and we felt our readers were entitled to all the relevant information that was made available to us.

Stan Hawkins chatted with Kavanagh after his visit to Jakarta and asked what he thought about the whole thing. Kavanagh gave his stock answer — that it was either a massive salting job, or Freeport had made some mistakes. "Now Hawk," Kavanagh said. "How can you salt 20,000-odd samples to the consistency that they got, to where it appears to be an orebody?"

"It's a good argument," Hawkins responded, adding that he, too, felt it would be difficult to salt so many samples undetected for all those years. "Still, in my view, there were seven holes, for chris- sakes, right in the heart of the orebody, right beside holes Bre-X had drilled. One [could have missed], or maybe two, but they should have hit *something*."

Hawkins had begun to think salting was the more likely expla- nation, and that it had started early on in the game. "I figured, eventually, that they honed up their [salting] skills on the Central zone, and then really moved into high gear on the so-called Southeast zone once they got it down to a science."

The world waits

Strathcona finished its drilling on April 7 and arranged for the core to be airlifted to Perth, where it had already made arrange- ments with Analabs Pty. Ltd., a large assaying firm, for space to fin- ish its work. Thalenhorst and Dumka, the long-suffering night shift, left for Canada on April 9, and perhaps found the 12-hour time change a relief. Farquharson flew to Jakarta and lined up the assay labs — Analabs, Indo Assay and Lakefield — for the next phase of the job. He instructed the labs to do both fire assays and cyanide leach analyses, and warned them that the project work was sensitive and would require both careful quality control and complete confidentiality.

Meanwhile, von Guttenberg, who was keeping an eye on the core in Balikpapan, got a taste of how closely the world was watching. Awakened by a late-night phone call to his room at the Dusit Inn, von Guttenberg received a torrent of abuse from a caller who accused him of trying to "ruin Bre-X."

Fourteen tonnes of core, together with Freeport geologists Don Chamberlain and Dave Potter, Nusamba's mining engineer Imang Suangdi, and Reinhard von Guttenberg, were flown out of Balikpapan on April 12 on a chartered Boeing 727.

Von Guttenberg started work at Analabs on April 13 and shortly found he had a shadow. A Normet employee had been sent over on instructions from John Felderhof to watch everything von Guttenberg did. Farquharson, who had joined von Guttenberg in Perth, found the intrusion unnecessary: "They [Normet] had been asked by Bre-X — by John Felderhof — to sit there all the time and monitor our movements. We put a stop to that." Quietly, but firmly, Farquharson had let it be known that he was far too tough to be intimidated by Felderhof's surveillance force.

Von Guttenberg started by examining the core and logging his descriptions; he then cut the core along its length using a diamond saw, and frequently took photographs of the cut core. Half went back in the box, which was sealed up again, and the other half, separated into its 2-metre intervals, was passed along to the sample preparation staff at Analabs for crushing. This yielded about 7 kg of core, which was divided off — just over a kilogram for each lab, plus a bag of leftover crushed material that was held in storage in case there were any problems.

To satisfy the minders, Farquharson and von Guttenberg held a daily briefing, then shooed them back out the door so that the logging and cutting could continue without interference. By April 19 the work was finished, and, two days later, the pair were back in Canada.

Disbelief and turmoil

In Vancouver, Placer Dome President John Willson was publicly struggling with the idea that something was seriously wrong at Busang. He told a reporter from the *Vancouver Sun* that he was greatly disturbed that Freeport's drilling had turned up only "insignificant amounts of gold," yet he could not fathom how Bre-X had been able to get consistent assay results for years. Willson was not alone; nothing like this had ever happened before in the mining industry. The possibility of salting thousands of samples was mind-boggling.

Halfway around the world in Jakarta, Australian geologists Graeme Chuck and John Levings were not surprised by the news of Freeport's drilling results. The two had been skeptical of Busang ever since drilling of the Central zone began yielding results that were much richer and longer than the mineralization they had seen during their days with Warren Beckwith's Westralian Resource Projects.

"We never believed it," Chuck said. "First, we knew the property, and second, we knew the people involved. We knew what kind of results we got and we knew we couldn't make any sort of resource from them.

"When they [Bre-X] started announcing long intersections, it was as though we were looking at two different deposits. In nature, that doesn't happen. A deposit doesn't change because a different person is drilling it."

Chuck admits he wavered when the excellent results began pouring in from the Southeast zone, though he was suspicious because there had been no alluvial mining activity in the area draining the Southeast zone. "But I thought, maybe it's true, though I'd have to say John Levings never wavered once. He didn't believe any of it for a second."

In Colorado, Birl Worley, de Guzman's former mentor, was dealing with the double whammy of the Filipino's apparent suicide and the disparity between Freeport's results and those reported by Bre-X. Mining is a small world, and when he heard rumors that the team at Busang was suspected of having tampered with the core samples, it hit him hard. These were his trainees and employees — men he had worked with for years.

Worley had planned to visit Busang in early 1997, at de Guzman's request. "Mike wanted me to come to Busang to go over the geology with him. He said he wasn't spending enough time at the site [and that] he had to spend too much time in Jakarta, and too much time making up papers."

He was somewhat surprised by the invitation, as de Guzman was normally self-assured about his geology and, since leaving Benguet, had never asked for advice. Worley never got to see Busang, though, as his plans were interrupted by a bout of illness.

While being treated in Jakarta, the American geologist heard that de Guzman had committed suicide by jumping from a helicopter. He was shocked and had trouble believing the story, as did most people who knew de Guzman.

Worley knew that disease would not make de Guzman jump; nor would four wives; nor would any of the normal reasons people have for ending their lives. The Mike de Guzman he knew loved life too much.

At the same time, Worley believed de Guzman might have killed himself under certain conditions. "He had reached the position where he was considered an oracle . . . that what he said about geology was right. If that was about to be taken from him, he would lose everything. It was more important to him than money, which he always threw away, mostly on wine, women and song."

Worley also knew that de Guzman's goal in life was to find one big orebody with which his name would always be associated. If Busang was not real, then that dream would have been impossible.

"He had some limited successes in life, some fairly decent successes, but there was no major ore deposit found," Worley explained. "You can destroy yourself so easily by chasing such a dream. In his mind he wanted to be the one, and maybe he came to believe that he had suffered too long from other people being the one. Maybe he said, 'It's my turn, and will you look the other way?' He was taught not to, but could he have? Yes."

For Worley, career disappointment is no excuse for scientists to forget what they have been taught or to abandon their professional ethics. "I'm sorry, but geology is a business where people have to be content to make contributions to finding mineral deposits. Finding one is rare."

Despite having described de Guzman as a meticulous, honest geologist who paid incredible attention to detail, Worley was unable to explain how his former employee could have ignored all the red flags at Busang. After all, de Guzman knew about salted samples from his experiences at Benguet. Not only that, Worley had passed along to all his students a basic part of his philosophy. "I told them never to fall in love with a pile of rocks. Question everything. And, most of all, if you have a suspicion that something is not right, go out and do the work yourself."

At first, Worley believed Freeport might have been engaged in some shenanigans, because the geologist he knew would never be involved in a scam. Later, though, as more information surfaced, his faith became badly shaken. He began to see another Michael de Guzman.

Worley said he could not understand why de Guzman allowed a sample preparation facility on site at Busang. "It is a red flag in itself. That alone would have said, 'Hey, something's wrong here.'" He was even more shocked to discover that Jerry Alo was in charge of that facility and, therefore, had custody of thousands of samples.

"Anyone who trusted Alo to do that needed his head examined, or was very new to the business," he said. "This is a guy who would not have been picked up anywhere in the Philippines, except by unscrupulous people, because everyone knew why I had asked him to leave Benguet."

Upon learning that Alo had been part of the Busang team with de Guzman's full knowledge and apparent consent, Worley was shaken. "If Mike put up with it, it was his fault, because he knew [about Jerry's past]. You have to take the responsibility for what is done under your name. He knew what he should have done, and he didn't do it."

Peter Munk's revenge

Life did not come to a standstill as the world waited for the Strathcona report. In Toronto, shareholders of Barrick Gold piled into a ballroom of the Royal York Hotel to hear what Peter Munk might say about his company's failed attempt to acquire Bre-X Minerals' Busang project.

The erudite industry captain did not disappoint. He apologized to shareholders for having wasted time and effort on the pursuit of the Busang deposit. Then, just in case the slow ones in the crowd didn't pick up on the hint, he made an impassioned case for the track record and accomplishments of the Canadian mining industry. The comments were made in response to public criticisms that had followed Freeport's no-gold announcement — criticisms that Munk knew had been levelled at the industry as a whole.

"No one deviant member, no one rogue operator can take away from the remarkable track record built up over the years by Canadian miners," Munk said. In a roundabout way that provided no problems for his lawyers, he had told the world the truth about Busang.

It wasn't long before David Walsh and John Felderhof caught wind of Munk's remarks. It took even less time for them to conclude that he had been referring to Bre-X and Busang, and to launch into their usual round of Barrick bashing.

Chapter Ten:
WITHOUT PRECEDENT

It was without a compeer among swindles.
It was perfect, it was rounded, symmetrical, complete, colossal.
Mark Twain, *Life on the Mississippi*

Lowering the boom

At Roly Francisco's request, Graham Farquharson headed for Calgary on April 23 to meet with Bre-X management. He didn't have much solid information to offer, since the labs were still working on the samples; but he tried hard to avoid giving any hope. It was the first time he had met Walsh, and he was surprised at how well it went. "David was good about it; he asked some good questions," Farquharson later said. Walsh, and Paul Kavanagh as well, "obviously believed there was still some gold there," but, in the absence of any numbers, Farquharson could tell them only that his geologists had seen nothing in the core to change their minds about Busang.

Back in Toronto, the Toronto Stock Exchange and the Ontario Securities Commission wanted to know more. Farquharson told them that what he outlined in his earlier letter still stood, and also that he recommended they *not* compel Barrick and Placer Dome to release the results of the testing they carried out on samples Bre-X had provided, since he feared those samples had been salted as well: "I just didn't want any more bogus information released to the public."

Farquharson had set up the testing so that all three labs would send him their results at the same time, on May 1. He was also expecting Lakefield to provide some descriptions of the gold in the crushed samples that had been sent from Indo Assay at the start of the audit program. On the evening of May 1, Farquharson,

Thalenhorst and von Guttenberg waited by the fax machine for the results. They worked until midnight on May 3, with von Guttenberg writing up the geology, Thalenhorst discussing the sampling, and Farquharson finishing the summaries. With 25 copies of the report in their hockey bags, Farquharson and Thalenhorst began their trip to Calgary.

Farquharson later told us that, thinking they might want something to read on the plane, the pair picked up a month's worth of *Northern Miners* before going out the door. "Reading them," Farquharson said, "we realized that you were right on our trail."

It was May 4 when the partners arrived at the Bre-X building, which was staked out by a mass of reporters from the dailies, and were quickly ushered into a meeting room. The whole board was there, except Felderhof, who was on the phone from Grand Cayman. Lawyers from Bennett Jones and Bre-X's U.S. counsel, Sullivan Cromwell, were there, sharpening their claws for the lawsuits Bre-X expected either to inflict, or defend. Staff from Kilborn SNC-Lavalin were there; so was Rod Stamler from Forensic Investigative Associates, which had been retained by Bre-X's professional wing, Coates and Francisco, to get to the bottom of the mystery.

"We walked in and made a few comments, and said we didn't have very good news for them," said Farquharson. "I didn't speak very long, and David said, 'Maybe you'd better leave us with your report for an hour or so.' The thing that surprised me most was that they had not anticipated that we were going to say there was no gold.

"They had based all their planning, and how they were going to handle the world on Monday morning, on the premise that Strathcona would come in and say there was not 70 million ounces; there's 30 million, or 20 million — that there's *some* gold there."

From early in his career, Farquharson has been a spin doctor's nightmare. His reports have traditionally been models of precision, leaving no wriggling room. He had left none in this report, and that hit the investor relations machine, which had been feeding on ambiguity for months, very hard. A two-paragraph letter preceding the summary said all that was required.

"We very much regret having to express the firm opinion that an economic gold deposit has not been identified in the Southeast zone of the Busang property, and is unlikely to be," Farquharson wrote. "We realize that the conclusions reached in this interim report will be a great disappointment to the many investors, employees, suppliers and the joint-venture partners associated with Bre-X, to the government of Indonesia, and to the mining industry everywhere. However, the magnitude of the tampering with core samples that we believe has occurred and resulting falsi-fication of assay values at Busang is of a scale, and over a period of time and with a precision that, to our knowledge, is without prece-dent in the history of mining anywhere in the world."

The news was devastating for Bre-X employees, officers and directors.

Farquharson was the first to leave. Stephen Ewart, a business reporter with the Calgary Herald, was told that when Walsh came out of the meeting, "he looked like he had been punched in the stomach." Brett Walsh came out next, ashen-faced and close to tears.

The executive summary of the Strathcona report went out on the wires Sunday evening, May 1. Few people had believed Strathcona's report would be so definitive as to be the junior's death blow. After all, they rationalized, the report was only "pre-liminary" and Strathcona had tested a mere 175 samples, com-pared with the many thousands of samples collected by Bre-X from Busang drill core.

Strathcona drilled 1,470 metres in the heart of the Southeast zone. The interim report was based on 350 metres of that core, or 175 samples. No values of economic interest were obtained, and Strathcona killed all hope of there being a gold resource at Busang by confirming that all of Bre-X's "mineralized" samples were salt-ed with placer gold. Strathcona's report even gave a backhanded compliment to the salting crew when it noted that the magnitude of tampering was "of a scale and over a period of time, [done] with a precision that is without precedent in the history of mining any-where in the world."

Mining analysts were no doubt relieved to read in the report that the Busang geological setting was found to represent a valid exploration target for gold. The site selected for the tampering scam, Strathcona noted, had been "well-chosen."

Bre-X falls apart

It was mid-afternoon in Calgary, the day after the gut-wrenching night before. David Walsh, Stephen McAnulty and Tommy Devlin were hiding from the press and packing away drinks at the Lord Nelson, a dark, wood-panelled, smoke-filled bar near the railroad tracks where people go to drown their sorrows, unnoticed and undisturbed. But the most famous men in Calgary were not about to have that luxury.

Steve Ewart had just received a telephone tip as to Walsh's whereabouts. The reporter dropped everything and found the boys from Bre-X seated at a small table in the middle of the almost empty bar. Ewart was surprised to find the multimillionaires in the working-class pub, though he realized that their newfound notoriety would have ruled out any chance of their being able to relax in the posh lounge of the Palliser Hotel.

The leather-top table was strewn with beer bottles — Molson Canadian and Coors Light; no Heineken or Corona for these boys. Walsh recognized the reporter and was cordial, in spite of his sudden reversal of fortune. "How did you find out we were here?" he asked.

Ewart mumbled something about a "mysterious phone call" and asked if he could sit down. Taking the non-committal grunt as a "yes," the reporter grabbed a chair and asked the waitress for a beer, setting his notebook a good distance away in order not to spook the already nervous group.

Walsh introduced Ewart to McAnulty, which was a tense moment for all as the Bre-X mouthpiece had sworn at the reporter several times and threatened a lawsuit at least once. Devlin said little, but kept a wary eye on the reporter and on the door. It was obvious he didn't think much of the press.

The sudden appearance of a *Calgary Herald* photographer startled Walsh, who warned: "If he takes our picture, I'll never talk to the paper again!" Ewart asked the photographer to leave, knowing full well that the last thing Walsh wanted was a picture on the front page of the local paper showing him and other Bre-X honchos hunched behind an array of beer bottles while investors were still counting the millions they had just lost in the scam.

The mood was sombre and the men appeared stunned by the turn of events. The Strathcona report was mentioned, and everyone agreed: "We have to accept it." They said it again, stumbling on the words after a month of repeating the company line that the gold was there.

Ewart watched closely but could not tell if Walsh and his cronies believed the line, or if they were merely trying to convince themselves that it was true. Over and over, they said they could not fathom the immensity of the salting that obviously had taken place. They argued their innocence.

"We used nothing but the best," Walsh moaned, as he and McAnulty verbally leapfrogged over one another, naming Kilborn and J.P. Morgan. "And Strathcona, Dr. Death," McAnulty bemoaned. At least they were right about Strathcona being one of the best.

Three cell-phones were on the table, and Walsh and McAnulty began taking calls. Walsh did not interrupt his smoking to do so, lighting up one after another. Being a multimillionaire chump and laughingstock of the business world is naturally hard on the nerves, Ewart thought.

Walsh and McAnulty discussed the "open access" they gave the analysts during visits to Busang. And they pointed out that Bre-X had not paid for their airfares, which meant the analysts had no sense of obligation to the company and could tell the story as they saw it.

"I guess we have to accept there is a fraud," McAnulty said, for the second or third time, his mood bordering on anger. Perhaps he was growing impatient for someone to tell him he really didn't have to accept the facts. Walsh picked up a call from his secretary, while McAnulty talked to Roly Francisco. Eventually, the Bre-X team got up to return to the office, so Ewart did likewise.

The Bre-X building was still surrounded by media anxious to know what Walsh would do next. Everyone knew it would not be business as usual.

On May 5, the TSE announced that the shares of Bre-X would not trade until the next day. Other exchanges followed suit.

When the markets opened on May 6, investors watched in horror as the value of their shares fell faster than Michael de Guzman. Paper millionaires were wiped out in minutes. Short sellers jumped for joy. After three years of hype and promotion, the Bre-X story was over, the stock valued at three pennies a share.

The TSE completed its no-brainer review of Bre-X's listing status on May 7, concluding that the Alberta basket case no longer met its listing standards. Bre-X was immediately de-listed. A few days later, it was yanked off the TSE 300 composite index.

Hugh Lyons resigned from the boards of Bre-X, Bresea and Bro-X, effective May 6. Paul Kavanagh resigned from Bre-X and Bro-X at the same time.

By May 8, David Walsh's trio of juniors received court protection against creditors. Price Waterhouse was appointed to monitor the assets and records of the three corporations. Shareholders were told that the role of Price Waterhouse was distinct from an ongoing investigation being conducted by Price Waterhouse and Forensic Investigative Associates. Another investigation, by the Royal Canadian Mounted Police, was also in progress.

Walsh said John Felderhof had resigned from the boards of Bre-X, Bresea and Bro-X "in response to a request from the companies." In effect, the minefinder was dumped in disgrace less than a month after winning the industry's highest accolade.

Felderhof told the world that he was not aware of any fraud. "Notwithstanding these revelations [in the Strathcona report], one does not lose faith in many years of professional work over night."

Felderhof also wrote a letter to David Walsh conceding that, in light of recent events, there was "very little to do" as senior vice-president of exploration. He resigned, but not before advising Walsh that he was reserving all his "legal rights and entitlements."

Roly Francisco resigned a day later.

The rest of Bre-X management resigned or disappeared. By June, the joke making the rounds in the mining industry was that Bre-X's press releases were being signed, on behalf of the board, by "Lance Crossfire, mailroom supervisor."

Bombshell in Indonesia

Deep in the bowels of Jakarta is a low-grade nightspot which became a favorite watering hole for the Busang salting crew to slake their thirst and chat up the bar girls when they came to the big city.

On the evening of the awful day the gold vanished at Busang, the salting crew was nowhere in sight. But the place was buzzing with its usual crowd of expats and Indonesians.

Suddenly, a hush fell over the crowd as a television news report flashed pictures of Busang's geological team, along with the news that Bre-X was a massive swindle — the biggest and best the world had ever known.

"There's Mike!" screamed one of the bar girls.

"That's Jerry," shouted another. "And Cesar!"

Le Low-grade Nightspot was no less shocked than Bay Street.

Felderhof's Waterloo

While David Walsh was suffering the slings and arrows of outrageous fortune, his partner John Felderhof was hiding behind the steel gates of his seaside mansion in the Cayman Islands.

Grand Cayman is a flat piece of land rising out of the tropical blue-green waters of the Caribbean Sea, south of Cuba, just far enough to plop down 570 banks, billions of dollars, and a colonial government that opted to make it a tax haven.

John Felderhof has three homes here, which is where he retreated when the Bre-X bomb went off in David Walsh's boardroom. Farquharson wasn't impressed by Felderhof's absence and, to make the point, gave Walsh credit for at least being there to take the bad news "like a man."

The *Calgary Herald*'s Steve Ewart was one of the first newshounds to arrive on the island and to see Felderhof before he retreated behind the ornate gates of the Vista de Mar housing complex, just outside the capital city, Georgetown. Tipped that

Felderhof drove a white Land Rover, Ewart hunkered down in a rented blue Suzuki, praying that Felderhof would soon emerge from the compound to get cigarettes. His patience was rewarded when a middle-aged white guy finally drove out in the white four-by-four.

A pursuit followed. "It was like the O.J. [Simpson] slow-speed chase," Ewart recalled. Felderhof then veered into a field to make a shortcut back to the compound. Ewart didn't get much for his efforts, except a few expletives from Felderhof's family, who made it quite clear what they thought about the press.

Felderhof's first comment on the collapse of Busang came on May 5, when he expressed his "shock and dismay" at Strathcona's conclusions. On May 7, prompted by Walsh's request, he issued a letter of resignation denying knowledge of any fraud. Felderhof released both statements through the Toronto office of law firm Heenan Blaikie; all his subsequent public statements have been made through his lawyers.

The world had to wait until July 25 for Felderhof to issue a longer reply to the Strathcona report. In it, he tried to establish his own innocence with a twelve-point summary of actions he said were inconsistent with having known about sample tampering at Busang. He had stopped selling Bre-X shares and still had a large number of them; he was still holding shares from converted options; he had gone back to Busang to face Freeport's music, taking his wife with him, and planned to have his son work at Busang that year; he had urged the Bre-X board to take on the surrounding ground and retain a majority interest at Busang.

None of those defences was necessarily inconsistent with involvement in the tampering scheme. Felderhof might still hold shares in Bre-X, but he had made $40 million already by converting options and selling shares. He had gone back to Busang to meet with Freeport, but if he behaved toward them as he had toward Strathcona, his presence would have been disruptive, not enlightening. And a bigger property meant more targets to drill and more core to salt at the ounce factory.

Felderhof made the misleading argument that Bre-X had invited a large number of mining analysts to the site. The analysts came back fooled. No less misleading was Felderhof's defence that he had invited Gregory Corbett and Terence Leach to the site to "assist Strathcona Minerals in understanding Busang's geology." As Farquharson and von Guttenberg recounted to us, it was Corbett and Leach who got the geology lesson.

Felderhof pleaded that Bre-X had hired "well-known and reputable experts" as consultants on the project. Bre-X had, indeed, hired well-known consulting firms, but all of them were engaged on limited terms of reference, terms those same firms later insisted had kept them from discovering there was a salt scam going on. And those terms were imposed by Felderhof, unless David Walsh decided to take a break from manning the boiler-room in Calgary.

Moreover, if Felderhof was going to tell the world how Bre-X's reputable consultants and labs showed he was innocent of any wrongdoing, he would also have to be able to claim that he was partly responsible for choosing the firms that worked at Busang. That ran headlong into another of his defences: Felderhof said he had simply been an administrative officer, rarely going to the Samarinda office and "only occasionally" visiting Busang. That is not consistent with accounts given by several geologists from other companies, all of whom had had close contact with Felderhof during their site visits to Busang. Wayne Spilsbury, for example, described Felderhof as "front and centre" when he and Jim Oliver visited the property in late 1993, and Stephen Walters dealt with Felderhof, as did his superiors at Placer Dome. Other geologists said they had dealt with Felderhof as well. Moreover, a number of internal company memos show that Felderhof had charge of the project.

And all the analysts and journalists who trooped through Busang in 1996 were shepherded jointly by Felderhof and de Guzman. If Felderhof wasn't thoroughly familiar with the project, he had no business giving guided tours, hectoring skeptics with his air of bullying omniscience, making eyeball resource calculations or accepting awards for discovering the deposit.

Strathcona, too, had direct experience of Felderhof's personal handling of the Busang project. After arriving in Jakarta to begin their audit, Farquharson and his team was stonewalled by the staff at Kilborn Pakar Rekayasa when they tried to get a look at the Busang project files. "Kilborn wouldn't talk to us when we came through there," said Farquharson. "We had a letter from Bre-X in Calgary, and it said we would get access to all data and information, and they came back at us and said 'We've been retained by John Felderhof, and that's the only fellow that can handle this.'"

If Felderhof was indeed Kilborn's principal contact, as Farquharson surmised when he went to Jakarta, then it is also Felderhof who bears responsibility for ignoring advice from Normet — printed in the metallurgical report and included in Kilborn's intermediate feasibility study — that twin holes be drilled for the express purpose of providing metallurgical samples.

Moreover, Felderhof would have to have been closely involved with the project for another of his propositions to have any weight. "Two well-respected laboratories, Indo Assay and Inchcape," he wrote, "never raised any concern with me about what they observed in the Bre-X core sample bags." If Felderhof was just a manager in Jakarta, why would a suspicious lab have bothered to phone him with queries?

What Felderhof told the world about Bre-X's sampling techniques, in his July 25 statement, was simply false. He insisted that assaying half the core ran the risk of producing an inaccurate assay. But half the core could have provided at least nine 750-gram assay portions, which were — on Felderhof's own showing — large enough to give reproducible results. His other contention, that gold might "fall off" if the core were to be sawed or split, is just plain absurd. Then again, maybe Felderhof is right on this point. The gold used to salt all that core at Busang did "fall off" in the metallurgical testwork — because it was never part of the core in the first place.

Then there was Felderhof's contention that samplers at the Kelian mine, 100 km southwest of Busang, took whole-core samples. Kelian, Felderhof's favorite example for skeptics, had indeed had grade control trouble that was eliminated by taking larger samples. But as Alan Roberts, the mine's manager, told us, Kelian saved half its core. Felderhof's "understanding" that Kelian analyzed whole core was something he could have checked quite simply by phoning Roberts.

The magic "K" word showed up in another element of Felderhof's defence. In response to the accusation that Busang cores should have shown some of the coarse gold that it was supposed to contain, he quoted, but did not reference, a geological description of the mineralization at Kelian to the effect that free gold there was rarely visible in hand samples. This was no more than a clumsy attempt to deflect the argument that sand-sized gold particles — which everyone at Bre-X said occurred at Busang — are visible to the naked eye, Kelian or no Kelian. And internal company documents refer to "coarse" gold being visible in drill core, including some written by de Guzman and Cesar Puspos to their boss, Felderhof.

Among the most damaging statements to have come from Felderhof was his insistence that he was "not alerted to, or even suspicious of, tampering until after Strathcona produced its interim report." Yet he also admitted he had learned that "bags were being opened in Samarinda" in early April 1997, a month before the Strathcona report came out. In fact, Felderhof had been told that there was a serious problem at Busang in early March by Jim Bob Moffett, a man not known to sugarcoat bad news. Moffett had to sit on his heels for 10 days until Felderhof finally made it to the site, wife and bodyguard in tow. Then Dave Potter and Steve Van Nort spelled out the details of Freeport's findings to Felderhof on

March 24 in Jakarta.

Felderhof backed away from that trap in August 1997, when he took a polygraph (lie detector) test at a hotel on Grand Cayman. In the course of the test, the examiner asked only, "Before March 1997, did you know for sure that there was tampering or salting of the Busang core samples?" Felderhof's reply was "no." The date had been moved back two months from the Strathcona report, and the level of certainty had been bumped up drastically from Felderhof's earlier assertion that he had not been "even suspicious" until May.

The reliability of the polygraph has always been questionable. Examinations are not admissible as evidence in criminal proceedings, though they have been admitted in some civil cases. The argument against them is that some people are very calm, accomplished liars who can tell falsehoods without sweat or tremor.

Polygraph examiner John McClinton, who presumably would not be in the business if he didn't believe the machine worked, told the *Miner* that the report of Felderhof's test, signed by John Galianos, a well-known examiner in Montreal, was a sound one, but that Galianos should have published a numerical score. Felderhof's principal counsel, Andrius Kontrimas of law firm Jenkens and Gilchrist in Houston, Texas, was not able to tell us the score, but assured us that the test had been scored "very conservatively."

Felderhof's protestations were ridiculed by his peers, for in the mining industry — which, at its best, is a true meritocracy — a man's career is a portrait of his character. The more Felderhof tried to defend his work at Busang, the more clearly was his character revealed. Felderhof had even less room than Walsh to suggest that the truth had been kept from him; he was closer to the project, was on site regularly, and de Guzman sent him a copy of every memo. The only way Felderhof could have been unaware of the salting scheme was to be even dumber than David Walsh.

"Felderhof was better off remaining incommunicado in the Cayman Islands than he was defending the idea that there is a gold deposit at Busang," wrote Bob Bishop, editor of *Gold Mining Stock Report*. "Whether he knew of the fraud or was, as he suggests, the unwitting victim of it, the problem is that he has no excuse for not knowing. I have trouble giving the benefit of the doubt to someone who can lose half of a 100-million-ounce deposit one week and have it grow to 200 million ounces with a wave of the arm the next, but the bottom line is this: If Felderhof wasn't in on the fraud, he has no plausible excuse for not becoming aware of it."

Others wondered how a man who had worked at numerous alluvial gold operations in Indonesia, during his days with Jason

Mining, could have missed all the red flags that screamed placer gold.

Kilborn's number-crunchers

Investors who put their faith in the reports produced by Kilborn SNC-Lavalin had a rude awakening after Busang went bust. Kilborn's professionals had been nothing more than clerks at the ounce factory's loading dock.

The Montreal-based firm started to put some distance between its Indonesian subsidiary and the project as soon as the bad news came out. On March 26 it issued a news release stating: "Kilborn Pakar Rekayasa did not drill, did not take the samples, nor did it assay those samples. The scope of its mandate from Bre-X relates to resource studies and modeling."

The consulting engineering firm that produced preliminary and intermediate feasibility studies was well aware that Bre-X did not split its core, but it had not verified the grades with its own drilling. It had sent an engineer to help Normet's metallurgist collect samples, and it incorporated the test results into its feasibility studies, so it should have been aware of the unusual results of the gravity and cyanidation tests, and the placer gold grains found by Roger Townend. Kilborn's work was a black eye for the profession.

The other engineering firm under scrutiny was Normet itself. Graham Farquharson had spoken to metallurgist Tony Showell and director Lincoln McCrabb while in Perth, asking for details of their study. "I think they found it difficult to answer some of the questions," recalled Farquharson, "They were a bit embarrassed."

Normet went into damage control after the Strathcona report, taking cover, as Kilborn had, behind the firm's terms of engagement. McCrabb sent out a news release on May 8 saying the firm had "never commented on the source of gold, as it is not in our area of expertise." His defence was better justified than Kilborn's, since, as metallurgical consultants, Normet had simply been asked to find the best extraction process for the gold. But this was the same firm that told the press that it had "confirmed a high-grade gold deposit," and the firm's managing director had insisted to the *Calgary Sun* that he would "certainly be hanging on" if he had owned Bre-X shares.

Nightmare on Bay Street

With few answers coming from Felderhof and Walsh about what went wrong at Busang, irate investors trained their sights on brokerage firms and mining analysts. The fallout on Bay Street the morning after Busang went bust was not pretty. There had already been a number of class action suits launched in Canada and the United States, naming Bre-X, its directors, and frequently Kilborn as well. But now it looked as if the investment houses, and even the Toronto Stock Exchange, might also be targets.

The TSE's volatile president, Rowland Fleming, defended the Exchange's actions in remarks he made to a congress of corporate secretaries on May 6. Claiming, incorrectly, that before May 3 there was "no confirmation that the Busang property was possibly a fraud," Fleming contended that the TSE and its listed companies had been unfairly wronged by press reports that criticized the Exchange for not examining Bre-X more thoroughly.

The core of Fleming's defence was that the TSE had taken all reasonable steps to prevent a scam stock from getting on the board, and he listed five facts in support of his view — that Bre-X, already on the Alberta Stock Exchange, had been granted a secondary listing; that the ASE had had no problems with the company; that Bre-X had met the TSE's listing requirements; that Bre-X had a prefeasibility report from a reputable engineering firm; and that Bre-X had plenty of working capital and equity, and a huge market capitalization.

Fleming was, quite reasonably, offended by some poorly researched articles that had appeared in the financial press, including one that featured some uninformed comment from U.S. analysts and executives on the undesirability of listing in Canada. Had the reporter been watching the Yasuo Hamanaka copper-trading scam, for example, he would have seen how quickly a U.S. commodities market can defame an overseas rival when a scandal erupts.

But Fleming was only half right in suggesting that "all exchanges . . . rely on accurate disclosure and the integrity of the listed company." They all rely on it, but some exchanges do more to compel it. The TSE had the Kilborn prefeasibility study, with the results of Normet's first set of metallurgical tests. The evidence was in front of it. And Bre-X's monstrous market capitalization was more reason, not less, to examine the company carefully.

The Street is a concrete jungle where you are only as good as your last deal, and Egizio Bianchini's last deal was a nightmare. While other analysts flirted with the Busang story, had a one-night stand, or a short-term relationship, Bianchini had married himself to it. He saw Bre-X as the next Barrick Gold.

The analogy never fit. It took Munk 10 years to build Barrick into a solid performer, and he did it by attracting professional mining people who attracted more of the same. John Felderhof never

Analysts at Busang examine core riddled with fool's gold.

allowed that to happen at Busang. His team remained small and not especially professional, no matter how large the deposit grew in size and importance.

Despite all this, the analysts who recommended Busang did so because they genuinely believed it was the real thing. Regulators believed it was the real thing. So did the financial press — after all, it had gone through a pre-feasibility study and an intermediate feasibility study, though neither was made widely available.

Analysts believed the same thing. They checked out the lab. The geology made sense and the rocks looked good. This bewildered investors even more. Through the days of doubt, watchers continually noted how too many people had seen the project for it to be fraudulent.

The Strathcona report laid out how the samples were doctored by the salting crew to give the illusion of a huge orebody. It stated that the property was well-chosen for the undertaking. But the report did not answer the biggest question of all: How did Bre-X's technical team manage to fool all those crackerjack analysts for so long, particularly the ones who visited the property?

The answer is surprisingly simple. They used the same tricks used by all con men. They aroused enthusiasm and sold a dream — a plausible, but non-existent, fantasy that was better than the real thing. And one of the salesmen did it the good old-fashioned Dale Carnegie way.

Shortcut to distinction

Ask mining analysts who sold them on Busang and none will say David Walsh. A few will say Paul Kavanagh opened the door and got them interested. But the real selling job was done by John Felderhof and Michael de Guzman.

Jerry Alo didn't sell anyone. He was the master mechanic who set up the ounce factory and made sure its assembly lines ran smoothly. Cesar Puspos didn't sell anyone either. He was too shy to do anything but stand in the shadow of the masters.

Some analysts were convinced by John Felderhof that Busang was the real thing . Others were sold by de Guzman. And to understand just how it was done, you had to have been there, and seen them both in action.

The histrionics were delivered by Felderhof, who described the "big picture." He was the structural geologist who applied the pumped-up "maar-diatreme" model to Busang and made it all sound plausible. Felderhof didn't talk about Busang. He raved about it. It was so big it was "scary." It was so remarkable it was "one of a kind in the world." It was so magical it had "secrets" that he could not tell anyone, because, if he did, Barrick Gold would know what he knew and beat him to the finish line. Analysts no doubt have their own opinions as to whether Felderhof's passions about Busang were real or contrived.

Other analysts were sold by Michael de Guzman, the perfect foil for Felderhof. He came across as sincere and hard-working. Felderhof was all ego; de Guzman appeared to have none at all, at least not in front of Westerners whom he deemed important. Employees below him in the pecking order were a different matter. There was a definite hierarchy in de Guzman's world.

Felderhof would wave his arms, make grandiose claims and tell analysts that Busang went on forever and that if he didn't stop somewhere and start developing a mine, his drills "would disappear over the horizon." He made people think big and believe they were visionary. De Guzman adopted a more low-key, scholarly approach. When the big picture was being described, the Filipino geologist anticipated what analysts were thinking and said reassuring things. "Yes, it sounds ridiculous, but we really have had to throw away all the books on this one. The geology dictates that we adapt to new concepts." He saved his really wild stories for gullible newspaper reporters.

Felderhof was volatile and would rant about "spies" and "claim-jumpers" and journalists who should "go back to school." He brow-

The Dale Carnegie Man points to his shortcut to distinction.

beat and bullied and shot down skeptics with scorn. De Guzman was even-tempered, reasonable and likable. He would argue geology with real interest. He still retained some of the qualities Birl Worley saw in him at Benguet.

De Guzman had kept another quality from Benguet. His training there included a Dale Carnegie course that was meant to help him gain the self-confidence to speak in public and make company presentations. It does not take more than a quick flip through Carnegie's bestseller, *How to Win Friends and Influence People*, to see that de Guzman had incorporated the fundamental tenets of the program — "shortcuts to distinction" — and used them in ways for which they were never intended.

The deepest urge in human nature, the book teaches, is "the desire to be important." De Guzman made everyone who came to Busang feel important. He remembered their names, where they worked and what they did. He submerged his own ego and stroked theirs. He aroused enthusiasm, told people what they wanted to hear, and dangled the prize in front of their eyes. He was a showman who was not afraid to dramatize anything, including geology, though he was rarely as brazen as Felderhof.

De Guzman was, as Birl Worley said, "a keen observer." He had an innate sense of human nature and human foibles. He preyed on self-importance but was sparing and subtle with the use of flattery. He was a great storyteller and a great listener at the same time. He threw down a challenge — in this case, the mysteries of Busang — and then coaxed geologists to understand its secrets, which he helped them find, one by one, with little hints and subtle sugges-

Alchemist Jerry, jungle trekker John, mischievous Mike and the ever-humble Cesar show off the rocks at Busang.

---

tions and lots of encouragement. De Guzman's best talent was knowing how to get people to meet him halfway. It was all one-on-one stuff too. The man really worked, which was why he was dubbed "the sorcerer," while his geologists were the "sorcerer's apprentices".

One Toronto mining analyst who never visited Busang later thanked his lucky stars that he was never invited, because everyone he knew who went there came back bewitched. He never got the sales pitch and he never got to see the rocks, which looked good enough to eat. He never got the one-two punch.

The mining analysts were handicapped, to a degree, by cultural values. "Canadians are basically honest," said a corporate lawyer with experience in the rough-and-tumble business world of Southeast Asia, "It was like sending in a bunch of boy scouts to visit a den of thieves."

But the *coup de grâce* was the remarkable consistency of the assay results. Most other salting scams had been detected fairly early in the game, because the assay results were wildly erratic or did not make sense relative to the underlying geology. Busang avoided both problems. Jerry Alo, an expert in his field, smoothed out all the telltale bumps with his experiments in the Busang salting shack. And the deposit was modelled based on what the drill cores revealed underground.

The beauty of it all was that there really was a mineralized system at Busang — a large pyritic hydrothermal system, complete with mercury staining and other mineral pathfinders that made it look prospective for gold. Busang is a huge deposit all right, but a deposit of fool's gold. And that fooled the geologists as well, because the real thing is almost always associated with its ubiquitous impostor.

The Busang scam itself was "without precedent," which meant that "Runaway Ron" Markham and a raft of other gold swindlers had to take a back seat to the Guzman crew, who executed the most daring gold scam in history by creating a near-perfect ounce factory.

'Runaway Ron' dethroned

"The gold is there. Lots of it," Ronald Markham said. "Our deposit is so big that any major company acquiring it would be in a position to control the world's gold market and price."

It was the spring of 1993. In those pre-Busang days, Markham's deposit was enormous. When the *Miner* decided to investigate, his Oregon property had 12 million oz. of gold, a staggering amount at the time. But it was still growing. As he often told investors, this was just the "tip of the iceberg." His company had nearby claims, not yet explored, which looked as rich as the ones hosting the deposit.

"We can't tell you the location," Markham said in hushed tones. "We don't want to start a staking rush."

Markham was a dashing, aging playboy promoter who trolled the society pages for suckers. He had long ago learned that deep wallets were to be found at charity balls, racetrack clubhouses and posh events. Until the Bre-X salting crew came along and toppled him from his throne, Runaway Ron was one of the world's best swindlers. He was of the old school, though. His company was kept private in order to bypass the scrutiny of securities regulators. His investors were mostly wealthy individuals. He was not technically skilled or sophisticated enough to pass the scrutiny of even the most junior mining analyst.

Markham was tall, dark and handsome, though his black wig appeared incongruous atop his tanned, aging face. He was charming, unflappable and always impeccably dressed. He knew how to charm women and was every bit the equal of Don Juan de Guzman. He had married a Filipino beauty queen, who at one time was a friend of Imelda Marcos, wife of the late, deposed dictator Ferdinand Marcos. Before that, Markham was married to a Chilean beauty queen. He had expensive tastes and a fondness for the world's largest everything.

At various times in his career, Markham claimed to have found King Solomon's mines, the world's largest kimberlite (hosting diamonds, of course), and the world's largest platinum deposit.

His latest venture, the world's largest gold deposit, was "discovered" on the same property that had previously hosted his huge platinum deposit. Markham was getting on in years and, rather than find a new property for his new gold scam, the Oregon claims had to suffice for both.

Before long, wealthy investors in Vancouver began buying into Markham's gold project. The deposit had fabulous assay results, every bit the equal of Busang's "glory holes." The results were so good that a few investors got nervous and hired Jan Merks to check things out.

Merks soon found that the wonderful assay results had come from an uncertified assay lab in Idaho, appropriately called Vortex Industries, a mom-and-pop operation that specialized in the "people-pleasing business." The price to carry out the "assays" was many times the normal price paid elsewhere, but, business was business, and someone had to pay for the gold that Vortex never failed to find.

Merks also learned that a mining company had taken its own samples from Markham's property. The samples that were sent to reputable labs showed no gold. The samples sent to Vortex showed lots of it. Vortex also reported fabulous gold values from rock samples a geologist had collected many miles from the property.

Merks did his calculations and concluded that the whole thing was a salting job perpetrated inside the lab. He openly accused the lab owner of salting the samples. The owner vanished and Merks did not see him again. Merks then asked the owner's wife how she always found the same grade in all the samples, close to 0.5 oz. gold to the ton. "She just smiled demurely," Merks recalled.

The investors were not smiling when Merks delivered the bad news. Some bailed out, but Markham found new clients. Merks, riled by all the nonsense, went to the press. The *Miner* investigated and reported that reputable labs could find no gold on the Oregon claims, and that the company's geologist had been involved in projects where gold had appeared and disappeared, depending on who did the assaying.

Markham was livid and so was his geologist, who turned out to be a shareholder and founder of a shadow company. The geologist threatened to sue, and did exactly that when no retraction was forthcoming. "Better be careful," they threatened on the phone. "You are being watched." The case was later abandoned. Markham continued selling shares in the ephemeral gold deposit.

Fortunately, Merks got other reporters interested in the story, and the news reports soon found their way to London. As it turned out, Markham had lived the high life in the British capital while selling shares in a Saudi Arabian gold mine to prominent socialites, lords and ladies, and various other minor nobility. He moved in the highest circles and even managed to have his daughter put forward to serve on a committee with Prince Edward. One of Markham's two daughters — both were beautiful young women instructed by their mother never to smile because it caused wrinkles — had a coming-out party at the Ritz Hotel, funded entirely by unwitting investors.

Markham raised millions of pounds before investors began asking why the Australian mining company that was supposed to buy the Saudi Arabian gold mine had not shown up. Questions like that always made Markham nervous. He fled to Dallas, Texas, with Scotland Yard on his tail. As the story goes, Markham managed to throw off his pursuers by having his "grieving widow" produce a phoney death certificate from the Philippines. He then continued selling shares in the Saudi Arabian gold mine to investors in Dallas. His list of clients included many prominent names.

When things got too hot in Dallas, Markham moved to Vancouver, where he promoted his platinum and gold deposits. This time, his own wife started causing problems. By this point, she had enough a grasp of how mining worked to demand why Markham wanted to do more work when he already had enough gold to put the mine into production.

"She was quite concerned about [her shares] in the project, and asked, Why drill more holes if you already have 11 million ounces of gold?" Merks recalled. He later learned the pragmatic beauty queen had a divorce settlement in mind.

Shareholders also began to wonder why no major companies were bidding on the project as promised. They worried more when they heard about the conflicting assay results. Investors were then told that the assaying technology was "proprietary" and represented an industry breakthrough. Skeptics were closed-minded members of the flat-earth society.

As time wore on, with no return on investment, the mood turned sour. Reports then surfaced about Markham's promotional activities elsewhere in the world. Securities regulators began receiving a steady stream of complaints.

A hearing was launched and Markham was asked to appear to respond to the complaints. True to form, Runaway Ron did not show up for the event. He had other business to attend to somewhere in the United States, where he was already touting another huge gold discovery.

Investors were shocked to learn that Markham had spent millions on such luxuries as a waterfront property, a woman's Piaget watch, and a Cadillac and Rolls-Royce for subsequent wives.

Markham, described by regulators as "the ultimate con man," was fined $100,000 and banned for life from trading in British Columbia and from serving as a director or officer of any company.

Runaway Ron had another claim to fame. His was the first lifetime trading ban ever imposed by the province's securities regulators. Only he wasn't around to appreciate it.

A weird moment

It was after the supper hour at the Busang property in late July 1996. The visiting mining analysts had already headed back to the guest house to grab a cold beer and watch the business news on television and find out how the markets were doing.

John Felderhof and Michael de Guzman were still seated at one of the tables in the camp kitchen, chatting about nothing in particular. Vivian Danielson was seated at the other side. She asked Felderhof if he knew an Australian geologist who claimed to have made a huge platinum-gold discovery in the southwestern United States.

"Oh sure," Felderhof replied. "He wanted us to get involved in that, but we turned it down."

"You should be really glad," she said, taken aback. "It's a scam. There's no gold."

Felderhof was visibly startled. But not de Guzman. He was as cool as a cucumber and kept the conversation going. "Oh really," he said. "How did they do it?"

Chapter Eleven:
WINNERS AND LOSERS

Let truth and falsehood grapple.
John Milton, in *Areopagitica*

The Exit Plan

F*ortune* magazine reporter Richard Behar experienced some weird moments, too, when he visited the Busang property in February 1997. A few "no gold" jokes were made at the site, but he had another "peculiar moment" in Jakarta, when the Freeport deal was announced.

The American reporter slapped the Filipino on the back and congratulated him, expecting de Guzman to be thrilled. "Instead he was stone cold," Behar said. "Grim. Icy. He didn't look at me. It was clear he wanted to talk to Felderhof alone."

De Guzman had every reason to be upset. A monkey wrench had been thrown in the Exit Plan. The story had to end, the salting gang knew, but not this way. Bob Hasan was not supposed to show up uninvited and bring in his partner of choice, the no-nonsense Jim Bob Moffett. No month of Sundays would ever convince that curmudgeon the gold was there. And Bob Hasan would not be the least bit interested in the maar-diatreme theory.

Bre-X was supposed to pick its own partner. And before it let anyone carry out a due diligence review, the potential partner would have to sign an extensive confidentiality clause that would prohibit disclosure of what was found in the technical data. But the ounce factory had found "too much gold," and the normal rules of the game had been thrown out the window. Business is done differently in Indonesia.

Both Barrick Gold and Placer Dome signed confidentiality agreements, which is why they cannot disclose what they found in the samples they were provided by Bre-X. The terms are believed to be in force for three years.

Confidentiality agreements provide a graceful way for companies to wriggle out of partnership discussions without having a loss of face. If the first party does not like the second party's property, the first party issues a news release stating the project "failed to live up to our expectations," or some such euphemism. The second party is then free to flog the property elsewhere and it becomes the next guy's problem.

Freeport, too, was supposed to play by those rules. "We were basically demanded by the Toronto Stock Exchange to release what we had or we would never had said anything," Jim Bob Moffett told reporters. "We'd have let Strathcona make [its] report because, in due diligence, we are not legally required to say anything as long as we don't tell anyone about it."

Small wonder some people at the ounce factory did not take kindly to the crew from Strathcona sticking its nose in everything. The interference from head office was not supposed to happen, which might explain rumors that Michael de Guzman and certain other parties had tried to browbeat Roly Francisco and put him in his place. David Walsh had always steered clear of the technical side of the business. He was just the money-raiser.

The ounce factory was supposed to wither on the vine when potential buyers saw that the goods were abnormal and defective. And Barrick was probably the first to get the treatment. A clue is found in the Strathcona report, which notes that Barrick got library core — thin slabs sliced from 2-metre sections of drill core — from Bre-X as part of the due diligence process at Busang.

That Bre-X provided Barrick with library core is telling. The salting crew knew the core was barren. The absence of gold was supposed to cool Barrick's ardor, but, to the junior's surprise, Barrick continued its hot pursuit.

Paul Kavanagh knew that his former employer had received the library core. How many slabs were received we don't know, but 20 or 30 may have been sufficient, statistically, to make sure things were generally as represented.

Barrick's hot-to-trot pursuit of Bre-X after it was given the library core convinced Kavanagh that the gold was there. He told Graham Farquharson that Barrick had "found gold" during the session of "unrelenting doom" in Jakarta.

As it turned out, Kavanagh was right. Barrick did find some gold. The Strathcona report shows that it wasn't much, only five hits, but it may have been enough to make some Barrick executives wonder if Bre-X was playing games and messing with their minds. After all, it was no secret that certain people at Bre-X hated certain people at Barrick. The mining industry was well-aware of the toxic brew of hate always kept hot in Bre-X's kitchen. The company's vilification of Barrick was an old, old story that began well before the Battle of Busang.

The few hits of gold in the library core were a quandary for Barrick's top honchos. The company also had crushed samples from Busang, and these showed plenty of gold. The company had not drilled any of its own holes. The technical information, therefore, would probably have been viewed as inconclusive — which is why Barrick might have retained a statistician like Jan Merks.

None of this was good news for Peter Munk, who wanted the ounces Bre-X claimed it had at its Indonesian project. We can only imagine the steady stream of bad news that Barrick's legal and technical team had already brought to Munk's attention, ever since he first cast his eye on Busang.

The lawyers probably led the procession of naysayers to the inner sanctum, and there was plenty of bad news to bring — that Bre-X Calgary was not much more than a boiler room of fired-up youngsters and a beer-swilling promoter who worked the phones all day, at least until Roly Francisco came along and tried to bring some professionalism into the picture; that Bre-X had an office in Jakarta but was not registered as the legal owner of PT WAM; that a Scotsman named William McLucas — not Bre-X — was the real foreign owner of PT WAM; that McLucas wasn't happy about the deal Felderhof had made to sell his property to Walsh; that PT WAM was operating on the Muara Atan contract of work under extension after extension; that the CoWs for II and III were stalled because Bre-X's Indonesian partner at Busang I felt he had been cut out of the deal and was complaining to the government; that paperwork was sloppy, and documents filed with regulators appeared to have been forged; that permits and underlying KPs had expired. And so on.

Life was not much better on the technical side. It was no secret in the mining community that Alex Davidson, a dour geologist impervious to the hype and arm-waving that excited many of his colleagues, was not overly keen on Busang. Davidson had enough grey hair and field experience to hold his own with the likes of John Felderhof. There was no maar-diatreming him.

Yet, Busang had all those ounces; those wonderful, low-cost ounces.

Major companies had to be interested, and the salting gang knew possible buyers would come around sooner or later. But, in the three years the factory operated, the owners never wanted a senior partner to help them explore or develop Busang. Equity deals were the way to go, David Walsh and John Felderhof told potential suitors; they wanted cash in the till. You have to buy a piece of us, not the property. That way, Bre-X would remain in the driver's seat.

The Exit Plan took on a new twist when Placer Dome entered the fray as a serious contender. The major must have obtained only doctored samples from Bre-X, as John Willson was hoping to beat out its longtime rival, Barrick. Talk on the street was that some investment advisors urged Willson to forget about due diligence and beat out Barrick by making a bid for Bre-X shares. Rumor is Willson thought they were crazy at the time and still does. He stuck to his rules.

The owners of Busang were no doubt disappointed that the euphoria did not induce mining executives to fork over cash, no questions asked.

But the big boys were too smart for that. Placer Dome and other majors always balked at buying shares of Bre-X. They wanted the asset, not the company, and they would not buy the asset without first seeing the goods. But the goods were gone, except for thin slices of library core.

Majors were not going to rely on the numbers flogged in Bre-X press releases. They had to drill their own holes. Freeport was the first major to sink its drills into Bre-X's Southeast zone. Had there been no Battle of Busang, Freeport would have walked away and, in compliance with the confidentiality agreement, said nothing about what it found. Busang would have been "the next guy's problem."

Bre-X's salting gang could have tried to explain things away by saying there was an "assaying problem," or that the deposit was "geologically complex." Another major might have drilled a few holes and walked, and so on . . . until Busang died gently in its sleep. But the ounce factory got too much attention from the wrong people. It found too much gold.

The salting gang had another problem. It was already late February, and everyone was booked to fly to Toronto in early March. The world mining community was there to see John Felderhof receive his award for discovering this fabulous gold deposit. It would have been spooky if any of the geologists from Busang had disappeared before the award was presented. The world would have known something was amiss, and the big boss would have been prevented from savoring his moment of glory.

'The Smell'

Bud Laporte calls it the 'smell.'
We call it that too, because even though work has stopped at the

Busang property and the phones are no longer ringing at Bre-X's Jakarta office, the smell of duplicity still hangs in the air.

In Laporte's case, the smell was associated with Bre-X's drilling contractor. After Busang blew up, the principals of PT Drillinti Tiko tried to sell the company to other contractors. Laporte and his Major Drilling team looked, as did many others, but no one wanted to buy, because of the smell of the company's books.

First of all, it had far more rigs than were ever put to use at Busang, yet Bre-X was its only client. The company had done little mineral exploration work before Busang came along. And there were longstanding rumors about the way business was being done behind the scenes.

Rumors had been floating around Jakarta for some time — rumors that certain individuals from the Busang salting crew were extracting kickbacks based on metres drilled. The speculation intensified when the owners of the drill company tried to sell the business after work at Busang ceased. As it turned out, only the rigs were purchased (by a larger contractor). The owners then moved on and, at the time of writing, were believed to be somewhere in South Africa.

The gossip was all the more intriguing to those who were aware that Benguet had had similar problems. The Philippine company had a core of professionals who tried to keep things on the straight and narrow. But the honest managers began hearing allegations from suppliers who complained, privately, that in order to make sales to the corporation, kickbacks, in the form of money or goods, were requested by certain personnel. One smart manager took the complaints seriously, and the corporation moved its purchasing office to Canada for a period to put an end to such practices.

The expat mining community soon learned that Bre-X's drilling contractors had been telling North American reporters that Michael de Guzman had bought placer gold from a Dayak who ran a small store at Mekar Baru. The story pitched was that de Guzman was a "regular customer" and had bought placer gold from the tribesman for three years. This was intended to prove that Busang was a "one-man scam" that began and ended in the Dayak equivalent of a 7-Eleven convenience store. How the one-man theory accounts for all those wonderful glory holes and bait holes, which were produced whenever the stock price was under downward pressure, is beyond comprehension. Perhaps De Guzman had a better grasp of stock market fundamentals than anyone imagined.

That story had too much of a smell to get past the geological community, even if the Dayak had sworn it was true. For starters, Mekar Baru was crawling with spies during Busang's heyday. One even tried to get into the camp by posing as a news reporter for *The*

Northern Miner. David Walsh called in a panic and the paper's lawyers had to send out a cease-and-desist letter to the snoopy geologist.

Had Michael de Guzman been waltzing into the store on a regular basis to buy gold in person, word would have spread quickly. Not only that, the gold recovered by Dayak tribesmen using basic sluicing equipment would likely have been far too coarse-grained for reliable use as a salting agent (though it occasionally may have come in handy in a pinch). The material de Guzman and the rest of the salting crew required was a concentrate from a genuine placer operation, one that used a shaker table or cyclone sizer; this more sophisticated equipment would have recovered gold in the 0.1-to-0.4-millimetre size fraction — the size that was ultimately found in the samples. And the owners of such operations do not sell their goods below cost in a corner store.

Alluvial operations are everywhere in Indonesia. De Guzman was familiar with a number of them, including the Tewah and Amphalit placer gold projects from the Jason and Pelsart days. The other possibility is that de Guzman, who was a capable panner, made a heavy-mineral concentrate, with gold in it. In either event, a concentrate could have been blended with some crushed rock to make a well-disguised salting mixture.

A smell taints other facets of Bre-X's Indonesian operations. Poor Stan Hawkins found that out when he allowed the company to "operate" work programs at his three joint ventures in Kalimantan.

"Dreadful accounting" and unexpected cover charges were one thing; but having no work done at all was quite another. The royal runaround by John Felderhof just added insult to injury.

And some Indonesian geologists are still wondering why 20 holes drilled more than a year ago at Bre-X's Sumatra property have never been assayed and are gradually being overtaken by jungle growth.

Poor Peter Howe got a whiff of it too. In 1996, he was telling shareholders of Diadem Resources that Bre-X would be operating work programs at three properties on the Indonesian island of Belitung. The project was a joint venture held 60% by David Walsh's Bresea and 30% by Diadem. An Indonesian partner held the remainder. The joint management committee consisted of John Felderhof, Mike de Guzman and Mike Bird.

It was great news at the time. Felderhof ranked all three areas as having the geological ingredients of a mine. "Sometimes, all it takes to find a new mine is original conceptual thinking," he said.

Fast forward to July of 1997: Diadem launches "independent investigations" concerning Bre-X's activities as operator, including a financial audit. "Preliminary information suggests that amounts invoiced have been substantially overstated," Howe tells shareholders.

Howe sent a Canadian consultant to Indonesia to conduct a geological audit. The geologist came back with more "disturbing facts." Core from the property was not being split, even though base metals, and not gold, were the commodity of interest. This kind of "conceptual thinking" was something quite new to base metals exploration.

Howe said he never approved the practice and was shocked to learn of it. "I guess somebody [at Bre-X] was trying to be consistent."

Peter Howe refused to pay the cash-call notices for work allegedly done by Bre-X and said Diadem would be seeking a partial refund of the $825,000 already paid. Stan Hawkins said he could understand why. "If the reporting was anything related to what we got, which was nothing, then yeah, I can understand Pete not wanting to pay anything. I never saw a report. I never saw anything."

The mists of Kalimantan

Clouds often enshroud Kalimantan, particularly the interior, where the Busang property is situated. There are other shrouds, too, which makes it difficult to get to the bottom of anything in Indonesia. "Things get swallowed up in the mists," as one Canadian visitor observed.

The truth also gets swallowed, and not merely because it can be bought and sold like any other commodity. Stories get told, along with variations on those stories. So much conflicting information has come forward about what really happened at Busang that the truth has become as elusive and rare as the gold.

Take but one example. Canadian reporters interviewed people who told them Michael de Guzman had been kidnapped in February 1997, ostensibly because he wanted to leave the project and was having fights with John Felderhof. It was interesting and colorful stuff. But others say Felderhof had suggested that Barrick might be behind the abduction to get information about Busang (everything was Barrick's fault, according to Felderhof). And reliable sources close to Bre-X Jakarta say there was no kidnapping, that de Guzman had disappeared for a few days with a lady friend and made the story up because he was supposed to have been somewhere else. Three versions of one event can not all be true.

Investigators are struggling to find answers, but many people are working at cross-purposes. Forensic Investigative Associates

(FIA), retained in April 1997 by Bre-X's board, has interviewed 150 witnesses and gathered more than 3,000 pages of documents related to the Bre-X fiasco. The firm's investigators have travelled to Alberta, British Columbia, Ontario, Nova Scotia, Indonesia, Singapore, the Philippines, Australia, the Cayman Islands, the United Kingdom and the United States.

But, at the end of the day, every individual interviewed who was in a "strategic position with regards to the core-handling process" denied any knowledge of, or involvement in, the tampering. We can only imagine the chorus of denials from Jerry Alo, Cesar Puspos, Rudy Vega and others.

David Walsh was right when he said that a "well-oiled misinformation campaign" had been orchestrated. But it was not orchestrated against the company; it was being orchestrated by forces *within* the company, as well as by forces associated with the company. The role of Walsh's own brother is but one example. Merrick Walsh wrote letters to politicians urging them to intervene when his brother's company was being beaten up by corporate bullies, and he regularly disseminated ludicrous information to the gullible Internet crowd. Telling investors to hold on to their $3 Bre-X shares was probably his worst call.

Some people who know plenty about what went on at Busang are now trying to make the world believe that it was a "one-man scam" executed by Michael de Guzman, with the help of a few accomplices. The theory does not wash in Indonesian or Canadian mining circles. When the Busang saga began, the Filipino geologists were nothing more than lowly paid field hands. They are now being portrayed as criminal masterminds of the world's biggest gold scam. Something doesn't quite add up.

Some of de Guzman's Indonesian friends agree. "No one is looking at the Canadians," said one of de Guzman's former bosses. "The Canadians pumped greed into these guys." That might be a naive comment, but the Busang swindle went way beyond a couple of field geologists trying to keep their jobs.

At the very least, De Guzman kept Bre-X's Jakarta office fully informed on the progress at Busang. One example is an internal memo, which the geologist wrote and erroneously faxed to a party that was not supposed to receive it. The document states who was authorized to discuss Busang samples if questions came up at the labs. "Communications pertaining to samples are to be addressed direct to the senior project manager [Cesar Puspos] and or to Jerry S. Alo, Project Chief Metallurgist, through our Jakarta head office," de Guzman wrote.

De Guzman also noted that Bob Ramirez, Manny Puspos and Rudy Vega were "authorized to communicate on behalf of Bre-X." The memo, entitled "Busang samples," was copied to John Felderhof.

FIA investigators have already found "reasonable and probable grounds" to believe that de Guzman and Cesar Puspos "conspired," together with Jerry Alo, Bob Ramirez, Manny Puspos and others, to defraud Bre-X and the public in Canada and elsewhere through the deceitful salting scheme.

They studied Bre-X records and found that some of these individuals profited substantially by exercising options and selling Bre-X shares during their employ with the company. Michael de Guzman pulled in $4.5 million, Cesar Puspos received $2.1 million, Jerry Alo raked in $1.2 million and Bob Ramirez made $378,125.

The investigators believe the tampering began in late 1993 in order to prevent closure of the site after the first two holes came up barren. And they believe de Guzman instructed Cesar Puspos to salt the first holes, which were crudely done, as man-made copper-gold alloy was found in the upper portion of hole 3.

Documents obtained by the *Miner* show that Jerry Alo was brought on board around this period. De Guzman already knew him from Benguet. Alo also was involved with both John Felderhof and de Guzman at Minindo when the Indonesian venture was being touted as quite the little profit centre. A stock scandal ensued when it proved to be quite the opposite. The three musketeers were thrown out of work until David Walsh came along and gave them another shot at success.

When drilling resumed at Busang in January 1994, Mike de Guzman and Jerry Alo went to work setting up the ounce factory. They were soon providing John Felderhof with progress reports relating to Alo's "experiments" to improve the "reproducibility" of the erratic assay results; the telltale signs of salting.

This is not, typically, the kind of work that goes on at an exploration site. John Felderhof frequently described Alo as "my metallurgist," which was somewhat strange as metallurgists are not normally employed at exploration sites. Metallurgists work in mills and processing plants at operating mines, or they work in laboratories that do testwork on ore samples. But Alo also was the site manager, and may well have had other duties besides trying to hide the telltale signs of salted core at the behest of his bosses.

Investigators state that de Guzman and Cesar Puspos "took advantage of a laboratory built at Busang" to salt samples of carbonate-altered core during the summer of 1995. Because the results were erratic, the Samarinda office was later used for the tampering, though how this would render results less erratic is not clear. A video of the Busang lab, shot in the summer of 1996, clearly shows that Jerry Alo was in charge of sample preparation and assaying procedures at Busang. The video shows crushed material

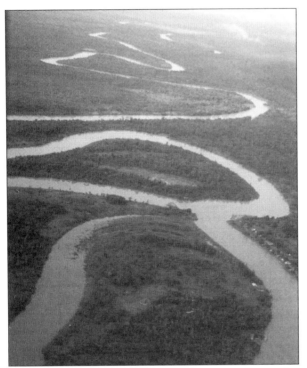

River of No Return? A jungle scene along the helicopter flight path to Busang.

bagged and ready for assaying, as well as metallurgical test-ing.

The actual salting may have been moved to Samarinda, however, as mining analysts were start-ing to visit Busang. But it is safe to say that plenty of salting was done right on site, because the Samarinda office was not obtained until later in the game.

Jerry Alo, the masterful alchemist, has already been rel-egated to a bit player in the sorry saga, by media and investiga-tors alike. He now lives somewhere in the Philippines, is financially comfortable and may never have to practise his black art again. "None of these guys are worrying," a source said. "They have protection."

'The stories one hears'

The mystery of what really happened during Michael de Guzman's infamous helicopter ride to his fantasy Eldorado also may remain enshrouded in the mist that hangs over Kalimantan.

FIA investigators report that they are satisfied "on the basis of information reviewed" that de Guzman committed suicide by jumping from a chopper on March 19. "We believe he killed him-self when faced with the prospect of having to be exposed for salt-ing Bre-X samples," the firm reported.

Others say that if de Guzman did jump, it was because he did not want to spend the rest of his life rotting in an Indonesian prison.

A few expats say they have talked with the owner of the heli-copter company, who told them "de Guzman definitely jumped."

Everyone has a theory, and speculation is rampant. But many people do not buy the official version of events.

Peter Howe says he doesn't know what happened, but admits the official story is full of "illogicalities." He said that de Guzman's handwriting appeared to be genuine, but the letters were uncharacteristically huge. (The Filipino geologist's handwritten field notes that we have obtained show small, condensed characters.) Howe believes the letters were written on the ground, probably in a motel room, as de Guzman left detailed notes on the work programs to be carried out at Bre-X's other properties, along with his suicide notes.

There also were reports that de Guzman tried to kill himself by taking pills, but, again, there are no credible witnesses.

Howe and many others found it strange that de Guzman did not move his family to Australia from the Philippines. During the 1996 site visit, de Guzman said he planned to move there because he feared family members would be kidnapped. He is believed to have obtained landed status in Australia in 1996 yet did nothing to make the move happen, even though he told people he and his family had been "threatened" that winter.

Michael Novotny, Felderhof's former bush mate, does not know what happened to de Guzman. "But, oh the stories one hears."

Indeed. We've heard them all. One version of events is that the boys from Busang trolled the bars, found a drunk who resembled de Guzman, offered him a job, and pushed him out a chopper before he sobered up — and before de Guzman went on his famous ride. De Guzman gets whisked away, a body is found after a few days, and presto: a one-man salting scam. Another scenario is that the whole crowd was under surveillance and the getaway plan was "rudely interrupted."

Quite frankly, we don't know. We have a hard time believing the suicide story. And we have an even harder time believing anything coming from Jerry Alo and the rest of the salting crew.

Alo was one of the last people to see de Guzman alive. He is reported to have brought a change of clothes to the Samarinda airport and later helped with the search effort. A team of Dayaks from Busang is reported to have found the body on March 24, which surprised the heck out of a team of searchers who, a year earlier, had failed to locate a chopper that had crashed in the jungle, 100 km from where the body was found. Anyone familiar with the jungles of Borneo, or the dank brown swamps, would agree that it would not be easy.

"If I had someone fall out of a helicopter in the middle of the rainforest, I'd give you, maybe, million-to-one odds of finding him using everything available," said Birl Worley. "Something appears

How fleeting is fame: John Felderhof holds up the Prospector of the Year award that he was later asked to return.

fishy from the word go."

Jerry Alo also identified the badly decomposed body. His assistant, Rudy Vega, then entertained reporters with accounts of how the gang had been in nightclubs singing "My Way" and other favorite songs before de Guzman decided to end it all because of the heartbreak of hepatitis B. We might believe the story too, if we hadn't been lied to by this gang before.

Cynic Bud Laporte thinks the soap opera is far from over. "The geologist is probably sitting somewhere with a bar stocked with the necessities. I trust he has enough salt left for his Bloody Marys."

Alo and Vega are, in our view, neither credible nor disinterested witnesses. It's a safe bet that mining analysts share the sentiment. After all, it was Alo's laboratory "experiments" that helped fool analysts into believing the assay results from Busang were remarkably consistent. And Vega was Santa's little helper.

The story becomes more and more bizarre. It appears that the will no longer exists in Indonesia to find answers to an embarrassing suicide now referred to as "the accident." The investigation by Indonesian authorities was shoddy and raised more questions than answers. Members of de Guzman's family said one thing one day and contradicted themselves the next. Some members told people they believe de Guzman was pushed from the chopper; other members have said they don't believe he is dead because they have not yet received "the power" — a cultural term for a form of spiritual energy that is supposed to descend upon the surviving family members. The fingerprints matched, and then they didn't. Some say the corpse had teeth, but de Guzman did not — his teeth were removed after having been badly weakened from childhood malnutrition. Things are not much clearer in the Philippines, where sympathy lies with the returning geologists who are now being blamed for the swindle.

The entire matter is now "classified," we were told by Philippine authorities. Perhaps too many issues of national honor are at stake for the government there to want to get to the bottom of a scandal that begins, in part, in its own backyard.

A loss of glory

After the Strathcona report was released, John Felderhof surrendered his Prospector of the Year award to the Prospectors and Developers Association of Canada.

Felderhof also agreed to surrender the Man of the Year award given him by *The Northern Miner* (though he kept the miner's lamp). In a letter to Publisher John Cooke, Felderhof said his decision was prompted by "uncertainty" cast by the Strathcona report. "I ask only that you are willing to consider returning it at an appropriate point in the future once the matters have been solved," he wrote. "As you know, I continue to believe that there is a significant amount of gold at Busang. This belief is based on the work in the area, as well as the structure, geology, mineralogy and alteration at Busang. This is shared by my site geologists, who have been publicly quoted in the press. As best I can tell, our work in the Central zone remains unchallenged. The Strathcona report dealt only with a section of the Southeast zone and there are many unsolved issues surrounding the report and our work in that portion of the deposit."

The ever-gracious John Cooke wrote back and informed Felderhof that, yes, we would reinstate the award once the lost gold was found. "And by the way, how is Ingrid?"

Nothing was heard from David Walsh until early September when a package arrived from Bre-X Minerals. After we debated whether or not to open it, curiosity prevailed. David Walsh had returned the brass miner's lamp, along with a letter stating that he felt obligated to return the award in light of the Strathcona report. The package had been sent in early May, but had gone astray and

David Walsh ponders his next big deal at his Nassau retreat.

was now being properly forwarded. Walsh also said the perpetrators of the Busang fraud "will be discovered and dealt with."

'Just a money guy'

It was April 22, 1997, and the world had gone mad. Or so we thought when David Walsh issued a press release containing results from a number of holes drilled on the Busang ounce factory. It was almost like old times.

Bre-X Minerals had not released assay results on a hole-by-hole basis for some time, having ceased that practice in favor of regularly updated ounce calculations from Kilborn. But here they were: a couple of pages of positive results followed by six dud holes. Some investors did not know what to think, and the investor relations team at Bre-X rushed to fill the void. "The gold is there. We will be vindicated." Yada, yada, yada. Some of the Internet shills even suggested that reporting dud holes proved the company's integrity, which, in turn, meant — wait for it — "the gold is there."

Strathcona later told the world that assays from drill core delivered by Bre-X to the lab since March 13 were "entirely negative." While the firm did not have time to trace the timing of "various stopping points en route to the lab," it was obvious, by this point, that holes drilled by Bre-X itself had returned the same completely negative results obtained by both Freeport and Strathcona. That will be a tough one for Felderhof to explain away.

Alarm bells should have gone off at Bre-X's Calgary office. And they may have for some people. But not for David Walsh. And not for Stephen McAnulty and the investor relations team. The pace of beer drinking may have picked up, but the we-will-be-vindicated rhetoric echoed as before.

Investors knew that Walsh did not trust Freeport's drilling. And Walsh may not have been terribly keen on Strathcona, especially if John Felderhof was still yanking his chain. But here were six dud holes from his own drills, one after another. What were the odds of that?

Instead of shutting down his promotional machine, Walsh kicked it into high gear, complaining all the while that corporate intrigue and a short-selling conspiracy were somehow behind his reversal of fortune.

Getting to the bottom of Walsh's role in the Busang story will not be easy. He was never keen on keeping a paper trail, and confessed to a reporter earlier this year that he "shredded sensitive documents" after a break-in at his Calgary office. Walsh was incompetent and, therefore, believable in the role of dupe, yet even his friends say he was as sharp as a whip when money was involved.

Others say Walsh may have been dealt a bad hand when he went to Indonesia and met John Felderhof and the team of innovative Filipino geologists. Barry Tannock said Felderhof showed little, if any, loyalty to David Walsh. "He always ran his own show and was always thick as thieves with de Guzman."

Walsh set out to follow a dream and found a nightmare of his own making. His lack of interest in the Indonesian projects, which he rarely visited, and his refusal to believe he had a problem in the face of compelling evidence are nothing short of mind-boggling.

Stan Hawkins does not believe David Walsh had anything to do with the salting scam at Busang, though he wonders why other directors, including Kavanagh, were kept at bay.

"I don't know if it was deliberate," he said, ever-generous to his old friend. "I know people came up to me and said, 'Now I know why they didn't want you to see the property.' But I think it may have had something to do with David's insecurity. He knew he was in way over his head. He put his faith in Felderhof."

At the March 1997 mining convention, Hawkins did not notice anything in Walsh's behavior that might suggest he knew something was amiss at Busang. "He did make the odd comment about 'that God damned Felderhof,' but was not specific about anything.

"He was a believer; that was my impression," Hawkins added. "He believed they had what they said they had, where they said they had it. When you know a person reasonably well over a period of time and you have drinks together, something will drop. Nothing ever, ever dropped and, being an old reporter, I'm pretty [attuned] to that short of thing. In my view, he was totally committed and he totally believed."

But the prevailing view in the mining industry is much harsher. Walsh was asleep at the switch mostly because he wanted to be asleep. The bottom line is that David Walsh never ran a junior mining company; he operated a Calgary boiler room that pitched smoke.

Many junior mining companies are headed by non-mining professionals. As one such executive remarked, "There are many geologists who will tell you: 'You don't know a thing about the industry, so just shut up and raise the money.' That's not good enough. Walsh was not strong enough to stop the money flow and ask for accountability."

When problems surfaced at Busang, Walsh's stock answer was: "I'm just the money guy," but in the next breath he would complain that people thought he was "stupid."

Walsh's defence always has been that he is not a "technical guy," which is true. But stock promoter Murray Pezim was not a technical guy either. In his heyday, "The Pez" raised millions of dollars for mining projects all over the world, and some fabulous discoveries were made from his efforts. But he always knew what was going on under his watch. If he didn't understand something, he asked. He had an incredible memory in his salad days and people were warned never to play poker with the man because he always remembered where the cards fell.

Pezim once told the story of a geologist he hired who tried to convince him "the gold is there" when the assay sheets said it was not. "The Pez" didn't want to hear about assay discrepancies and reproducibility problems. He chased the rogue geologist out of his office screaming, "What the hell are you trying to do, give me a God damn heart attack?"

Walsh is dumping all over "that God damn Felderhof" now, but it's a little late. Bashing de Guzman for being a pathological liar won't help much either.

David Walsh only acts like a loser; which is precisely what he needs to do to come out a winner.

'Troppo' John

The Australians call it "going troppo." The Dutch, who had been in Indonesia for decades, both before and after independence, called it "*mata glap.*" Both terms describe a strange phenomenon that afflicts some Caucasians who have been in the tropics too long and are forever marked by the experience.

Some of John Felderhof's friends speculate that this is what happened to him. He certainly cultivated the air of a half-mad jungle trekker as he sold the idea of Busang to investors, analysts, mining executives and the world at large. He smoked heavily, drank heavily, was quick to ignite, and slow to forgive. At the height of his fame, people tiptoed around him, as though his very rage could bring them harm. It was bad luck to cross John Felderhof; he had the evil eye.

The mining industry believes Felderhof deserves an Oscar for his performance during the awards ceremony at the March 1997 mining convention. That would add another to the two awards that still grace his mantlepiece. "Either he has the balls of an elephant or he was ignorant of what was going on," said one observer.

Others were impressed that Felderhof went to de Guzman's funeral in Manila, and then back to the Busang site after he was first summoned by Jim Bob Moffett. "That took guts," said one, "even though it took 10 days to find them."

Felderhof's believers were those who knew him as a young man, as a solid citizen and member of an upstanding family. Many of these people admit they rode their Bre-X shares down to pennies because the John Felderhof they knew would never have engaged in fraudulent activities. His detractors are, by and large, those who knew him in Indonesia, just before Busang became news. They remember a jaded, cynical and bitter soul who had gone over to the dark side.

Mining analysts have a lot to say about Felderhof, but none of it is fit for print. Some hope Felderhof's next project will see him studying sulphurous formations at the roots of his maar-diatremes deep in the Earth's mantle. Others want vanity licence plates custom-made by the great man himself.

Don't ask mining men if Felderhof ought to have known about the salting at Busang. They will think you're crazy. "He'd have to be pretty drunk not to know," is a typical comment.

Stan Hawkins, who always tells it as he sees it, is harshly critical of Felderhof. "I think he knew [about the salting]. How the hell could he not know, if he was any kind of engineer? There was no surface show, so what would make him think anything was there?"

But some old friends are more understanding.

Felderhof's workmate Mike Novotny, who had been through a salting scandal himself, told us he believes Felderhof is just as innocent as he was. "I would be very surprised if he had anything to do with the salting," he said. "But, you know, people do have secret lives, even professionals."

William Burton says he remembers Felderhof as being dedicated to the industry. "I would not then, or now, suspect tampering or any other unprofessional behavior." And he believes that Felderhof's acceptance speech at the PDAC convention was heartfelt. "Knowing his background, I can't believe that he put that whole thing on. I think he felt the thing was there. He might have had questions in his mind on some issues that had come up in the prior few months, but I still think, professionally, he wanted to find a big deposit.

"He must be having some tremendous personal problems trying to place himself into the context of this, because his whole life was this industry. That's another reason I don't think he was involved. I can't see him jeopardizing his position in this industry — the only industry he has ever known."

Burton said he "very much doubts" that Felderhof put a plan together and instigated the tampering that took place at Busang. "But when he might have known, or whether he ought to have known, that's a tough one."

Many people say Felderhof's experiences in Indonesia left him bitter. Burton does not disagree that, over that period of years, Felderhof was exposed to a different way of doing business that may have progressively eroded the values and standards he had learned as a young man in Canada, to the point of acquiring a blind eye.

"When you are that long in that environment, I guess I would say it is a possibility," Burton said, with a hint of sadness.

"He fell into difficulties and would have loved to get back at the industry for a lot of the failures that happened to him down in Kalimantan, especially after the 1987 market crash, which left him holding the bag on a lot of issues, especially with Jason [Mining]," he said. "But I can't see him organizing any sort of retribution on the industry such as this."

In public, Felderhof still maintains that the question of gold at Busang is open. "I continue to believe that there is a significant amount of gold at Busang," he wrote in his major statement to the press in July 1997. He has told friends that people are still interested in Busang as a valid target and that he will be issuing a full criticism of Strathcona's final report whenever it is released. He is certain they did a lousy job.

Some people have listed Felderhof as one of the losers in the great game of Busang; they say he will spend the rest of his life with his lawyers, that he is exiled on Grand Cayman, that his status as a pariah in the mining industry has taken away any hope of fulfilling his big dreams. Cynics say he cares for none of these things. He has a mountain of money protected by good lawyers, bank secrecy, and the tax laws of the Cayman Islands. He is unlikely ever to face criminal charges over the Busang fraud, and cannot be compelled to answer civil suits. And from a fortress in a tropical sea, he vents his spleen on better men, and is well-satisfied with himself. *Mata glap* he may be, but a mining man he is not.

The prodigal son

When Graham Farquharson lowered the boom on Busang in Bre-X's Calgary boardroom on May 4, Paul Kavanagh knew it was over.

"Paul threw in the towel at that point," Farquharson said, with a touch of sympathy in his voice.

Kavanagh believed in Busang, perhaps more than anyone. His faith and support were horribly betrayed and, at the end of the day, he probably knew he had been used to window-dress a sordid story.

There are different reactions to Kavanagh's role in the Bre-X affair. Some, on the money side of the mining business (brokers, analysts, fund managers and the like), are mad as hell. "I blame him for a lot of it," said one money manager during a black-tie charity event. "You don't bring shit like that [Bre-X and Busang] to a room like this," he said, pointing to the obviously monied crowd gathered at one of Toronto's poshest hotels.

That was not just big money talking, it was lost money talking.

Many in the mining side of the business who know Kavanagh well are more forgiving. They understand his foibles and weaknesses and the highly emotional side of his character. At the same time, they have no doubts about his honesty and integrity. They know Kavanagh believed in Busang with his heart and soul. Their only criticism is that his sharp mind should have been brought to bear as well.

Kavanagh knows all this and carries a heavy burden. Some industry people have reached out to him in the spirit of friendship, including those who lost money and face in the Bre-X fiasco. They know mining was Kavanagh's life and they are trying to give him some semblance of his life back. The real mining industry — the doers — is a small family, and Kavanagh had earned his place in that family long before Bre-X came along. He made real contributions to building companies and building mines. He encouraged young people to pursue careers in science. But he is now the industry's prodigal son.

The legal aftermath

The lawyers were lined up with their yellow pads long before Graham Farquharson pulled the plug on the Busang ounce factory.

Bre-X shareholders began threatening to sue during the height of the Battle for Busang. At first, their sights were trained on Barrick Gold, which many believed was engaged in a covert, underhanded operation to "steal" Busang.

"Putting that slant on it was completely wrong," says Dale Hendrick. "If Barrick hadn't gone in there, the thing might have gone on forever. During the anger and denial phase of all this, Bre-X shareholders were snarling at everybody."

The lawyers turned their guns around when the Strathcona report made it clear that Bre-X Jakarta had not been telling the whole truth about what was going on at Busang. The irate investors were not deterred by the notion that the managers could not have known what was going on because they were on a Caribbean beach. It was their job to know; that was what they were paid the big bucks for.

Bre-X and its entire team of officers and directors have been named in several class-action lawsuits.

On May 9, a class-action suit was filed against Nesbitt Burns, arising from the company's activities related to Bre-X Minerals. First Marathon and analyst Kerry Smith were named in a separate lawsuit announced on June 4. The suit alleged that the company "acted negligently, in conflict of interest, and in breach of their fiduciary duty." First Marathon responded with a statement that it intended "to defend itself vigorously."

By July, shareholders had banded together in a lawsuit naming Bre-X, Bresea, John Felderhof, David Walsh, Jeannette Walsh, Stephen McAnulty, John Thorpe, Rolando Francisco, Hugh Lyons, Paul Kavanagh, J.P. Morgan & Co., PT Kilborn Pakar Rekayasa, Kilborn Engineering Pacific, SNC-Lavalin Group, Nesbitt Burns and Lehman Brothers. A number of the respondents, including Bre-X, the Kilborn companies, Nesbitt and Lehman, had pooled their resources to fight the suit.

Some of the people and companies named above were victims of the Busang swindle, too, making this one of the rare cases where victims are suing other victims.

Lawyers will be the really big winners in the Bre-X fiasco.

'The Accident'

Indonesia's minister of mines, Ida Bagus Sudjana, came back to Canada in the summer of 1997. The trip was sponsored by the Indonesian Embassy and the Canada-Indonesia Business Club. The purpose was to mend fences with the Canadian mining industry.

And there *were* problems. The minister had tried to introduce onerous provisions into the latest generation of CoWs that would make it near-impossible for juniors to raise money. The minister's role in the Bre-X fiasco was still being whispered about. "Who wants to go and find a big orebody if it is going to end up with a scramble like that?" one geologist asked.

Next, in early May, the government made an unprecedented request to Newmont Mining through Sudjana. Would Newmont be so kind as to reduce voluntarily its 80% interest in the country's second-largest mining project?

Newmont's banks were horrified by it all as the Batu Hijau gold-copper deposit was nowhere near as rich as Busang was claimed to be. Some intense backroom discussions were held and Newmont prevailed. It is building the mine today with its existing Indonesian partner, Jusuf Merukh. "It didn't happen, and that was good for everyone" said the president of a Canadian-listed company working in Indonesia.

These incidents, combined with Bre-X's problems, had made mining companies wary of Indonesia. The delegation came to Canada to reopen a dialogue.

Appropriately, the meeting was held in Calgary, a known hotbed of fundraising for Indonesian mining ventures. The officials opened the session by stating that there would be no discussion of Bre-X as the matter was under investigation. It did come up, but with typical Javanese obliqueness, the delegation simply referred to it as "the accident." and changed the subject.

Officials said "the accident" had caused great concern about junior companies. The junior sector was needed and still welcome, but mining executives were told that the next generation of CoWs would call for greater emphasis on community development, socio-economic agreements, and the like.

After the delegation left, the mining executives bemoaned how Bre-X and subsequent scams had made it difficult to raise money to explore projects in Indonesia. The funds had dried up.

But some Australians believe the Canadians have some house-cleaning to do before investors will show interest in their projects. "Some of the companies here are still only worried about the market," said an Australian geologist working in Indonesia. "They are not worrying about increasing the company's wealth by finding and mining an ore deposit. No wonder the investors are going away in droves. They have every reason to be fed up totally with it all."

A representative from Inco made the point that Bre-X's problems working in Indonesia were largely of its own making. The company had carried out non-permitted activities under its SIPP. There were other ownership problems, and these led to the government intervention. Inco representatives made the same points at a luncheon meeting in Toronto in early 1997. Business can be done in the country, and companies don't have to compromise their principles when they go there. Inco had been in the country since the second-generation contracts of work and was now embarking on an expansion program at its huge nickel mining complex on Sulawesi. And it did all this the old-fashioned way — by building friendship and trust over a period of 30 years.

Among Indonesians, the consensus is similar. "Life goes on," said Theo Van Leeuwen of the Indonesian Mining Association. "There are still good prospects to explore."

Fool's gold rush

The success of Bre-X Minerals was a godsend for Mike Novotny, Laurie Whitehouse and Armand Beaudoin.

John Felderhof's former colleagues all came out winners. They made fortunes wheeling and dealing properties to the flock of Canadian juniors that came to Indonesia hoping to find the next Busang.

Novotny and Whitehouse found, however, that the ghost of Karpa Springs haunted them as they tried to do deals with some juniors, particularly when they attempted to sell the properties for cash and shares. Things were smoothed over when the partners obtained letters from the Crown prosecutor in the trial acknowledging their "co-operation" in the case.

"The people who muddied my name were jealous because I had got the best properties," Novotny said.

Novotny and Whitehouse did get some decent prospects, mostly because of their previous experience exploring in Kalimantan. They knew when the best targets were being relinquished and were first in line. Today, both men are large shareholders of several Canadian juniors.

Armand Beaudoin bounced back from the Minindo mess and become comfortably wealthy from his property dealings. He tied up huge tracts of ground, which he vended to a number of juniors, including some of the highest-profile companies active in the Indonesian land rush. He has since turned his attention to Mongolia, of all places.

Here we go again

Brian Mountford and Morris Beattie delivered the bad news to shareholders of Delgratia Mining on May 19. The Josh property in Nevada, which was reported to have fabulous grades of gold over impressive widths, was a bust. It was a tough blow for those who bought the story and the stock late in the game, when it had already climbed to over $30 from about $5.

"We conclude that there are insignificant amounts of gold contained in the Josh deposit and that any gold detected beyond background amounts was introduced into the samples after they had been collected at the drill," the geological auditors told shareholders.

Delgratia President Charles Ager was horrified, albeit relieved that the "audit" done by Mountford and Beattie had absolved everyone in his company. The problem stemmed from the lab that had done the assays. "It is now clear that the company has been the victim of data falsification," Ager said.

He tried to give shareholders some hope. "I personally believe that the ultimate determination of whether or not there is significant gold in the Nevada project will have to await further work."

Shareholders did not agree. They sued Ager, and other directors of Delgratia. Ager's pleas of being a "victim" were falling on deaf ears.

For starters, Ager was wearing too many hats. Through companies owned by family members, Ager was the vendor of the property, which he agreed to sell to Delgratia for more than US$5 million. But he was also the president of Delgratia, the purchaser. And he owned Cactus Mining, which was paid a fee to carry out the exploration programs.

Ager also had his own sample preparation facility on site, and he retained a lab that was not qualified to do assays. In the past, the lab's owner had had some securities problems that regulators were none to happy with.

And there were questions about the audit itself. Mountford and Beattie decided to include Ager's own assayer as part of the exercise. The fellow was "sworn to secrecy" and then asked to help get to the bottom of the phoney assays that he may have had a hand in creating.

Shareholders were then told that the tampering had taken place in the unlicensed labs. But the irate investors knew these labs had all been hand-picked by Ager. And some were still suspicious that the assays might have been cooked up in a row of crock pots housed in Ager's in-house lab.

But most investors thought Ager's plea of "victimization" was the real crock. The lawsuit was ongoing at the time of writing, and Ager has resigned.

A short while later, two juniors exploring in Ghana told their shareholders that, oops, their high-grade gold samples may have been tampered with, too.

A mirror for the industry

Every major swindle in history has been a mirror for the time and place in which it operated. Busang was no exception. Some investors came face-to-face with their own greed as they hung on in hopes of ever-increasing riches.

It was a mirror for the mining industry, which had become too promotional and too tolerant of its own miscreants. It was a mirror for the brokerage and investment sector, which took institutional money to places it was never intended to go, thereby propelling a low-grade scam into the pension plans of thousands of Canadians. Bre-X always was a highly speculative stock, and, in the old days, it would have known its place.

Bre-X and Busang were a mirror for the business reporters, who picked up the story and made it all sound magical and exciting. Mining analysts saw themselves reflected as people more interested in the sizzle than the steak. Investors saw regulators asleep at the switch.

Bre-X will change all that, for a while at least.

John Kaiser, author of the newsletter *Kaiser Bottom-Fishing Report*, says the Busang bust will bring market valuations of juniors back to earth and set the stage for a round of intelligent speculation based on rational analysis of project potential and risk-reward leverage. "It will be possible to make money through thoughtful research instead of playing the greater fool momentum game."

Kaiser sees investors demanding better-quality research. Bre-X fallout has already hit the analyst community. Musical chairs are being played, and some of the larger brokerage firms have brought on fellows with more grey hair and more field experience. The idea of "star analysts" is falling by the wayside, too.

"Things will have to change," said one mining executive. "Because if they don't, the funds will get their own analysts and these guys at the houses will be glorified salesmen."

Others predict that market forces — that fine balance between buyers and sellers — will bring about changes. The pendulum had swung too far in favor of sellers; now it will be the other way round. Investors will refrain from buying until the quality of the merchandise improves.

Busang also was a mirror for gold, and the hype and promotion it always seems to attract. Birl Worley says gold does strange things to people. "I've been around gold for so long and have seen it happen, time and time again. Gold makes people dishonest."

Others say that neither gold nor the mining industry is bad. It is

This was it: The now-abandoned exposure of the Southeast zone that convinced geologists that Busang might be the mother of all gold deposits.

the rogues who are bad, and the mining and investment industries need to clamp down on them. "It is the responsibility of the mining and investment industries to protect investors, and themselves, from the worst of their own kind," one said.

If Busang was a mirror for an industry, the reflection was unsettling for many. One American fund manager, who refused to buy into the Bre-X story, saw his side of the industry reflected and didn't like what he saw. He later told friends that he had been taken to task for not getting the returns others were getting from their Bre-X shares. But he held firm, because he didn't like the story and didn't like the people. When it all blew up, he resigned. "It was more than the scam that bothered me," he told friends. "It was the incompetence that allowed it to happen. The hardest thing to see in all this was the incompetence."

Publicly, mining executives are loath to criticize Bay Street's high-powered mining analysts and brokerage firms for their part in the Busang fiasco. Privately, they could talk for hours.

"Bay Street was waiting for the second coming of Christ," said one. "They missed Voisey's Bay, and they were determined not to miss the next one. But why did they have to chuck aside everything they were taught in school to bet the barn? They were out of control at ninety miles an hour."

Said another: "If principles were kept, this would not have happened. Bay Street did not scrutinize any of these guys. No matter what went wrong in Indonesia, what went wrong here is more troubling."

Chapter Twelve:
SEE THEM COMING, NOT GOING

The dust will not settle in our time.
And when it does, some great whirling machine
will come and whirl it all sky-high again.
Samuel Beckett, *All That Fall*

Samuel Beckett was not talking about Bre-X Minerals. He was talking about human nature and the propensity of mankind to forget the past and make the same mistakes over and over again. After the New Cinch scandal of the 1980s, salting scams were expected to go the way of the dodo bird. We were at last too smart to fall for those tricks again. Well, here we go 'round the mulberry bush — again.

Voluntary, or premeditated, salting is, of course, the stratagem of scoundrels. But equally culpable and equally serious is the involuntary form by which perfectly honest but misguided individuals unknowingly affect results.

Involuntary salting is not common, but is equally misleading. When it does occur, it is usually the result of an engineer or sampler leaving out mineralized areas or sections which had not thought would run (i.e., yield a high value), but do.

It seems wise to compile some advice from scam-busters and industry experts on measures to ensure that the industry itself sees fraudulent operators coming, not going. The most fitting place to start is with the man who pulled the Busang fraud apart without seeing a single rock.

Making sense of the numbers

Jan Merks
Statistician, Matrix Consultants
Vancouver, British Columbia

When you can measure what you are speaking about, and express it in numbers, you know something about it; but when you cannot express it in numbers, your knowledge is of the meagre and unsatisfactory kind.
Lord Kelvin

Only a fraction of Bre-X's samples and assays on which Kilborn based its geostatistical estimate of 70.95 million oz. of gold would have been enough to prove beyond reasonable doubt that Busang was a fraud, and would have proved it long before John Felderhof was honored by his peers. Analysis of variance would have shown that the intrinsic variability of the gold was indeterminate — as it ought to be in a phantom deposit — and that preparing test samples of drill core added most to the variance of the measurement chain. Analysis of variance can also be applied to quantify the probability that the mineralization between measured values is continuous.

Analysis of variance is widely used in science and engineering, but in geostatistics it is as popular as Darwinism is in the Bible Belt. Whether neologisms such as "deterministic geostatistics" and "applied probability" are the promises of brilliant innovation or oxymorons coined by a bankrupt science is an intriguing question, not only because kriging enhances spatial dependence and creates it where none really exists, but (even more so) because kriging variances are mathematical aberrations. The geostatistical theorist ought to explain how it is possible to develop a model based on widely spaced exploration data when closely spaced drill hole grades do not display a significant degree of spatial dependence.

Confidence limits are reported for Gallup polls, but not for grades and contents of gold deposits. Confidence limits quantify the risks that arise when prospects are advanced to producing mines. It makes sense to calculate confidence limits for grades and contents of resources and reserves. Therefore, an International Standards Organization technical committee on resource and reserve definitions and calculations would be in the best interest of the mining industry and of the investment community.

For the general reader, a precis of Jan Merks's opinion may be helpful:

Busang demonstrated that conventional statistical methods — the kind of calculations many university students learn in their second year, then forget for a lifetime — could have shown that the data from Busang were artificial. It was possible to tell, by looking at the statistical distribution of the individual assays from Busang, that the main source of the differences between one Busang core sample and the next was sample preparation — the step that included a trip to the salting shack.

Jan Merks aims his remarks at professional, not general readers, but, for both, there is much to learn in what he says. The discipline of mathematical statistics is used in many industries and professions. It is the near-universal language of those who work with measurements of any kind. Put a pollster, a cancer researcher, a crop breeder and a geochemist in a small room, and they will find that they have that one body of knowledge in common.

Mining stands alone among the world's industries in having felt the need to develop its very own brand of statistics, a system called geostatistics. Nobody ever demonstrated that the statistical techniques used throughout the other physical, biological and social sciences were not up to the task of calculating mineral resources and controlling grade in operating mines. Nor did anybody ever explain why our industry can use standard mathematical statistics to ensure quality control in a flotation mill or an assaying laboratory but cannot use the same methodology when we are trying to describe the shape, form and grade of an orebody.

Geostatistics had no direct part in the fraud at Busang. But a particular habit of thought is common to those who accept geostatistical models uncritically and those who were taken in by the Bre-X fraud. A ready acceptance of what one is told, whether by a computer screen or by a geologist with big ideas, is a step on the way to becoming a mark.

George Cross is a long-time observer of the Vancouver market scene and has witnessed many a fraudulent deal in the mineral exploration business. His views on human nature stem from that experience; every Vancouver market watcher keeps a mental list of the "usual suspects" to watch for in scams. Old Southeast Asia hands were well-acquainted with some of the *dramatis personae* of Bre-X, in particular "metallurgist" Jerry Alo, and their judgment of Bre-X grew out of their experience with the people they saw associated with it.

His second point, the implementation of procedures that already exist, is important: after the Bre-X bust, how many people brought up the argument that others *should have known* there was a scam going on?

George Cross is right. The fact is that Bre-X broke many of the industry's conventions yet still was given the benefit of the doubt by a large number of people. As Cross points out, any independent consultant worthy of the name would have recommended wholesale changes at Bre-X.

Fraud in mineral exploration

George Cross
Publisher, The George Cross Newsletter
Vancouver, British Columbia

In mineral exploration or any other business, it is seldom *what* you know — it is almost always *who* you know. Since it is impossible or meaningless to legislate honesty, the important factor is the quality of employees. What motivates a man to go bad after years on the straight and narrow? The best protection against a fraud, after carefully selecting the people, is the implementation of operating procedures and regulations now in place — regulations that were, in Bre-X and other recent cases, neglected, avoided or ignored. Only in very special cases are "eyeball assays" meaningful. There have been several recent instances where company share prices have gone wild on eyeball assays alone. The eyeballs were not fraudulent; they were just wrong, bad eyeballs.

After sampling, strict controls are necessary to ensure that the opportunity to tamper is prevented. This can be accomplished by running duplicate and blank samples as checks, and by using various labs to run checks, to obtain results that can be considered reliable.

In retrospect, it seems that a diligent, qualified, independent, arm's-length consultant would have changed the sampling procedure at Bre-X in a flash, had he been asked. The industry knows what to do to minimize the opportunity to create a fraud, and how to do it. For a variety of reasons, these normal industry procedures were not followed. The responsibility for this lack of proper procedures rests at a number of corporate, management, regulatory and professional levels.

Pierre Lassonde's guide for investors, *The Gold Book*, was published by *The Financial Times* in 1990. The book included an excellent discussion of the "dirt-pile" swindles used by confidence tricksters, which usually operated with private investors, off the stock markets. His emphasis on the role of the outside directors of the firms is especially intriguing in light of the way Bre-X management used the company's outside director, Paul Kavanagh, and its professional staff, Bryan Coates and Roly Francisco, as window-dressing for the scam.

Scams, frauds and Bre-X

Pierre Lassonde
President, Franco-Nevada Mining Corporation and
Euro-Nevada Mining Corporation
Toronto, Ontario

Over the past twenty years, I have accumulated a very special file of all the scams and frauds I have witnessed in the mining industry. Bre-X, with a market capitalization of $6 billion, is the grand dame of them all. The lesson, in each case, is deceptively simple.

All the regulatory hurdles in the world will not deter con artists from trying to profit from man's most formidable vice: greed. In the Bre-X case, it collectively blurred the critical judgment of the most respected mining analysts, whose opinions millions of investors rely upon — not to mention the regulators, who, because the stock proved to be a bonanza to them as well, didn't venture to ask *the* questions. Reason, in the form of critical scientific analysis, was suspended by the vision of tens of millions of ounces of gold, and billions in new wealth and commissions. It's the closest thing to the famed South Sea Bubble of 1642 our generation will ever see.

Can the mining industry regulate itself? Certainly. It has already moved to adapt standard systems for cost-reporting and reserve/resource definition. It can do more. Reserve calculations and reporting are management's primary task for junior exploration companies. However, the independent directors should bear the burden of providing a "reality check." In the Bre-X case, it is one of a glaring unanswered question; "Where were the outside directors?"

Perhaps the time has come for the creation of a formal reserve audit committee of outside directors of natural resource companies. It would raise the standards, but not prevent frauds.

I believe it would be inappropriate to have our industry shackled by a rash of new rules and regulations by those who, in my mind, compounded a deceptively simple scam into a billion-dollar fraud.

Immediately following the exposure of the Busang fraud, there was a body of opinion that held that Canadian resource and reserve classification schemes were not stringent enough, and that we needed a system like the Australian code. Poorly informed reporters joined in the clamor, and it is satisfying to record Michael Lawrence's much more subtle opinion here. What he stresses is not the classification of reserves and resources but the importance of having professionals take personal responsibility for the work they do, and the need for investors to insist on regular and understandable reports from mineral exploration companies.

An Australian perspective

Michael Lawrence
Managing Director, Minval Associates
Sydney, New South Wales

While small-scale sample-tampering and deliberate deception can never be ruled out, the enormous scale of the systematic deception at Busang is much less likely with proper surveillance systems in place. The systems require accredited technical professionals, who must follow best-practice codes and guidelines — both in reporting reserves and resources, and in assessing and evaluating mineral projects — or face significant ethical sanctions from their professional body. The Australian codes are initiatives of the Australasian Institute of Mining and Metallurgy, endorsed and supported by the Australian Stock Exchange and the Australian Securities Commission. The Australian capital market has come to expect periodic independent verification of technical results, even where it is not required by law.

Hence, what the Busang scandal has emphasized is the urgent need for a *national* Canadian securities watchdog and a *national* stock exchange, which would adopt most of the Australian initiatives in order to minimize future market fraud. Also required is a nationally co-ordinated Canadian accreditation scheme for mining professionals, with enforceable ethical codes, which would also assist the global mobility of Canadian resource professionals.

The advantage of codes and guidelines is that they ensure consistency and accountability. They provide a test of whether what was done was reasonable, forming the basis of a due diligence defence, and protecting those on both sides of a transaction — the author and the recipient of the data. To be credible, the codes, guidelines and accreditation schemes must be strictly enforceable — though regulators must devolve the task of creating and enforcing guidelines to an appropriate professional body, because it is there that peer pressure is most effective.

There is no easy solution; one protective measure alone will not be enough. More should have been done at Busang to preserve the integrity of samples between field collection and assaying, but the real lesson of the Busang affair is that such tampering can be discovered and exposed, and the damage minimized — if the right systems are in place, if they are being supervised, and if the right ethos exists among all the participants.

A more strategic way to avoid another Busang affair would be to have better and more detailed project assessment standards. Under the Australian codes, a reserve/resource report must state the name and position of the individual who prepared it and who must sign it. Professional peer pressure on individuals can make them perform to the highest ethical standards. Also, there should be continuous, detailed disclosure requirements like those of the Australian Stock Exchange, particularly for technical matters.

One can forget, in the hype, that Bre-X focused on reporting contained gold in global resources, and some analysts even called them "reserves." It ignored the natural attrition of resources when they are converted into minable tonnes and grades that reflect revenues, costs, dilution and mining loss. Also, in view of the different tenements covering the whole Busang "deposit," Bre-X should have reported the resources by tenement, as well as, separately, its own share of those resources. Analysts were wrong to quote a share value based on the gross *in situ* value of the "deposit," computed simply from contained ounces multiplied by the gold price, and divided by the number of issued shares.

It is to be hoped that the Canadian Mining Standards Task Force will force changes on the operation of Canadian explorers and exchanges. There is no simple solution, and no one solution will solve everything. You need more than a code. You need a national approach and a capital market that demands independent high standards of disclosure.

Coincidentally, the Canadian consulting firm of Watts Griffis & McOuat played a role in developing the Australian codes. Ross Lawrence of WGM offers his apologies to talk-show host David Letterman for offering his own top-ten list of fraud indicators.

Salting, did you say?
The Watts Griffis & McOuat list of sure-fire fraud indicators

Ross Lawrence, Geologist
Watts Griffis and McOuat
Toronto, Ontario

If you read a press release that contains some or all of the following concepts, watch out!

10. In Ghana, our company has found a gold deposit at or near surface, with resources equal to the total gold reserves of Ghana.

9. Artisanal miners recover only 40% of the total gold. Therefore, when our high-tech dredge begins operation, our company will have an operating margin of 160%.

8. Our junior company has done a deal with Megamine Inc., which dilutes our interest in the Brewtang deposit to one-third. But not to worry — our reserves just increased by a factor of three.

7. Our chief geologist has just returned from a flying visit to Ouagadougou to report that our partners in Burkina Faso have recently completed a trenching program on the De Gaulle vein. This work, under the direction of geologist Pierre Orpailleur, who recently graduated from the University of Ouagadougou, indicates that channel samples from the De Gaulle vein had an average grade of 0.5 oz. per ton.

6. Metallurgical work from samples on our property has indicated the presence of coarse, gravity-recoverable gold which has never before been identified in drill core. The testwork gave 85% recovery of gold in a gravity circuit.

5. The company is pleased to announce the discovery of a new style of mineralization on the property, which was not recognized by the previous operators. Due to the presence of coarse gold, assay results from this new style of mineralization are highly variable.

4. Previous work on our Mexican property returned very low silver values. However, new samples have just been assayed by Unknown Black Box Assayers Inc., using a revolutionary new assay technique. Our new assays from Black Box show significant silver values in the samples.

3. Surface sampling results have just been received from our Ipanema project in Brazil, where tropical weathering is extensive. The grade of the samples is an average of 5 grams gold per tonne. If this mineralization extends to a depth of 300 metres, a potential

resource of 2 million oz. would be present.

2. Our latest consultant has a remarkable new tool, which will allow us to explore our huge exploration concession in short order. The new equipment, for which patents have just been applied, utilizes aerial photographs which are fed into a special slot in the device. The operator then sets a dial to the mineral being sought, and a special pen marks the location of all deposits of this mineral directly on the aerial photograph.

1. Salting on such a massive scale is beyond belief; therefore, there is no salting.

Douglas Leishman has carved out a reputation as one of the country's most independent and critical mining analysts, and was known for his free-thinking comments during the progress of the Bre-X scandal. He points out the need for a "clear chain of command," which was, of course, lacking at Bre-X. That has allowed any number of people to claim that they knew nothing of the fraud.

Leishman's comments about "globalization" are worth marking. In many salting scams in the past, the company was based in one jurisdiction and the property in another. This made the scam easier to run, because the activities, and often the people themselves, slipped through the jurisdictional cracks. Busang was the archetype of the offshore scam. Because the project was in the Kalimantan jungle, any number of tales could be spun about government interference, logistical problems — and whatever other excuses, conspiracy theories and cover stories served the ends of the ounce factory.

No more Three Stooges

Douglas Leishman
Mining Analyst, Yorkton Securities
Vancouver, British Columbia

B re-X has been a costly experience for the investment and mining communities, as well as for private investors. The onus is on professionals from both sides of the industry to learn from this mistake and to prevent it from happening again.

The globalization of the junior resource industry poses new challenges to industry due diligence. Many of problems are related to people; and their individual professional, ethical and moral values. The "people aspect" is of paramount importance, but the most difficult to evaluate.

All industry professionals should regard any red flags associated with the technical aspects of projects with open and obvious suspicion. Proprietary assay and analytical techniques from a non-recognized or certified laboratory should not be accepted. Companies presenting what appears to be acceptable data, but which cannot accurately confirm or detail the chain of custody of how the samples were collected, should be viewed with suspicion. Any deviations from normal industry practice should be viewed with suspicion. Whole core analysis, as practised by Bre-X, should be relegated to the history books. New geological concepts or models should be regarded warily. A clear chain of command and the inherent responsibilities associated with such (between remote centres of operation and home office) should be established. Passing the buck is not a viable defence. However, even if all the above are eliminated, we must still rely on the professionalism, the integrity and the values of the people involved.

Investors have the right to demand that work programs be carried out to high professional standards. The financing of such programs should be contingent upon the involvement of professionals acceptable to us — the project financiers. The Bre-X fraud and those associated with it have attempted to destroy my profession and my ability to make a living. The Three Stooges belong on Saturday morning television, not on the board of a public company.

Keith McCandlish's firm, Associated Mining Consultants, acted for the Alberta Stock Exchange in investigations of Naxos Resources and Timbuktu Gold. His call for professionals to accept direct responsibility for their conclusions echoes the provision in the Australian code requiring reports to be signed by a "Competent Person."

Taking professional responsibility

Keith McCandlish
Associated Mining Consultants
Calgary, Alberta

Busang, the most financially significant tampering case involving Canadian companies operating internationally, was not the first or most recent. Since then, considerable, and somewhat public, soul-searching has been done by securities industry regulators and investors who lost money.

Would tighter listings requirements or disclosure rules prevent the occurrence of fraud? Absolutely not. Would they result in earlier discovery of sample tampering or inflated exploration results? Possibly, although the Bre-X results should have raised more questions long before they did.

Strangely and disturbingly silent in all this have been the mining sector and the brokerage houses, yet it is precisely these groups that have the most to lose. Conferences are already touting ways to raise new funds in the aftermath of Bre-X, but there is very little discussion of what has occurred and what needs to be done to restore confidence in the Canadian mining sector.

Many mining companies, junior and senior, may believe that their disclosure is technically correct and adequate. Sadly, many of the press releases I have seen indicate that this is far from the truth. As a simple example, the Canadian Institute of Mining, Metallurgy & Petroleum has a perfectly adequate set of resource/reserve definitions and guidelines. Yet companies misuse existing terms and invent new ones.

Numerous highly reputed analysts made outrageous predictions, based on inadequate and incomplete information, of the resource base at Busang. The public relied on them, with very serious consequences. While I feel sorry for the many investors who lost money, it must be remembered that many also made money. No new wealth was actually created; it was merely transferred.

Brokerage houses, by their very nature, are not truly independent. Should investors expect objective advice from the analysts employed by these houses? Analysts cannot be correct all the time, but the investing public has a right to reports prepared with adequate due diligence. The courts may decide this issue in years to come, and I suspect there will be changes to the way brokerage house reports are distributed, and to whom they are distributed.

Where do we go from here? Truly independent consultants will be used more frequently to review exploration results, particularly where feasibility studies lead to the publication of reserve estimates. Disclaiming professional responsibility for the conclusions will no longer be acceptable. Increasingly, geologists and mining engineers will be forced to accept the kind of public responsibility for press releases that directors already bear. And investor relations personnel should have no input into the technical content of public disclosures.

Geologists must increase their knowledge of sampling and assay procedures, to understand, more fully, the limitations of the data they receive. We must also learn, accept and use the available resource and reserve definitions. Regulators will have to increase their knowledge of the technical aspects of mining, to know when they must intervene or request clarifications. The financial press will need to become more aware of technical issues before commenting on press releases. Exchanges must co-operate with geological and mining technical societies to advance everyone's education.

Brokerage house analysts should think about whether publicly issued reports ought to be restricted to country- or commodity-specific studies, without emphasis on one company's mining project. Explicit "buy" or "sell" recommendations should be restricted to sophisticated private clients; while it is naive to think recommendations will not be circulated, it at least puts the onus on investors to research their choices.

Ultimately, confidence in the Canadian mining sector will be restored. There are so many good projects, and so many good people working on them.

George Poling, for many years a professor in the Department of Mining Engineering at the University of British Columbia, is a recognized authority on gold sampling and analysis. Naturally, both he and assayer Ralph Pray (whose comments follow Poling's) make the case for careful mineralogical examination and grain size analysis to detect species of gold that do not "belong" — and it was precisely these kinds of tests that brought down Bre-X.

Preventing fraudulent or incompetent valuation of gold deposits

Dr. George Poling
Rescan Environmental
Vancouver, British Columbia

Valuation of gold deposits demands special attention to ensure that samples are adequate to represent a larger entity and are not contaminated or salted, and that analyses are accurate. In addition, samples should be split, to leave a duplicate — in secure storage — for possible later independent analyses.

Too small a sample is generally without value. The problem of adequate sample size is particularly acute in dealing with precious metals, because "ore grades" can be around one part per million. As well, one part per million by weight is equivalent to about one-tenth of a part per million by volume, because gold is so much denser than the silicate minerals surrounding it.

For example, if a low-grade ore has an average gold content of 1 gram per tonne, and a significant proportion of its gold is in grains coarser than 0.15 millimetres, then the minimum sample size to achieve a precision of plus or minus 10% is over 2 kg — a sample size very few procedures can accommodate.

What does this mean for drill evaluation of a lode gold deposit? First, drill layouts must be designed by experienced geological professionals, with geological structures in mind, to learn the maximum information about grades and reserves. Among other things, this means that holes drilled down the centre of a narrow, gold-bearing vein do little to establish real gold reserves. Instead, they were probably drilled to hype a stock play.

Second, drill cores should have a large enough diameter to provide reproducible samples even after splitting or sawing.

Third, experienced, independent ore microscopists should carefully examine the gold particles in the core samples taken from a deposit. Physical appearances or morphologies of individual gold grains can often tie down the origin of gold grains. A detailed elemental analysis, with an electron microprobe, will add more evidence.

Fourth, as we have learned (again, all too recently), sample preparation is a dangerous time for samples, so using independent, certified laboratories and keeping cores away from current owners can help prevent salting.

Fifth, "metallics" assaying, where coarse gold is screened from the pulverized sample, can give a more accurate total gold assay and provide valuable information about the size of the gold grains.

Fire assay procedures for gold, coupled with instrumental analysis, have become nearly standard in this industry. Myths about the inapplicability of fire assay techniques to certain materials are simply myths; their mere mention should raise concerns about the competency of an assayer.

Crooks who salt samples to defraud investors are, thankfully, few and far between. Unfortunately, the law seems woefully inadequate in bringing this line of crooks to justice. Fortunately, meticulous application of modern technology, and constant vigilance, can detect nearly all gold frauds at an early stage. The gold mining industry, particularly the junior exploration companies, needs to employ independent experts on each and every potential gold discovery before inviting investors in. Frauds and incompetents should not be tolerated.

Ralph Pray, known to a number of fraud artists as "that s.o.b. from L.A.," has spent four decades working as an assayer and analytical chemist. The curiosity in which he sets such store is itself an essential characteristic of professional responsibility: it is another name for the spirit of inquiry that drives all good science.

Suspicious gold samples

Dr. Ralph Pray
Assayer, Scam-Buster and Mining Expert
Monrovia, California

The proper analysis by fire assay of a mineral sample always yields an acceptably precise value of the sample bag's contents. Technical competence is a "given." The first judgment of the assayer determines the general rock type, whether oxide, sulphide, carbonate, etc., to permit proper flux addition. This is a visual approximation and is some of the "art" part of the fire assay procedure, which is best performed by experienced lab people.

The curiosity required to identify a fire assay sample before fluxing may take only a second of time. But it is this trait — curiosity on the part of the assayer and the exploration geologist — that nails down the most meaningful early economic description of the sample.

If the sample from the new show yields gold, the assayer goes back to the unpulverized sample for a quick look. A few coarse particles have the dust blown off and get examined under the glass for a hint about the host. To answer the question, "Are the values higher in the fines?" a 14- or 20-mesh screen provides two new samples for assay.

If the fine material is high, and the coarse material trace, it's time to look at the fines in the gold pan. The red flag goes up when specks of brown precipitated gold are visible; or when tiny black points of nitric-parted gold stick to the pan; or when smooth, flat placer colors form a brilliant tail; or when grains of gold-bearing white quartz pan out of a material with no white quartz; or when a sulphide mineral pans out but can't be found in the coarse; and, finally, when the panned concentrates show nothing while the fines assay like crazy, indicating gold-chloride salting.

These samples are all promoterite.

Few field geologists seem to be satisfied with initial fire assay reports of good gold mineralization from a new show. They ask the assayer and the metallurgist, "Where is the gold in the rock?" "Is it disseminated?" "Along fracture lines?" "On cleavage planes?" "Native or in sulphides?"

These questions, and their answers, are the greatest defence against the introduction of spurious ore-grade information to the public. There should be a built-in suspicion about anything said to be very large and very good, particularly a story about gold. It takes one man only a few hours to measure the merits of a few dozen rock samples, but there has to be curiosity somewhere along the line. World-class laboratories are not the arbiters of truth without someone peeking over the edge or receiving instructions to extend their investigation.

The comfortable part of all this is that the vast majority of ethical professionals far outweigh the scoundrels among us, and that good choices prevail.

Queen Isabella didn't have these options when Columbus, the first big New World storyteller, insisted before he left on his second trip, "Just give me enough money to find the gold. I know it's there."

David Robertson, who has run a prominent Toronto mining consultancy for many years, also sees individual responsibility as the main issue to address.

Fraud and salting

Dr. David Robertson
Mineral Consultant
Toronto, Ontario

The exploration area of the mining industry seems to have been particularly susceptible to fraud throughout its history. Australia, Canada and the United States have each had their embarrassing "scams" and each has reacted with stiffer rules and regulations that have had only limited success in curbing fraud. No single scam, however, has been so successfully carried out through such a long period of time as the Bre-X fraud.

What are the processes by which these frauds are created? How can a Bre-X run for years? How can they be prevented?

Fraud in the mining industry, in my experience, generally takes the form of deliberate salting to produce false results, the use of black-box assaying techniques to produce supposed assay results not producible by standard methods, or the drawing of improper inferences by exaggerating the meaning of results. All three processes have been used by certain promoters through time. The last one, the drawing of improper inferences, commonly lies in the hands of financial analysts, advisors and technical professionals.

This sometimes is deliberate and sometimes arises through inexperience and ignorance.

Accidental salting, through improper sampling, carelessness in sample preparation, and so on, is preventable with care and well-designed procedures. Prevention of deliberate salting probably is not possible, although detection requires only simple check procedures, such as independent sampling by qualified persons and careful control of samples from collection through to assay. Any project that appears to be developing a substantial resource should have a check sampling process in place.

The occasional suggestion that gold or platinum metals cannot be measured properly by standard assay techniques should trigger instant suspicion. "Black box" assaying methods require instant checking and stock exchanges should not accept them as a basis for stock trading.

The more subtle and more common fraud — that of improperly suggesting that a certain assay result, or geophysical anomaly, or geological similarity guarantees or implies an economic future for a project, is widespread in the more promotional areas of the exploration business. Historically, the professional integrity of the mass of geologists and geophysicists has been a bulwark against the wider spread of such activity. But it is a common tool of some promoters, used either deliberately or through ignorance, and when supported by financial analysts and stock salesmen it can be economically damaging to those prone to speculating.

At the corporate level, it can be met by monitoring of press releases by the exchanges; among financial analysts, by a strong education in the meaning of integrity. At the sales level, no one can protect the greedy.

Technical professionals face an especially difficult task. To deal with exploration results and make sound recommendations, they need a high degree of judgment based on knowledge and experience. Geological interpretations thought to be proper can change profoundly as more information comes in, and there is always room for some divergence of opinion.

Nevertheless, the pressure of a client's needs can persuade some technical experts to deal with their reporting almost as part of a game, rather than as an expression of their independent professional judgment. When ore reserve numbers are involved, the concept of a "competent person" taking responsibility for the numbers could be useful. Ore reserves and resources are the bedrock on which any mining enterprise stands. It seems to me that confirming them deserves as much care as does confirming financial statements — keeping in mind, of course, that development of reserve numbers needs good geological understanding and proceeds by assumption and extrapolation, and that neither of these processes are mechanical.

At the exploration level, it seems that sanctions by a recognized body, such as the organization of Professional Engineers, could be applied to improper recommendations for expenditures that have been made in a fashion such as to elicit investment.

As authors, we are determined to have the last word. Perhaps we should be prepared to bring ourselves and our colleagues to account a little more often. The one measure that would do the most to force deception into the open is the competent person rule: that anyone making claims of resources, reserves or value must shoulder the responsibility for every digit.

If a single thread runs through all the opinions in this chapter, it is that professionals and investors alike must shake off the comforting notion that we can let others do our thinking for us. We should start and end every day knowing we are our own competent person.

Acknowledgements

The leaves on the trees were small, fresh and green when we started. They were brown, shriveled and dying when we were done. The Bre-X story was like that too, starting and ending the way it did.

It was not easy to write a story we were part of, and more difficult still to write a story involving people we know well. We know that the topic is a painful one for some investors, as well as for many people in the mining and investment industries. It was not a pleasant experience for us, either. But there are lessons to be learned from the whole affair, and that is why this book was written.

We have tried to use sources we believe are credible and avoid the rest. We are grateful to the most credible sources of all, Graham Farquharson and Reinhard von Guttenberg, for the time they spent with us going over their experiences on the Bre-X audit.

We would like to thank John Cooke and Doug Donnelly, executive publisher and mining group publisher of *The Northern Miner*, and Bruce Creighton, president of the Southam Magazine and Information Group, for their support.

Thanks also go to Mark Heinzl and *The Wall Street Journal* for providing transcripts of interviews that fleshed out the story, and to Steve Ewart of the *Calgary Herald* for a detailed description of the Bre-X implosion, and his newspaper for the use of two file photos of David Walsh.

Theo Van Leeuwen's account of Indonesia's mining history also proved useful, and we thank him for allowing us to make use of his detailed chronology.

We want to thank the mining professionals who contributed to our final chapter their thoughts on how to ensure that history does not repeat itself, and to Stan MacEachern who would have contributed but was too ill to do so. Most particularly we thank Jan Merks for his consistent support. A number of other friends in the mining industry were prevented, by pressures of time and circumstance, from contributing, and we thank all of them for gracious replies, which invariably came with useful suggestions.

We are also indebted to Frank Kaplan — the kind of mining reporter they don't make 'em like any more — for reviewing a number of chapters and providing helpful comments, insights and inspiration.

As the Busang story unfolded, and later as we worked on this book, a number of people close to the situation came forward with information and assistance. Chief among them was Birl Worley, whose insights into the difficult days at Benguet were most enlightening.

And the old files at the *Miner*, where mining ghosts live on, provided a world of information.

This book is the product of many hands at *The Northern Miner's* Toronto bureau. We thank Thom Loree for his tireless copy-editing and valuable comments, Tom Brockelbank for his production contributions, and Mike Attenborough for his help with copy-editing and proofreading; Mike also ventured out into Toronto's bars and clubs on the trail of Mandy and Candy, a service above and beyond the call of duty.

Also above and beyond the call of duty were the contributions of Dean Spicer and Karen Whyte, whose patience, encouragement and interest were the water canteens that sustained two enthusiastic adventurers on their long search for the Lost Dutchman Mine.

Glossary

Alloy – A compound of two or more metals.

Alluvium – Relatively recent deposits of sedimentary material laid down in river beds, flood plains, lakes, or at the base of mountain slopes. (adj. alluvial)

Alteration – Any physical or chemical change in a rock or mineral subsequent to its formation. Milder and more localized than metamorphism.

Anomaly – Any departure from the norm which may indicate the presence of mineralization in the underlying bedrock.

Andesite – a volcanic rock common in island arcs and mountain ranges.

Anticline – An arch or fold in layers of rock shaped like the crest of a wave.

Assay – A chemical test performed on a sample of ores or minerals to determine the amount of valuable metals contained.

Basalt – An extrusive volcanic rock composed primarily of plagioclase, pyroxene and some olivine.

Base metal – Any non-precious metal (eg. copper, lead, zinc, nickel, etc.).

Bit – The cutting end of a drill frequently made of an extremely hard material such as industrial diamonds or tungsten carbide.

Breccia – A rock in which angular fragments are surrounded by a mass of fine–grained minerals.

Bulk mining – Any large-scale, mechanized method of mining involving many thousands of tonnes of ore being brought to surface per day.

Bulk sample – A large sample of mineralized rock, frequently hundreds of tonnes, selected in such a manner as to be representative of the potential orebody being sampled. Used to determine metallurgical characteristics.

Calcite – Calcium carbonate, a mineral often introduced by mineralizing solutions.

Capitalization – A financial term used to describe the value financial markets put on a company. Determined by multiplying the number of outstanding shares of a company by the current stock price.

Carbonates – A group of minerals, all containing the carbonate radical (CO_3), common in veins and in altered rocks.

Channel sample – A sample composed of pieces of vein or mineral deposit that have been cut out of a small trench or channel, usually about 10 cm wide and 2 cm deep.

Chip sample – A method of sampling a rock exposure whereby a regular series of small chips of rock is broken off along a line across the face.

Cinnabar – A vermilion–colored ore mineral of mercury.

Collar – The term applied to the timbering or concrete around the mouth of a shaft; also used to describe the top of a drill hole.

Concentrate – A material produced in metallurgical processes, containing the greater part of the valuable mineral in an ore.

Contact – A geological term used to describe the line or plane along which two different rock formations meet.

Contact metamorphism – Metamorphism of country rocks adjacent to an intrusion, caused by heat from the intrusion.

Core – The long cylindrical piece of rock, about an inch in diameter, brought to surface by diamond drilling.

Core barrel – That part of a string of tools in a diamond drill hole in which the core specimen is collected.

Country rock – Loosely used to describe the general mass of rock adjacent to an orebody or to a body of intrusive rock.

Crust – The outermost layer of the Earth; includes both continental and oceanic crust.

Cut value – Applies to assays that have been reduced to some arbitrary maximum to prevent erratic high values from inflating the average.

Cyanidation – A method of extracting exposed gold or silver grains from crushed or ground ore by dissolving it in a weak cyanide solution. May be carried out in tanks inside a mill or in heaps of ore out of doors.

Cyanide – A chemical species containing carbon and nitrogen used to dissolve gold and silver from ore.

Dacite – A volcanic rock similar to andesite, but normally containing more quartz.

Day order – An order to buy or sell shares, good only on the day the order was entered.

Debt financing – Method of raising capital whereby companies borrow money from a lending institution.

Development – Underground work carried out for the purpose of opening up a mineral deposit. Includes shaft sinking, crosscutting, drifting and raising.

Development drilling – drilling to establish accurate estimates of mineral reserves.

Diamond drill – A rotary type of rock drill that cuts a core of rock that is recovered in long cylindrical sections, two centimetres or more in diameter.

Dilution (mining) – Rock that is , by necessity, removed along with the ore in the mining process, subsequently lowering the grade of the ore.

Dilution (of shares) – A decrease in the value of a company's shares caused by the issue of treasury shares.

Dip – The angle at which a vein, structure or rock bed is inclined from the horizontal as measured at right angles to the strike; also, the angle at which a drill hole is inclined, measured from the horizontal.

Disseminated ore – Ore carrying small particles of valuable minerals spread more or less uniformly through the host rock.

Drill–indicated reserves – The size and quality of a potential orebody as suggested by widely spaced drill holes; more work is required before reserves can be classified as probable or proven.

Due diligence – The degree of care and caution required before making a decision; loosely, a financial and technical investigation to determine whether an investment is sound.

Dyke – A long and relatively thin body of igneous rock that, while in the molten state, intruded a fissure in older rocks.

Epigenetic – Orebodies formed by hydrothermal fluids and gases that were introduced into the host rocks from elsewhere, filling cavities in the host rock.

Epithermal deposit – A mineral deposit consisting of veins and replacement bodies, usually in volcanic or sedimentary rocks, containing precious metals, or, more rarely, base metals.

Equity financing – The provision of funds by buying shares.

Erosion – The breaking down and subsequent removal of either rock or surface material by wind, rain, wave action, freezing and thawing and other processes.

Exploration – Prospecting, sampling, mapping, diamond drilling and other work involved in searching for ore.

Fault – A break in the Earth's crust caused by tectonic forces which have moved the rock on one side with respect to the other.

Felsic – Term used to describe light-colored rocks containing feldspar, feldspathoids and silica.

Fence – A pattern of drill holes along a line.

Fine gold – Fineness is the proportion of pure gold or silver in jewelry or bullion expressed in parts per thousand. Thus, 925 fine gold indicates 925 parts out of 1,000, or 92.5% is pure gold.

Fissure – An extensive crack, break or fracture in rocks.

Float – Pieces of rock that have been broken off and moved from their original location by natural forces such as frost or glacial action.

Flotation – A milling process in which valuable mineral particles are induced to become attached to bubbles and float, and others sink.

Flow-through shares – Shares in an exploration company that allow the tax deduction or credits for mineral exploration to be passed to the investor.

Fold – Any bending or wrinkling of rock strata.

Footwall – The rock on the underside of a vein or ore structure.

Fracture – A break in the rock, the opening of which allows mineral-bearing solutions to enter. A "cross-fracture" is a minor break extending at more-or-less right angles to the direction of the principal fractures.

Free milling – Ores of gold or silver from which the precious metals can be recovered by concentrating methods without resort to pressure leaching or other chemical treatment.

Galena – Lead sulphide, the most common ore mineral of lead.

Gangue – The worthless minerals in an ore deposit.

Geochemistry – The study of the chemical properties of rocks.

Geophysics – The study of the physical properties of the earth.

Geophysical survey – A scientific method of prospecting that measures the physical properties of rock formations. Common properties investigated include magnetism, specific gravity, electrical conductivity and radioactivity.

Glory hole – In the Busang context, a drill hole with spectacular grades.

Gossan – The rust-colored capping or staining of a mineral deposit, generally formed by the oxidation or alteration of iron sulphides.

Grab sample – A sample from a rock outcrop that is assayed to determine if valuable elements are contained in the rock. A grab sample is not intended to be representative of the deposit, and usually the best-looking material is selected.

Granite – A coarse-grained intrusive igneous rock consisting of quartz, feldspar and mica.

Grubstake – Financing furnished to a prospector in return for an interest in any discoveries made.

Hangingwall – The rock on the upper side of a vein or ore deposit.

Head grade – The average grade of ore fed into a mill or metallurgical process.

High grade – Rich ore. As a verb, selective mining of the best ore in a deposit or theft of ore from a mine.

Host rock – The rock surrounding an ore deposit or intrusion.

Hydrothermal – Relating to hot fluids circulating in the Earth's crust.

Igneous rocks – Rocks formed by the solidification of molten material from far below the Earth's surface.

Institutional investors – Pension funds and mutual funds, managing money for a large number of individual investors.

Intrusion – A body of igneous rock formed by the consolidation of magma intruded into other rocks, in contrast to lavas, which are extruded upon the surface.

Jaw crusher – A machine in which rock is broken by the action of steel plates.

Jig – A piece of milling equipment used to concentrate ore on a screen submerged in water, either by the reciprocating motion of the screen or by the pulsation of water through it.

Kimberlite – A variety of peridotite; the most common host rock of diamonds.

Leachable – Extractable by chemical solvents.

Leaching – A chemical process for the extraction of valuable minerals from ore; also, a natural process by which ground waters dissolve minerals, thus leaving the rock with a smaller proportion of some of the minerals than it contained originally.

Lode – A mineral deposit in solid rock, as distinguished from a placer.

Log – To examine drill core and record observations.

Magma – The molten material deep in the Earth from which rocks are formed.

Marcasite – An iron sulphide mineral, a low-temperature relative of pyrite.

Mineable reserves – Ore reserves that are known to be extractable using a given mining plan.

Native metal – A metal occurring in nature in pure form, uncombined with other elements.

Net profit interest – A portion of the profit remaining after all charges, including taxes and bookkeeping charges (such as depreciation) have been deducted.

Net smelter return – A share of the net revenues generated from the sale of metal produced by a mine.

Nugget – A small mass of precious metal, found free in nature.

Open pit – A mine that is entirely on surface. Also referred to as open-cut or open-cast mine.

Option – An agreement to purchase a property reached between the property vendor and some other party who wishes to explore the property further.

Ore – A mixture of valuable minerals and gangue from which at least one of the metals can be extracted at a profit.

Ore reserves – The calculated tonnage and grade of mineralization which can be extracted profitably; classified as possible, probable and proven according to the level of confidence that can be placed in the data.

Oreshoot – The portion, or length, of a vein or other structure, that carries sufficient valuable mineral to be extracted profitably.

Outcrop – An exposure of rock or mineral deposit that can be seen on surface, i.e. that is not covered by soil or water.

Oxidation – A chemical reaction caused by exposure to oxygen that results in a change in the chemical composition of a mineral.

Pan – To wash gravel, sand or crushed rock samples in order to isolate gold or other valuable metals by their higher density.

Participating interest – A company's interest in a mine, which entitles it to a certain percentage of profits in return for putting up an equal percentage of the capital cost of the project.

Pay streak – Unusually high-grade strips in a placer mineral deposit.

Placer – A deposit of valuable minerals, particularly gold, in alluvial sand or gravel.

Plug – A small body of intrusive rock, typically cylindrical or pipe-like in shape. Often a remnant "feeder" for a volcano.

Plunge – The vertical angle a linear geological feature makes with the horizontal plane.

Plutonic – Refers to rocks of igneous origin that have come from great depth.

Porphyry – Any igneous rock in which relatively large crystals , called phenocrysts, are set in a fine-grained groundmass.

Porphyry copper – A deposit of disseminated copper minerals in or around a large body of intrusive rock. Commonly also contains gold, molybdenum, or tungsten.

Possible resources – Valuable mineralization not sampled enough to accurately estimate its tonnage and grade, or even verify its existence. Also called "inferred resources."

Primary deposits – Valuable minerals deposited during the original period or periods of mineralization as opposed to those deposited as a result of alteration or weathering.

Private placement – Sale of shares to individuals or corporations outside the normal market, at a negotiated price. Often used to raise capital for a junior exploration company.

Probable resources – Valuable mineralization not sampled enough to accurately estimate the terms of tonnage and grade. Also called "indicated resources."

Prospect – A mining property, the value of which has not been determined by exploration.

Prospectus – A document filed with the appropriate securities commission detailing the activities and financial condition of a company seeking funds from the public by issuing shares in the company.

Proven resources – Mineralization that has been sampled extensively by closely spaced diamond drill holes in enough detail to give an accurate estimation of grade and tonnage. Also called "measured resources."

Pulp – Pulverized or ground ore in solution.

Pyrite – A yellow iron sulphide mineral, normally of little value. It is sometimes referred to as "fool's gold".

Pyrrhotite – A bronze-colored, magnetic iron sulphide mineral, a high-temperature relative of pyrite.

Quartz – Common rock-forming mineral consisting of silicon and oxygen.

Reconnaissance – A preliminary survey of ground.

Recovery – The percentage of valuable metal in the ore that is recovered by metallurgical treatment.

Refractory ore – Ore that resists the action of chemical reagents in the normal treatment processes and which may require pressure leaching or other means to effect the full recovery of the valuable minerals.

Rejects – In assaying, crushed or ground material in excess of what is needed for assaying; usually stored or returned to the client.

Replacement ore – Ore formed by a process during which certain minerals have passed into solution and have been carried away, while valuable minerals from the solution have been deposited in the place of those removed.

Reserve – The calculated amount of material that can be mined from a mineral deposit, based on dense drilling and sampling and on technical assessments of minability.

Resource – The calculated amount of material in a mineral deposit, based on limited drill information. A less precise figure than a "reserve," giving no assurance that all the material is minable.

Rhyolite – A fine-grained, extrusive igneous rock which has the same chemical composition as granite.

Royalty – An amount of money paid at regular intervals by the lessee or operator of an exploration or mining property to the owner of the ground. Generally based on a certain amount per ton or a percentage of the total production or profits. Also, the fee paid for the right to use a patented process.

Salting – The act of introducing metals or minerals into a deposit or samples, resulting in false assays – done either by accident or with the intent of defrauding the public.

Sample – A small portion of rock or a mineral deposit, taken so that the metal content can be determined by assaying.

Sampling – Selecting a fractional but representative part of a mineral deposit for analysis.

Scintillation counter – An instrument used to detect and measure radioactivity by detecting gamma rays; also called a "scintillometer."

Secondary enrichment – Enrichment of a vein or mineral deposit by minerals that have been taken into solution from one part of the vein or adjacent rocks and redeposited in another.

Sedimentary rocks – Secondary rocks formed from material derived from other rocks and laid down under water. Examples are limestone, shale and sandstone.

Shear or shearing – The deformation of rocks by lateral movement along innumerable parallel planes, generally resulting from pressure and producing such metamorphic structures as cleavage and schistosity.

Shear zone – A zone in which shearing has occurred on a large scale.

Shoot – A concentration of mineral values; that part of a vein or zone carrying values of ore grade.

Silica – Silicon dioxide. (Quartz is a common example.)

Siliceous – A rock containing an abundance of quartz.

Skarn – Name for the metamorphic rocks surrounding an igneous intrusive where it comes in contact with a limestone or dolostone formation.

Sludge – Rock cuttings from a diamond drill hole, sometimes used for assaying.

Sodium cyanide – A chemical used in the mill of gold ores to dissolve gold and silver.

Sphalerite – A zinc sulphide mineral; the most common ore mineral of zinc.

Split – To divide a sample into portions, taking care that the portions, whether equal or unequal, are identical in composition.

Step-out drilling – Holes drilled to intersect a mineralization horizon or structure along strike or down dip.

Stratigraphy – Strictly, the description of bedded rock sequences; used loosely, the sequence of bedded rocks in a particular area.

Strike – The direction, or bearing from true north, of a vein or rock formation measured on a horizontal surface.

Stringer – A narrow vein or irregular filament of a mineral or minerals traversing a rock mass.

Strip – To remove the overburden or waste rock overlying an orebody in preparation for mining by open pit methods.

Stripping ratio – The ratio of tonnes removed as waste relative to the number of tonnes of ore removed from an open pit mine.

Sulphide – A compound of sulphur and some other element.

Syncline – A down-arching fold in bedded rocks.

Tailings – Waste material from a metallurgical process after the recoverable minerals have been extracted.

Trend – The direction, in the horizontal plane, of a linear geological feature (for example, an ore zone), measured from true north.

Tuff – Rock composed of fine volcanic ash.

Vein – A fissure, fault or crack in a rock filled by minerals that have travelled upwards from some deep source.

Visible gold – Native gold which is discernable, in a hand specimen, to the unaided eye.

Volcanic rocks – Igneous rocks formed from magma that has flowed out or has been violently ejected from a volcano.

Vug – A small cavity in a rock, frequently lined with well-formed crystals.

Wall rocks – Rock units on either side of an orebody. The hangingwall and footwall rocks of an orebody.

Waste – Unmineralized rock, or sometimes mineralized rock that is not minable at a profit.

Working capital – The liquid resources a company has to meet day-to-day expenses of operation; defined as the excess of current assets over current liabilities.

CONVERSION FACTORS FOR MEASUREMENTS

SI	Multiplied by	Gives	Imperial	Multiplied by	Gives
LENGTH					
1 mm	0.039	inches	1 inch	25.4	mm
1 cm	0.394	inches	1 inch	2.54	cm
1 m	3.281	feet	1 foot	0.305	m
1 km	0.621	miles (statute)	1 mile (statute)	1.609	km
AREA					
1 km^2	0.386	square miles	1 square mile	2.590	km^2
1 ha	2.471	acres	1 acre	0.405	ha
MASS					
1 g	0.032	ounces (troy)	1 ounce (troy)	31.103	g
1 kg	2.205	pounds (avdp)	1 pound (avdp)	0.454	kg
1 t	1.102	tons (short)	1 ton (short)	0.907	t
CONCENTRATION					
1 g/t	0.029	ounce (troy)/ ton (short)	1 ounce (troy)/ ton (short)	34.286	g/t

Index